For Families Only

Tyndale House
Publishers, Inc.
Wheaton, Illinois

J. ALLAN
PETERSEN,
EDITOR

For Families
Only

Answering
the tough
questions
parents
ask

Library of Congress
Card Catalog
Number 77-072437.
ISBN 0-8423-0880-6.
Copyright © 1977 by
Tyndale House
Publishers, Inc.,
Wheaton, Illinois.
All rights reserved.
First printing,
September 1977.
Printed in the
United States of
America.

To Genevieve Frew

*One of God's choice and talented servants:
an able speaker, gifted writer, heartfelt singer,
a loyal critic, and my warm friend. She has
been the most significant contributor to the
development of this book.*

CONTENTS

Teen Problems

School Review

Critical Issues

Acknowledgments

"Are Our Convictions Contagious?" by Howard G. Hendricks is reprinted from *Heaven Help the Home*, © 1974 Victor Books, Wheaton, Ill. Used by permission.

"Should Dad Be More Than a Breadwinner?" by Kathleen Davis is reprinted by permission from the April 1976 *Parents' Magazine*, New York, N.Y.

"To Be Fair, Must Things Be Equal?" by Alice Schrage is reprinted from the September 1975 *Family Life Today*, © 1975 by Gospel Light Publications, Glendale, Calif. 91209. Used by permission.

"Can We Make Chores Exciting?" by Dorothy Mauldin is reprinted from *Home Life*, January 1974. Copyright © 1974 The Sunday School Board of the Southern Baptist Convention, Nashville, Tenn. All rights reserved. Used by permission.

"Should Outgrowing Parenthood Scare Us?" by Margaret Ross is reprinted from *Home Life*, February 1972. Copyright © 1972 The Sunday School Board of the Southern Baptist Convention, Nashville, Tenn. All rights reserved. Used by permission.

"What Is Our Children's Number One Need?" by Richard L. Strauss is reprinted by permission from *Confident Children and How They Grow*, © 1975 Tyndale House Publishers, Inc., Wheaton, Ill.

"How Can We Build Family Self-esteem?" by James Dobson is reprinted from *Hide or Seek*. Copyright © 1974 by Fleming H. Revell Company, Old Tappan, N.J. Excerpts used by permission.

"What Helps Teens Toward Social Maturity?" by Ellen McKay Trimmer is reprinted from *Building Interpersonal Relationships*, © 1972 Moody Press, Moody Bible Institute of Chicago. Used by permission.

"Am I My Child's Crutch?" by Marguerite and Willard Beecher is taken from *Parents on the Run: A Commonsense Book for Today's Parents*. Copyright © 1955 by Marguerite and Willard Beecher. Used by permission of Crown Publishers, Inc., New York, N.Y.

"What Marriage Preparation Is Necessary?" by Anthony Florio is reprinted from *Two to Get Ready*, © 1974 by Fleming H. Revell Company, Old Tappan, N.J. Used by permission.

"Should Our Teenager Marry?" is reprinted from *Seventeen*, New York, N.Y.

"Is Sex Education Necessary?" by Letha Scanzoni is taken from a paper written for the Continental Congress on the Family.

"Can Sex Really Be Taught at Home?" by Dr. Kenneth Gangel is reprinted from *The Family First*, © Kenneth O. Gangel. Published by HIS International Service, Minneapolis, Minn. Used by permission of author.

"How Do I Answer Those Sex Questions?" by W. Cleon Skousen is reprinted from *So You Want to Raise a Boy*, © 1962 Doubleday & Company, Inc., New York, N.Y. Used by permission.

"Is Our Child a Homosexual?" by Barbara Wyden is reprinted from the July 1970 *Family Circle*, New York, N.Y. Used by permission.

"Is Masturbation Sinful?" by David A. Seamands is taken from a paper written for the Continental Congress on the Family.

"What Marks Us as a Christian Family?" by Francis D.
Breisch is reprinted from the chapter "Family and
Neighborhood" in *The Family That Makes It,* © 1971
Victor Books, Wheaton, Ill. Used by permission.

"How Can We Get Next to Our Neighbors?" by Philip E.
Armstrong is used by permission of the author.

"What If Our Neighbors Are Relatives?" by Mary Alice and
Harold Blake Walker is reprinted from *Venture of Faith,*
Harper and Row Publishers, Inc. and is used by permission.

"Have We Forgotten Hospitality?" by Joy A. Sterling is
reprinted from the October 1975 *Eternity,* © *Eternity*
magazine, 1716 Spruce Street, Philadelphia, Pa. 19103.
Used by permission.

"Are We for Real?" by Winnie Christensen is reprinted from
Caught with My Hands Full, © 1970 Harold Shaw
Publishers, Wheaton, Ill. Used by permission.

"How Should We Choose a Church Home?" by Stanley C.
Baldwin is reprinted from the September 1975 *Moody
Monthly.* Copyright 1975, Moody Bible Institute of
Chicago. Used by permission.

"Are We Serving the Church but Losing Our Children?" by V.
Raymond Edman is reprinted by permission from the
January 1965 *Christian Life,* copyright 1965 Christian Life,
Inc. Gundersen Dr. and Schmale Rd., Wheaton, Ill. 60187.

"How Can We Succeed with Family Worship?" by Tenis C.
Van Kooten is reprinted from *Building the Family Altar,*
copyright 1969 by Baker Book House, Grand Rapids,
Mich., and is used by permission.

"Can We Claim Our Family's Salvation?" by Theodore H. Epp
is reprinted by permission from the November 1966 *Good
News Broadcaster,* copyright © 1966 by The Good News
Broadcasting Association, Inc., Lincoln, Nebr.

"Am I My Child's Biggest Problem?" by S. Bruce Narramore
is reprinted from *Help! I'm a Parent.* Copyright © 1972 by
The Zondervan Corporation, Grand Rapids, Mich. Used by
permission.

"Do I Have to Be Perfect?" by Keith Miller is reprinted from
the August 1976 *Eternity,* © *Eternity* magazine, 1716
Spruce Street, Philadelphia, Pa. 19103. Used by permission.

"Which Answers Never Change?" by Stanley E. Lindquist is
reprinted by permission from the June 1962 *Christian Life.*
Copyright 1962 Christian Life, Inc., Gundersen Dr. and
Schmale Rd., Wheaton, Ill. 60187.

"What Makes Mealtimes Fun?" by Merla Jean Sparks is taken
from *The Creative Christian Home,* reprinted by Baker
Book House, Grand Rapids, Mich., and is used by
permission.

"How Can We Have a Happy Family Vacation?" by Bernice
K. Gregg is reprinted from *Home Life,* March 1969.
Copyright © 1969 The Sunday School Board of the Southern
Baptist Convention, Nashville, Tenn. All rights reserved.
Used by permission.

"How Can Parents Get Away—Alone?" by Valerie Sloane is
reprinted from *Creative Family Activities.* Copyright
© 1976 by Abingdon Press, Nashville, Tenn. Used by
permission.

"How Is College Affordable?" by Frank L. Keegan is used by
permission of the author.

"Can We Escape the Debt Trap?" by George Fooshee, Jr. is
reprinted from *You Can Be Financially Free.* Copyright
© 1976 by George Fooshee, Jr. Published by Fleming H.
Revell Company, Old Tappan, N.J. Used by permission.

Preface

Good family life these days is not easy to come by. It never has been. But in this late twentieth century, it seems to be tougher than in earlier times.

The recent major study on families and children, the first since World War II, indicates the American family is increasingly falling apart and children are suffering unbelievably. This social upheaval is likened to that during a global war, or the Great Depression. One of every six children lives in a broken home. One-third of all children are at risk socially and medically. Eighty percent of children in low-income city areas are from single-parent families. A whole generation is growing up with no experience in "caring." "A person, even a girl, can graduate from high school without having ever cared for the sick, held a baby, or been responsible for someone else." Divorce is becoming as common as the cold.

More than ever, thinking Christian parents have some hard, practical questions for those of us in a family helping ministry. And the neat, easy, idealistic answers are not sufficient any more. Every month in our Family Affair Seminars across the continent, these concerned questions are asked—same problems, different city. Across my desk every week come similar questions from our widely scattered radio listeners and readers.

Some of these questions have been asked for hundreds of years, others reflect the unique problems of our society—its rootlessness, permissiveness, and fragmentation. For me or anyone else to attempt to adequately answer all of these would require what one man does not possess—the wisdom of Solomon. I would rather arrange for others—well-known or

unfamiliar, professional or layperson—to
share their wisdom in one volume to the
greater helpfulness of many.

So, you've asked the tough questions and we
have found some answers that combine the
spiritual, practical, and common-sense
approach of Solomon. My very capable
secretary, Cheryl Brokering, commented
excitedly as she typed up the manuscripts,
"This material will help so many people in
such a practical way." There is no *question*
about that!

J. Allan Petersen
Family Concern, Inc.

Are our convictions contagious? *Howard G. Hendricks*

What do you want for your child? Here's a principle: you can achieve only that for which you aim. If you aim at nothing you will hit it every time. You must have the target clearly in focus. Many people have a very fuzzy idea of what they want to inculcate.

Beware of
inconsistency

One real roughie that manifests itself in at least four areas is inconsistency. First, your standards are different from the contemporary society of which you are a part. So, your children are always asking, "Why do we do this? How come we're different?" There are many Christian couples who can't choke this down. They are afraid to be different. Distinctively so.

Second, your standards are different from the Christian community. Many of us are patterning our lives after the general run of Christians, and the Christian community is going downhill. The standard of Christian experience is not the Christian community; it's Jesus Christ. If you have to break with the accepted practices of the Christian community in order to conform yourself to him, do it.

The standards of Christians are usually cultural. Christian standards are always biblical. Some parents will send a kid to hell for two inches of hair. Oooh, they make this a federal case! I knew of a Christian couple who chased a son out of their home and told him never to return until he went to a barber shop. He never returned. They're still looking for him—and wishing they had made a better decision. If you're going to take a stand, be sure you take a stand on the crucial issues!

Third, your future standards will be different from your present parental convictions. Give yourself ten years and a couple of teenagers, and what you think now are convictions may become unfortunate prejudices. What you thought was relatively trivial suddenly becomes pivotal, absolutely central. Beware of being insensitive to the Spirit of God, because you ought to be in the process of growing. And so should your convictions!

Fourth, there is inconsistency because your standards are often different from those of your parents. There is inherent danger in this. You see, we tend to react against the negatives of our parents while failing to reproduce the positives. I asked a student what turned him off about his parents. Without a moment's hesitation, he gave me five things—very clearly thought through. "I don't want to produce that in my kids!"

"That's good," I agreed. "What do you want to produce in your children that your parents produced in you?" Then his thinking was not so clear.

If you happen to have spent the bulk of your teen years dumping disapproval on your parents, then you have a lot of hard, constructive thinking ahead. You have to get rid of the garbage and go back and determine what your parents did that was very good, that you want to reproduce in your children.

Set clear objectives and priorities

List some things that you definitely want to develop in your family. These may include:
Respect for authority.
Selective friendships.
Learning to take responsibility.
Systematic giving to the Lord.
Obedience. A disciplined walk with the Lord.

A positive self-image.
A responsible use of time.
Giving without expecting return.
Treating the body as the Lord's.

Looking over this suggested list, I am impressed with what it is going to take to put each item into action. The model you provide will be the primary means for communicating your convictions.

Relationships always precede rules. In fact, they are more important than rules. The principle: a child tends to accept your ideas, your philosophy, because he accepts you. And he tends to reject your ideas and philosophy when he rejects you.

Let love be supreme

Without love, the child reacts rather than acts. Deprivations of loving discipline in childhood leave deep scars of pathological anxiety—even if he has received spiritual and moral teaching.

This lack is my explanation for why many kids reared in Christian homes kick over the traces. The home did not lack clear-cut moral teaching, but the moral teaching took place in a context lacking meaningful love (in which the parent does that which is best for the child).

Love always acts in the child's best interests, even if the child does not understand at that particular point in time. You are not interested in how he feels and reacts now as much as how he feels and reacts ten to fifteen years from now. True love treats the child now in terms of the future. "Now" love should be alive with activity.

On Thanksgiving Day, a young mother was seated in the den of her home with a group of friends and relatives. Her six-year-old daughter came in and whispered in her ear, "Mommy, I need to tell you something."

"OK, Honey, tell me."

"I can't tell you here," she whispered frantically.

"Oh, yes, you can, just say it out loud."

"No, Mommy, I can't."

And that was the end of the dialogue.

Three or four days later, the young woman heard (from a friend in whose home her little daughter had visited) of an incident that had taken place involving moral implications. "Your daughter was pretty upset," the friend told her.

Later, when the woman asked her daughter why she hadn't told her about the incident, the little girl responded, "Mommy, I tried to, but you wouldn't listen, and Uncle Jack was sitting there, and I couldn't say it in front of him!" That mother learned a hard lesson; she lost a choice opportunity for communicating. "From here on out," she said, "when my child is ready to talk, I'm ready to listen."

Live your convictions consistently

Children are not looking for perfect parents; but they are looking for honest parents. An honest, progressing parent is a highly infectious person. Your convictions are much more caught than taught. A child unconsciously patterns his life after a model in his environment. Unfortunately, many children do not have adequate models. I believe the primary problem with rebellious teens is the lack of reliable models.

Dr. Thomas Harris warns against inconsistency in parents of small children. "When they say 'don't lie,' and then the child hears them lying, this produces confusion and fear, and the child tries to tune out the discordance." Harris illustrates the principle with an algebraic equation: "A plus times a minus equals a minus. It does not matter how big the plus was, or how little the minus was.

The result is always a minus . . . The effects in later life may be ambivalence, discord, and despair." Christian parents need to be certain that what they say and what they do harmonizes.

Feed your children responsibility

You can't become a responsible person overnight; it requires a process. Feeding responsibility is risky. It means we have to allow children to do some things that we would probably rather do for them. Sometimes they are going to fall — where you think they shouldn't fall.

Responsibility is developed over a lifetime. We are all in the process of developing. Give your children the privilege of an early start, so that when they step out of home, they have a background of living with their own decisions.

Houseclean your attitudes

Atmosphere, climate, is paramount in communicating convictions. I would suggest that the most important thing you contribute to a child is to allow him the luxury of a mistake. Let him know he is free to fail.

Failure has a rightful place in the Christian home. It is sometimes necessary to lose minor skirmishes in order to win a lifetime struggle.

Share personal failures. It is a great encouragement to children to know that Mom and Dad failed sometimes, too—that they sometimes strike out, even now.

Seek God's will, not your own

Getting a child to conform to the will of the Lord is probably the ultimate goal of all Christian parents who have themselves experienced the pleasure and satisfaction and fulfillment of living in God's will. Reiterate to your children: "It is not so important how you relate to us, as how you relate to Christ." As our children have grown older, this has taken on new meaning for them.

When they are young, they follow their parents. Paul wrote, "Follow me as I follow Christ." Our first principle was "sharpen your personal convictions." Your children will imitate you as the beginning of the process which leads to imitation of Christ.

What do you really want your child to be? Something that will reflect most favorably upon you? Or something that will reflect most favorably on Jesus Christ?

Inculcating Christian standards is like building a fire in the rain. It requires willful determination, against all odds, to do what seems impossible. It calls for expertise— know-how which understands the nature of the child and the nature of a hostile world. It demands a stubborn perseverance to keep fanning the flickering flame, to keep protecting the hot coals. A warm young life, glowing for Christ, is the most needed commodity in the damp, depressing chill of the marketplace today.

A well-known Bible teacher stated that the Lord spoke to him one day and said, "You may travel all over the world with your briefcase and preach to thousands of people and have them flock to the altars when you finish, but if your home is not in order—in my eyes you are a failure."

A former president of Wheaton College said that in looking back on the way he brought up his children, if he had it to do all over again, he would spend much more time with them in simple, nonreligious activities. He said he found out that the things his grown children remembered most were the informal times of just being together.

Get your family in order. Those you touch, those your children touch will be brought into your home—not to be preached at—but to know and experience the love of God; to see a living example of people knit together in love in a world that is falling apart. MRS. WILLIAM RADCLIFFE

Should Dad be more than a breadwinner? *Kathleen Davis*

Jenny looked absurdly tiny and dear standing on the arm of the sofa, her bare toes curled over the edge. Her father sat on the floor, three or four feet away, facing his year-old daughter. Jenny balanced on her perch for a moment, as though savoring the thrill of her daring. Then she lifted her arms wide, and with a happy cry she "flew" into the outstretched arms of her father.

This was Jenny's favorite game—one she played every evening with Daddy.

Jenny's trust in her father has been growing since she came home from the hospital when she was four days old. On Jenny's very first morning at home, her father had bathed her and put on her tiny shirt and diaper. If his hands were clumsy, they were also firm and gentle, promising his child love and security in her new world.

Jenny is my granddaughter, and I had come to visit and to help right after her birth. But to my surprise and deep pleasure, Jenny's dad, Michael, who is my son, had graciously declined my offer to look after the baby. He was very happy to have me take over the running of the house while my daughter-in-law, Lee, rested, but when it came to the baby-care tasks, Michael was eager to take over. And so he did, using several days of his vacation in order to share with Lee the responsibility and joy of looking after their newborn infant.

Now, a year later, as I watched Jenny and her father, I was deeply thankful that Michael was experiencing fully the joy of parenthood.

It wasn't like that when I was a young

mother. When Michael was born, most mothers were the sole homemakers, fathers the sole breadwinners. Almost all of the advice I read then on infant care was addressed only to mothers. So I quickly assumed the role of the important parent in our son's life. Rarely did my husband even get to hold the baby, though Michael's father, like so many others, I'm sure, would have liked to play a more active part in fathering. But most men in those days were embarrassed to ask in the face of their wives' discouragement.

I was adamant about Michael's schedule, which required him to be fed and in bed for the night before his father arrived home from work. On weekends, I maintained my baby-care routines. The books told me it was best for the baby to have one familiar person on whom he could depend for all his needs, and I followed them to the letter.

So Michael's father never experienced the giving of love through the care and handling of his baby son. And in losing the opportunity of really knowing his son as an infant, my husband also lost out on vital preparation for later stages of fatherhood when a man has much to offer his son.

I didn't fully realize all this until Michael was grown. One evening shortly before his marriage, he talked to me about his regret at not having been closer to his father during his early boyhood. Mike told me then that when he became a father, he was resolved to experience parenthood fully, right from the beginning.

Michael kept that resolution. Fortunately, he had his wife's cooperation. During the months of Lee's pregnancy, they attended childbirth classes together, so that both would be able to help at the time of delivery. Since Lee recovered well, and Michael was prepared to help take care of Jenny at home, Lee and Jenny were able to leave the hospital three days after the baby's birth.

At home, Lee nursed the baby and Michael took on the job of changing Jenny's diapers, bathing her (a thing most men are afraid to do), and sharing with Lee the satisfaction of comforting their baby when she cried.

After Michael went back to work, he still spent time with Jenny every evening. Usually they had a quiet playtime together while Lee prepared dinner. Sometimes, when Jenny was in a fretful mood, Michael would rock her until she fell asleep.

Surprisingly soon, Jenny learned to recognize signs of her father's arrival, listening intently as the front door opened and closed, and squirming eagerly at the sound of his voice.

On the basis of my own mistakes, and from seeing the value of my son's close relationship to his daughter, I would offer some suggestions to fathers-to-be.

Naturally, a father's relationship to his child will be different from that of a mother's. But an infant—boy or girl—can only benefit from having a tender relationship with both parents. A son who grows up knowing and trusting his father should have no trouble identifying with him, respecting him, and establishing his own masculine identity. A daughter's early loving relationship with her father will help her to understand those mysterious creatures, men, and to relate to them comfortably and naturally.

For the father, early involvement with his child means his paternal feeling will develop most readily. He won't feel left out or jealous of the baby as so many new fathers do. And for mothers, the benefits are immense. There's practical help when it's most needed, and above all, the chance to share with their husbands this profound experience with its ups and downs, joys and blues. I even believe there would be fewer cases of postpartum depression if husbands truly shared this experience with their wives. Then women would no longer feel the isolation so many do as they realize their lives have changed forever, and they are responsible, really responsible, for the existence of another human being.

Here then are my suggestions to fathers who would like to take an active hand at parenting during the first months of their children's lives:

1. Assure yourself of your wife's cooperation by letting her know in advance that you want to be involved with your baby. Ask her about ways in which you can help. Attending pre-childbirth classes together is an advantage. One way to dive into your role as a father is to assist at the baby's birth, if you and your wife wish it and your doctor and hospital permit. Some hospitals even allow fathers to room in, thus getting a head start in sharing instead of being shut out.

2. Have confidence in yourself as a father. Remember that no one except your baby's mother is as important to him or her as you are. No one can take your place. Your infant needs to sense that you are his strong and powerful protector. Your confidence in your ability to take care of your baby will build his growing confidence in you. From the beginning, help your child to be aware that there are two important loving people in his life he can count on to minister to his needs.

3. Take over some of the physical care of your infant. Never mind if you're slow and clumsy putting on a diaper. What's important to your baby is that you're touching him with love.

Even if your attempts to take care of the baby seem awkward to your wife at first, she'll soon be thankful for your help. And the more you help with this newcomer, the more time your wife will have for you.

4. Talk to your baby when you hold him in your arms. An infant will soon respond to your loving voice. And look at your child when you talk to him. Long before he can understand your words—and he'll understand them much earlier than you may think—he'll realize you're communicating with him, and he'll delight in it.

5. Pay attention to your relationship with your wife. Find a reliable person to take care of the baby so that you and your wife can go out together at least once a week. If problems arise between you, try to talk them out. If this fails, seek help from your own pastor or a family counseling service. A good relationship between you and your wife is vital to you, but it's also important to your child, whose feelings of security will be strengthened as he senses the harmony between you.

To be fair, must things be equal? *Alice Schrage*

They were twins, but they were different from birth. They even looked different. The elder was wrinkled and red and hairy, and like an old man weathered by the elements. In contrast, his brother was white and smooth.

These twins grew up to be very different men. Esau was a hunter who loved the open air and a rough life. Jacob became a settled "homebody" type.

Isaac, the father, ended up loving Esau. Rebekah, the mother, loved Jacob. How the parents played their respective favorites, and how it all led to misunderstandings, trickery, deceit, and tragedy is recorded in Genesis 25 through 33.

An obvious lesson in this story is "don't play favorites." God loves us all equally, and the Christian way is to love our children equally too.

It's an excellent principle, but I have found it takes constant effort to put it into practice. "Loving equally" and "making things fair" is not always the same as "making everything equal."

My children, Susi, nine, and Tina, seven, are as different as Jacob and Esau. I feel differently about each of them. Can I love them equally when they are so different? How can I be "fair" when Susi has one set of needs, Tina another?

For example, Susi's life is more settled and ongoing while Tina lives in the present moment. Susi enjoys occasional solitude, but Tina wants someone nearby to chatter to constantly. Susi can follow directions and finish a job; Tina rarely listens or finishes alone.

I have had to learn that because I feel

differently about the two girls does not mean I love one more than the other. By nature I appreciate Susi's more quiet, organized personality. I have felt guilty on many occasions when Tina's "whatever will be, will be" approach has made me feel judgmental and irritated. I am beginning to see, however, that the response of my personality to my child's personality is not something to feel guilty about; it's something to understand and deal with. I'm even beginning to appreciate the many differences in Susi and Tina and to deal with each child individually, according to strengths and weaknesses, without feeling guilty and like an "unfair mother."

Of course, there are times I treat my two daughters alike to show I love them equally. I give them the same number of cookies for snack. I give them the same cereal or let each choose. But there are other times when treating them exactly the same is depriving one or putting too much responsibility on the other. Fair does not always mean equal. Equal is not always fair!

When Susi says, "May I ride my bike around the block, Mommy?" I usually let her. But I don't let Tina ride around alone. Susi is responsible enough not to loiter or stop at someone's house. Given the same privilege, Tina could be gone hours without thinking.

Nor can I insist that the girls go to bed at the same time. Susi, still wide-awake, would keep Tina up, and the next day Tina would be tired and miserable.

For us, loving our children equally has come to mean accepting them as individuals. It means making allowances for differences in personality and ability. If I ask Susi to set the table, for example, she will finish it without supervision. Tina, though very excited about helping, may just get started before being distracted by the cat as he walks through the room.

I've learned that one way to help Tina complete a task is to give her one-step-at-a-time instructions. This keeps us talking and planning together while she works and also gives me opportunities to praise her for what she's doing. I usually save the part of the job Tina enjoys best for the last step. For example, when setting the table Tina thinks filling the glasses is special fun.

Taking time to deal with each girl's individual problems and needs sometimes results in one child getting more attention than the other in certain situations. When we moved last year, we tried to prepare the girls very positively. After the move Susi adjusted quickly, while Tina needed extended support. To help her, we assured and reassured Tina that this wasn't just another of our many moves, but we really intended for this to be our very own house for a long time.

Also, we asked for and used Tina's suggestions for fixing up her room. And often, even in the midst of all of the moving activities, we took time to hold and love Tina, to share a snack with her, or to read for a little while from one of her favorite storybooks. We explained Tina's special needs to Susi and she helped by spending time playing with Tina.

And how do our daughters respond to our "individual treatment?" Do they see this as equal love? How do I convince them they each have a fair share?

I think the most important thing we do is try to impress them with their uniqueness. We tell our children that they are very special people, created by God, that we love them each in a very special way.

No, our children don't always feel we are being fair with them. I think there will always be questions no matter what approach we use. But I believe they will feel satisfied more often if they are treated as individuals.

Our children are unique. We recognize they're different and have different needs. In our family, whatever happens about "equal or fair," we are trying not to play favorites. Our goal is to love each child in a very special way, as a very special person, created by God himself!

A LOVING TIME

A few years ago when I returned to teaching, I was assigned a first grade class. I was apprehensive, as I had always taught upper grades.

One of my first actions was to eliminate the "Show and Tell" period, since I felt that the children who had something to talk about did not require practice in communication, and that the shy ones who needed to speak out were reluctant to do so.

One of the shy ones was a small curly-headed girl named Teresa. After my announcement Teresa came to me with a request:

"Instead of 'Show and Tell,' can we have a loving time?"

I asked her to explain. I hope the years will never allow me to forget her answer: "Every once in a while you could love us and give us a hug, and we could tell you something important. It wouldn't take long."

From that day on, whenever a child needed "loving," he would stand close to my desk and receive a hug, a pat, and a few moments of my undivided attention while he told something "important." We had such a good class that year; it was the year my students taught me.
MYRTLE W. SILVA

Can we make chores exciting? *Dorothy D. Mauldin*

The first time I met my daughter's third-grade teacher, she said, "I'll bet Amy has regular chores to do at home."

"Yes," I answered. "How did you know?"

"Oh, you can always tell," she smiled.

We have lived on a farm since our first child started school, so there have been many useful chores to keep our children busy. They were quite young when they began learning responsibility for feeding and watering the cows, horses, rabbits, chickens, as well as the dogs and cats. Now they're raising their own livestock and have numerous FFA and 4-H projects.

My husband has accepted the biggest responsibility for assigning outside chores. However, I feel that to be independent, reliable individuals, even the boys need indoor chores as well.

A college boy I know wrote home, "Mother, please send recipes for low-cost meals, with explicit directions. My budget won't reach for cafeteria food, and I'm awfully tired of Sam's macaroni and wieners. Could you send washing instructions for clothes too? I could save on laundry bills as well, but I goofed somehow and shrank my good blue sweater. Please advise what to do."

I was certainly glad that my husband had some knowledge of cooking and housework when our children were little.

To know they need this training is one thing. To see that they have it is something else, especially if you happen to be a tense and harried mother, as I often am.

**Start
early**

When Amy first showed an interest in cooking, but was still too young to be much help, I would let her get the utensils, ingredients, and cookbook for me. I also started her watching the toast in the broiler to brown it just right. Later I showed her how to measure. Before she could use the electric mixer, she was able to assemble all the ingredients and prepare the pans for a cake. My three boys weren't quite as interested as Amy, but they learned much the same way.

Amy is now twelve, and though I haven't let her prepare complete meals alone for our large family, she does most of the baking, broils meat, and fries eggs—anything that doesn't pop and spatter grease too much.

Children can learn gradually and be helpful at the same time. While I cook the main dishes, Amy is a great help when she sets the table, fixes the salad, makes the tea and coffee, puts ice in the glasses. As she becomes more adept at cooking, we will trade places, and she will have learned it all.

What about cleaning up the mess? Amy does that quite well, too. I discovered early that she didn't take too kindly to dishwashing. But when we were building our present farm, I specifically asked for a window over the kitchen sink. From it, we have a lovely view of mountains and our pond with a pair of white ducks (often wild ones, too). Sometimes our horses and cows come into view, too. Now Amy says, "It's almost fun to do dishes here where I can look out."

Our eldest son is married now. The next oldest is sixteen and has so many outside activities, as well as working with his dad, that he isn't home a great deal. However, he still likes to cook (and eat). So from time to time, we are treated with his talent for making cakes, cookies, pancakes, even doughnuts.

Sometimes he does the supper dishes when the rest of the family goes out for the evening. He can iron pants and shirts when those he wants to wear are not ironed.

Interesting jobs

So often we parents expect the children to do the routine jobs while we complete the more creative and interesting chores. The promise of more important and exciting jobs can lend incentive to do the more menial tasks. I've found that children don't mind doing dishes so much when they learn to do them well and in a short period of time. Actually, timing them can help. Being called back to do something over again helps them do a better job next time.

I've noticed, too, that assigning one specific job—like dusting or picking up scattered items —is much easier for a child to manage than something general, like cleaning the living room.

Work together

Working with the children makes it more enjoyable for both you and them. Demonstrate how "many hands make light work." Naturally, these times provide excellent opportunities for talking and listening to your youngsters.

Recently, my nine-year-old son and I had a whole Saturday to ourselves. I had several tasks to accomplish and felt the need to keep active little Nathan occupied. I hit on the idea of listing what I wanted to do and wanted him to do. All my children like to make lists— what to take on a trip, items for a picnic. His list included picking up toys, sorting school papers (to see which ones to throw away), carrying out the trash. We added some fun things for him to do alone, and things we would do together.

We had numerous interruptions, and he did his fun things so quickly that we had to think up some more. We finished the day by making candy; and while it cooled, we worked a jigsaw puzzle. Incidentally, he wouldn't let me go to bed that night until I put my hair up, an item on my list.

This experiment was so rewarding that I decided to expand the idea. Amy has joined in with her list, and we have after-school chores and those for Saturdays, including school homework. I added some to their allowance; and when everything is done for the week, they receive the full amount.

There are special jobs they can do for extra credit. Fun things include more cooking for Nathan, and sewing and learning to crochet for Amy. My contribution is reading to them at night and, time permitting, a table game or puzzle. Nathan delights in working with me in the yard, even pulling weeds, as long as we do it together. Amy is learning to iron, can operate the automatic washer, hang out and bring in the clothes and fold them, as well as other housecleaning activities.

Of couse, the children don't always work well together. Occasionally I must separate them or work with them to keep peace.

Contrary to the way many believe, work is still exciting and wonderful when you have the proper attitude.

Norman Corwin wrote of children in these terms: "One child makes a home a course in liberal education for both himself and parents; two children make it a private school; three or more make it a campus . . . All in all, the home is the great staging ground for the family's traffic with the world, as well as a fortress against the world's intrusions."

Should outgrowing parenthood scare us?
Margaret Ross

"Say, Mom, can I go on a fishing trip overnight with some of the guys?"

"Overnight!" I exclaimed. "I should say not! Think of all the things that might happen."

"Like what?" John challenged.

"You might get lost. Or hurt. Or get in a wreck," I explained. "How were you planning to go?"

"Brad's driving his dad's pickup," John said.

"Brad! That child!"

"Mother, he's sixteen," John explained.

"Nonetheless. . ." I began; at which point John muttered a rude, "Forget it!" and stomped out of the house, banging the door behind him.

"He is fifteen, Mother," nineteen-year-old Sue reminded me.

"Fifteen or not, it's still my duty to take care of him," I argued.

"Mom, do you remember when John was a little boy about three years old?" Sue asked.

"Of course I remember. What has that got to do with an overnight fishing trip?"

"Quite a bit, really. You remember how you and Dad put a low fence all around the yard?"

I nodded.

"You told John that he must not go beyond that wire. We all watched to see that he didn't."

"He was good about it, too," I remembered, "once he got the idea that outside the fence was off limits."

Sue said, "Things happened to him inside the fence. I remember he fell off the porch and cut his chin. And once he got stung by a bee."

"And one day a stray cat came into the yard and scratched him across the face," I added.

Sue laughed. "I had forgotten about that. Boy, did he set up a howl! But nothing very bad happened to him. And he did learn something about the world because you gave him room to move around—clear out to that fence. Then, later on, you let him outside the fence to go around the block."

I must have looked puzzled because Sue said, "What I mean is, it's not much different now. John is growing up, but he still needs limits. Only he wants the limits to keep moving outward."

Wonderful, wise daughter! I thought. Still. . .

"Oh, Mom, I know you're afraid something is going to happen to John. Something might, too. He will probably break his leg or something," Sue predicted cheerfully. "Things do happen to people, but that just makes 'em readier for what comes next."

Not a very cheering philosophy, I thought. But maybe that was the way things had to be.

"Here comes John now," Sue said, looking out the window. "Old Grumpy himself!"

"Call him in," I said with a sigh. "I guess I'll reverse my decision and give him a little more room to grow."

In every neighborhood are those who did not outgrow childhood because their parents did not outgrow parenthood.

Thirty-five-year-old Melissa, a stenographer, lives with her widowed mother. All last winter Melissa made plans and saved money for a trip to Hawaii with a fellow stenographer.

Sometime during the week prior to the trip, Melissa's mother became ill, so Melissa stayed home. Emergencies of this sort happen in all families, but in Melissa's case the mother's illness is a way of life.

Looking back, Melissa remembers her mother was not well at a time when she was considering marriage—her mother's health would not allow her to move the year that she was in line for a job promotion that would involve transferring to another state—her mother was not well enough to live alone when she entertained the idea of sharing an apartment with two young women her own age. Melissa's mother never quit being a parent, and Melissa never quit being a submissive daughter.

Harold, age forty-one, is an alcoholic. He began drinking heavily after the death of his wife. Finally out of work, out of money, and in difficulty with the law for drunken driving, he moved back home with his aging parents.

Harold's father supports him and his two children. His mother cares for the children. When Harold is hauled into court for some infraction of the law, his father buys his way out. His mother makes excuses for the grandchildren's truancies, just as she made excuses for her own son when he was a schoolboy.

To Mom and Dad, Harold is still a little boy to be loved, protected, and forgiven for irresponsible behavior.

Not all cases of arrested development in parents are as obvious as these. What about us parents who merely want the best for our offspring, and who feel that we are equipped to insure that "best"?

Suppose our boy wants to join the military instead of going to college. It takes extraordinary maturity to be the kind of parent who can allow the high school graduate to make his own choice when that choice may throw him into danger and into situations not considered desirable by the parents.

Suppose our teenagers conceive a child and decide to get married. We are tempted to take the responsibility out of their hands, not only to keep on being parents to our young people, but to be parents to their children.

How do we justify this clinging to parenthood? By insisting we want the "kids" to get an education. We must support them and take care of their baby until they are on their own feet.

All too often, the "kids" do not find their own feet. The marriage dissolves. Dad has his little girl home again. And Mom has not only her little girl, but her little girl's baby. There is a long stretch of parenthood ahead for this rather typical middle-aged couple.

Suppose our boy is one of those rebellious little characters who like to make up their own minds about things. What if he decides to play high school football, even if it is dangerous? What if he signs up for auto mechanics at school instead of advanced math? What if he takes on a job after school instead of studying? What if he decides he does not want to go to college? What if he spends his allowance the first week of the month and has nothing left for the remaining three weeks? What if he gets poor grades in high school and is barred from the college of his parents' choice?

Few parents of teenagers have matured to the point that they can sit by and watch their children make unwise choices and then let them suffer the consequences.

But the growing-up process for parents must begin long before their children become teenagers. I look back over my own parenthood and remember how difficult it has been to ease out of that role. I wonder if I can become a mature adult by the time my own offspring are adults.

The wise parent knows that helping children to grow up involves more than simply turning them loose into new situations or allowing them all of their own choices. Growing up emotionally occurs only when the individual has a sense of responsibility for his own behavior in terms of his welfare and that of his society.

Thus, the parent is constantly faced with the perplexing problem of giving the child responsibilities which are appropriate to his age. This must begin when the child is old enough to learn that some behavior is acceptable and some is not.

"What would you do if you learned that you had only a year to live?" the family doctor once asked me.

"I would worry about my children," I said.

"Well, sure," he agreed, "but what would you do about it?"

"I suppose I'd help them to outgrow their need for me," I said. "Teach them to be parents to themselves."

"Exactly!" the doctor agreed. "Statistically, your chances of living to age seventy-two are excellent. But there is no better time than right now to start training those children of yours to be good parents to themselves."

Good parents to themselves! I have been working at it for years, and it has been harder on me than on the children. Every now and then, though, I find those individuals who were once my children acting like mature adults.

They really might outgrow their childhood someday, and I might even outgrow my parenthood!

2

Confident
Children

What is our children's number one need? *Richard L. Strauss*

Here we are, faced with the awesome responsibility of molding our children into spiritually dynamic, well-adjusted adults that will bring joy to God's heart and to ours. How are we going to do it? One thing stands above all else. It represents what may be our children's greatest need, and the one which parents can fulfill better than anyone else. Children need to be loved by their parents. That's the way God deals with us. "For the Father himself loves you dearly . . . ." "See how very much our heavenly Father loves us . . . ." And that's the way he wants us to deal with our children.

Every child has the right to be conceived in love, carried with love during those nine months of pregnancy, and warmly welcomed into this world as the prized possession of loving parents. After the baby is born, loving surroundings are even more important; he needs to be cuddled, caressed, and cooed.

As a child grows older he still needs to be assured over and over that he is loved, not for what he does or doesn't do, but just for himself. He needs that assurance with gentle words and with physical closeness. With it he will develop healthy emotional patterns of acceptance and security. Without it, he may become withdrawn, insecure, hostile, or neurotic. Some doctors have discovered that a lack of affection can actually stunt a child's growth. Others have concluded that lack of parental love can cause homosexuality, frigidity, and other aberrations.

A dedicated Christian father told me that his ten-year-old daughter was becoming cold

and indifferent toward him. As he evaluated
the situation he realized that he was cuddling
and carrying her younger brother who was
handicapped, but pushing her aside with
comments like, "You're a big girl. You can
take care of yourself." When he began to
demonstrate openly and enthusiastically his
love for her, she blossomed into a very warm
and loving little girl who enjoyed snuggling up
to her daddy. It is our inescapable conclusion,
both from the Word of God and from human
experience, that a child has the divinely
bestowed right to feel secure in his parents'
love. It is God's way of getting him started on
the road to healthy emotional growth. It is
God's security blanket for children.

Almost all knowledgeable authorities agree
that the most potent cause for antisocial
behavior, for rebelliousness, disobedience, and
discipline problems of all kinds is a lack of
affection. Children who know they are loved
and accepted, who have no fear of being
rejected or abandoned by their parents, do not
need to act up to get attention or establish
their individual importance and worth. They
are important to someone and they know it.
They have been accepted, and that assurance
brings an inner satisfaction and security. The
love they feel from their parents inspires love
in their hearts, just as God's love for us
inspires us to love. And their love then
encourages them to obey us just as our love for
God encourages us to obey him. Because they
love, they want to please. Rather than inspiring
rebellion and disobedience, love restrains it.

Camp counselors have told me of problem
boys, starved for affection, who respond
beautifully when they become aware of
someone who really cares for them and shows
it. Unfortunately, many of these love-starved
children are from Christian homes and are

proving to be discipline problems in Bible-believing churches. Maybe we must conclude that the children of Christian parents do not always feel the love God wants them to have. And if that is the case, maybe we should explore some ways of communicating our love so that our children will enjoy this essential God-given right.

Just how should our love for our children be expressed? One way is by words. Some parents, possibly deprived of love in their own early years, find it impossible to tell their children they love them. They want to, but those tender words will not come out. To force them would seem contrary to their whole makeup and nature. If that is your problem, will you thank God right now for his verbal expressions of love to you in his Word, and will you ask him to help you tell your children that you love them? You may see an immediate improvement in their behavior.

But words alone won't do it all. Those words must be backed by actions. Children are amazingly perceptive. They know when our words are empty and meaningless. "Let us stop just saying we love people; let us really love them, and show it by our actions."

We need to back our words with time spent with them. The Lord does. He is with us always. We really do love our children, but how often we communicate just the opposite with "I don't have time for that now. Go away and leave me alone." We would have more time eventually if we would give them a few minutes of our undivided attention now. That doesn't mean we must drop everything and run every time they want us to do something with them. They can be taught to wait when that is necessary. But for some children, the attention they ask for and wait for never comes. So they develop less acceptable means of getting it, much to their parents' time-consuming embarrassment and dismay. Every time we carelessly push our children aside because they are interrupting something we want to do, we add another scar to their sensitive spirits, and another obstacle to overcome in their growth toward emotional maturity and wholesome adjustment to the world around them.

It isn't just time we're suggesting, however. It's the right kind of time. Quality counts more than quantity. Showing interest in the things that interest them will help build a sense of companionship and confidence that will make it easier for them to talk to us in the critical teen years.

It is often the pious, super-spiritual, heavenly minded Christians whose children are the greatest discipline problems in the church. Evidently they are so preoccupied with spiritual things that they don't have time to let their children know they love them. The best investment we can ever make is the investment of quality time in our children.

Not long ago I talked to a missionary friend who has eight brothers and sisters, all but one of whom are in the Lord's work, and that one was still in school at the time. I asked what his parents did that so influenced their lives. "The one thing that sticks in my mind is the time they spent with us," he said. "Mom sometimes turned down jobs in the church because they would interfere with being a good mother. We all worked for dad in his business, but sometimes he would suggest taking off for awhile in the middle of the day and we would all go out and shoot baskets or play some other game. We had fun together." Times of family fun say, "We love you. We enjoy being with you. You are our most important treasure in this world."

Another way of showing love is by praise and appreciation. Every time we let them know that their performance was not quite as good as it might have been, we chip away a little more of their confidence and make them a little more apprehensive about their adequacies and abilities. We always need to be looking for things a child does well, complimenting him for them. That will build in him a sense of confidence and help him overcome the "I can't do anything right" syndrome that could affect most everything he puts his hand to. And it may help convince him that we really do care for him, approve of him, and are glad that he is our child.

We can also help our children feel our love by being understanding. Every child is an individual, different from every other child in looks, personality, intelligence, aptitudes, and emotional responses. Each one has the right to be accepted as such and not forced into a mold. God's love shows no partiality, and he expects ours to be the same.

In order to help us really understand, we need to listen to what our children are saying. We often jump to conclusions, offer advice, or give lectures without ever hearing our children out. Then we wonder why they stop confiding in us. We need to listen, think, try to understand what they are feeling at the moment, then express words that let them know we understand. Let me illustrate. Suppose your child loses a prized possession such as a brand new baseball. How do you react? "Well, if you had been more careful, you wouldn't have lost it." "You'd lose your head if it weren't screwed on." "When are you going to learn to take care of your things?" "Baseballs don't grow on trees, you know." "Don't gripe at me about it. I didn't lose it." And there may be a hundred other possible retorts designed to convince the child that we really don't care about him, and that a two-dollar baseball is far more important to us than he is. We do need to teach him the value of money and proper care of his belongings. But why not first try something sympathetic like, "And that was your favorite ball, wasn't it?" Or something helpful like, "C'mon, we'll look for it together. Where do you think you had it last?" Or something encouraging like, "Maybe we'll find it when we clean out the garage." Then you will convince him that you really care for him, that you are his friend rather than his antagonist and critic.

showing the disappointment

We express love to our children by respecting them too. They are persons whom God has made with value and eternal worth, and they should be treated accordingly. That means we should never laugh at their weaknesses or ridicule their idiosyncrasies. "George, you throw a ball like a girl." "Well, how's my little butterball Becky today?" "Just innocent fun," we say, but it damages their sensitive spirits, destroys their fragile self-image, and puts another strain on their struggle to maturity.

Love will be communicated by our tone of voice likewise. You may say you love your children, but they are not feeling love when you scream, "Stop that this instant," or whine, "You kids are getting on my nerves today." Sometimes we need to be reminded that children are people who have the right to be talked to kindly and pleasantly just as we would talk to any other person we cared for.

"But they can be so exasperating and irritating." Yes, and we need to admit that our love is not enough, that it wears thin and finally explodes. Then we need to yield our wills to Christ and let his Spirit express his love through us. The natural product of that

Spirit-filled life will be God's kind of love. Then we will be able to communicate our love to our children even when they are acting like children. And they will be able to relax in our love and get down to the business of growing up instead of expending their energies trying to get our attention or establish their importance by one unacceptable means after another. And we will begin to experience the joy God intended us to have in our children.

Many Christian parents, viewing various expressions of the child through their adult eyes and experiences, interpret natural phases as a demonstration of the "old nature." Natural forms of "attention getting" are interpreted as the expression of "natural selfishness." Curiosity, particularly of a sexual nature, is interpreted as perversion or inappropriate sexual behavior. Expressions of self-will are categorized as the beginning of a self-centered life.

There is no doubt that the sin nature comes into play early in life. But studies have demonstrated that these childhood expressions during the first three years of life are natural phases that are essential for normal development. They must be treated accordingly. For example, to withhold attention from a child only increases the desire for attention. To bear down hard on exploration of sex as unnatural and perverted only draws attention to the sexual nature of the child and may create perversion. To try to break the will of a three-year-old by "beating it out of him" may create a "spineless" person or may drive his feelings inward, resulting in repressed feelings of hostility which will eventually reveal themselves in teenage or even adult rebellion. Some Christian parents then actually create the opposite results of what they are attempting to achieve.

Every Christian parent needs to pray for wisdom to rear children according to their natural growth patterns, both physically and psychologically. This seems to be the true meaning of Proverbs 22:6. There must be control, but not over-control. There must be discipline, but not over-discipline. There must be standards, but not so high that they frustrate the child and "provoke him to wrath" (Ephesians 6:4). GENE A. GETZ

How can we build family self-esteem? *Dr. James Dobson*

Dear Docter Gardner

What is bothering me is that long ago some big person it was a boy about 13 years old. He called me turtle and I know he said that because of my plastic sergery.

And I think god hates me because of my lip. And when I die he'll probably send me to hell. Love, Chris

Can't you feel Chris's loneliness and despair? How unfortunate for a seven-year-old child to believe that he is already hated by the entire universe! Yet Chris is merely one more victim of a stupid, inane system of evaluating human worth—a system which stresses attributes which cannot be obtained by the majority of our children.

So what are we to do? How can we, as parents, build strong egos and indomitable spirits in our children, despite the social forces which prevail? What are the steps necessary to reverse the trend?

Examine the values in your own home

Are you secretly disappointed because your child is so ordinary? Have you rejected him, at times, because of his lack of appeal and charm? Do you think he is dumb and stupid? Does he embarrass you by being either too loud and rambunctious or too inward and withdrawn?

A sizable proportion of your child's self-concept emerges from the way he thinks you "see" him. He watches what you say and do with interest. He is more alert to your "statements" regarding his worth than any other subject, even reading your unspoken (and perhaps unconscious) attitudes. It is very easy to convey love and disrespect at the same time. You are tense and nervous when he starts to speak to guests or outsiders. You butt in to explain what he was trying to say or laugh nervously when his remarks sound foolish. You reveal your frustration when you are trying to comb his hair or make him "look nice" for an important event. He knows you think it is an impossible assignment. He reads disrespect in your manner, though it is framed in genuine love. The love is a private thing between you—whereas confidence and admiration are "other" oriented, having social implications to those outside the family.

Sensitivity is the key word. It means "tuning in" to the thoughts and feelings of our kids, listening to the cues they give us and reacting appropriately to what we detect there.

Help your child to compensate

Some children have much greater handicaps than others and are almost certainly destined for emotional trouble during adolescence. Perhaps a child is particularly ugly or he might have a severe learning problem. For whatever reason, everybody can see that he is going to get clobbered by life. What are his parents to do?

First, we must be realistic. Some books on self-esteem naively assert that parental love, if vigorously expressed every day, is all that a child needs to develop self-confidence. I wish that were true, but in fact, a child's view of himself is a product of two important influences: 1) the quality of his home life; 2) his social experiences outside the family. There is no emotional armor which will make your child impervious to rejection and ridicule in his social contacts. It will always hurt to be laughed at, snubbed, ignored, or attacked by others. But our task as parents is not to eliminate every challenge for our children; it is to serve as a confident ally on their behalf, encouraging when they are distressed, intervening when the threats are overwhelming, and above all, giving them the tools with which to overcome the obstacles.

One of those vital tools involves a process called compensation. It means the individual counterbalances his weaknesses by capitalizing on his strengths. It is our job as parents to help our children find those strengths and learn to exploit them for all the self-satisfaction they will yield.

Perhaps he can establish his niche in music —many children do. Maybe he can develop his artistic talent or learn to write or cultivate mechanical skills or build model airplanes or raise rabbits for fun and profit. Regardless of what the choice is, the key is to start him down that road early. There is nothing more risky than sending a teenager into the storms of adolescence with no skills, no unique knowledge, no means of compensating. When this occurs, his ego is stark naked. He cannot say, "I may not be the most popular student in school, but I am the best trumpet player in the band!" His only source of self-esteem comes from the acceptance of other students—and their love is notoriously fickle.

Help your child to compete

A parent who strongly opposes the unfortunate stress currently placed on beauty and brains, as I do, must resolve a difficult philosophical question with regard to his own children. While he recognizes the injustice of this value system, he knows his child is forced to compete in a world which worships those attributes. What should he do, then?

Despite the injustice of this system, my child will not be the one to change it. I am obligated to help him compete in his world as best he can. If his ears protrude, I will have them flattened. If his teeth are crooked, I will see that they are straightened. If he founders academically, I will seek tutorial assistance to pull him out. He and I are allies in his fight for survival, and I will not turn a deaf ear to his needs.

What discomfort is your child experiencing in silence, today? Isn't it our obligation, within the limits of financial resources, to eradicate the flaws which generate the greatest sensitivity?

Discipline without damaging self-esteem

Does punishment, particularly spanking, break the spirit of the child? It is very important to understand the difference between breaking the spirit of the child, and breaking his will. The human spirit is exceedingly fragile at all ages and must be handled with care. It involves a person's view of himself, his personal worth, and many emotional factors. A parent can damage his child's spirit very easily—by ridicule, disrespect, threats to withdraw love, and by verbal rejection. Anything that depreciates his self-esteem is costly to his spirit. However, while the spirit is brittle and must be treated gently, the will is made of steel. It is full strength at the moment of birth, as any midnight bottle-warmer knows. We want, then, to shape the will of a child, but leave his spirit intact. This is done by requiring reasonable obedience to predetermined commands, and then winning the battles he chooses to initiate. If you permit your youngster's will to remain unbridled, the result is often extreme self-will, which makes him useless to himself, others, or even to God.

Keep a close eye on the classroom

What will we do for the self-esteem of the slow learner? Approximately 22 percent of the children in America have IQ's between 70 and

90. Before they even enter first grade, it can be predicted that most of these children will soon develop feelings of inadequacy and inferiority.

I offer two strong recommendations to the parents of a slow learner: First, de-emphasize academic achievement as a value in your home. There are some things in life which are more important than success in school, and self-esteem is one of them.

Secondly, a parent should not allow the school to "fail" his slow learner after kindergarten. I can think of few circumstances which justify an incapable child being retained in the same grade twice. What can he conclude, other than that he is incredibly stupid? What self-hatred this archaic educational practice has wrought in the lives of its victims.

The slow learner needs parental help in finding his compensating skills, coupled with the assurance that his personal worth does not depend on success in academia.

Avoid over-protection and dependency

From about three years of age, your little pride and joy begins making his way into the world of other people. It now becomes very difficult for Mom to control his environment. Other children may mock him and laugh at his deficiencies; he may be incapable of competing in their games; or he might even be crippled or killed in an accident of some kind. This initial "turning loose" period is often extremely threatening to his compulsive mother. However, her intense desire to help may actually interfere with his growth and development. Certain risks must be tolerated if a child is to learn and progress.

I have observed that the process of "letting go" during late adolescence is much more difficult for parents with deep religious convictions than for those without them. Christian families are more likely to be aware of, and be concerned by, the spiritual dangers their child will face with increasing independence and freedom. They have greater reason to fear the consequences of premarital intercourse, marriage to a nonbeliever, rejection of the Christian ethic, and other departures from the faith they have taught. Everything they have said during the first eighteen years will either be incorporated into the values of the new adult, or it will all be rejected and thrown overboard. The importance of this decision, then, causes too many zealous parents to hold on tightly to their maturing child. The result is often tremendous resentment on the adolescent's part, leading him to defy them just to prove his independence.

The biblical story of the Prodigal Son in the book of Luke is a brilliant guide to follow at this point. The father knew that his boy was going to squander his money and live with prostitutes. He knew he would make many mistakes, and possibly destroy himself in the process. Yet he permitted the young man to leave home! He did not chain him to a tree, or even condemn him verbally. Nor did he bail him out when he ran aground in the distant land. The love with which the father said good-bye made it possible for his son to return after making a mess of his life. We would do well to follow the father's loving example.

In summary, our final task in building self-esteem for our children is in transferring responsibility from our shoulders to theirs, beginning with the rudimentary skills of infancy, and terminating with their emancipation during the late teens or early twenties. Letting go is not an easy task, but good parenthood demands it.

What helps teens toward social maturity? *Ellen McKay Trimmer*

Many people enter adulthood dragging their teens behind them. They are socially immature. To help our children become mature adults, we need to teach certain concepts by precept and example.

Self and others

At birth every human being is the center of his world—the pivot upon which everything turns. Before we become socially mature, we must learn to view ourselves as a cog, not a pivot. We need to learn cooperation with others.

We do a child an injustice when we fail to teach him consideration for others by restraining his selfish acts. Although our expectations must be suited to the age and disposition of the child, "other-centeredness" can be taught. When a child learns to be thoughtful of others, he has opened a door to lifelong satisfaction in happy social relationships.

Mine and yours

"Other-centeredness" will create respect for the possessions of others. There will be a clear line between "mine" and "yours" when children are trained in this concept from the cradle.

One afternoon while riding a bus, I observed a chattering four-year-old with her mother. Suddenly she sighted a sparkling broken earring. "Mommy, look what I found!" she shrieked. Her mother smiled and said, "That's nice, dear, but that belongs to someone else. I think you should take it to the driver."

The girl made her way reluctantly to the front of the bus and gave it to the driver. He examined it carefully and put it back in her hand. "I don't think anyone will want that. It seems to be broken," he said. "You can have it."

Perhaps without knowing it this mother was teaching her child to respect the property of others. Mature unselfishness places the emphasis on giving, not taking.

But there are other ways of stealing which are much more damaging than taking another man's possessions. We can steal his right to be an individual and to develop in his own way. How many parents or marriage partners have done this? Every person has a right to be different and separate from all other individuals.

How often we have heard parents say in anger, "Why can't you be like your brother?" Or perhaps more often, "Why can't you be like your sister?" Or conversely they say, "You're just like your Aunt Lucy!" and the child knows that Aunt Lucy is the skeleton in the family closet. To force a child into any mold—whether the mold be good or bad—is wrong. Domination is never justified.

Dependence and independence

At birth a child is totally dependent on its mother, emotionally and physically. As he grows, that dependence diminishes until adulthood when the apron strings should be completely cut.

A parent can help a child move from complete dependence to independence by refraining from doing anything that he is capable of doing for himself. The other side involves not expecting him to do for himself what he is incapable of doing, thus destroying his self-confidence. To establish his capabilities at various ages, you may need to talk to other parents and children. Books are also helpful, especially *The Gesell Institute's*

Child Behavior by Frances L. Ilg, M. D. and Louise Bates Ames, Ph.D.

Normally an emotionally secure parent will gradually withdraw his control from a child as he grows older. It is unfortunate that some young people have to stage a major revolt before their parents discover that they have been holding the reins too tightly. No wonder the prophet Jeremiah said, "It is good for a man that he bear the yoke in his youth."

Now and later

A young child cannot project his plans or desires into the future. If you offer him the choice of a small sucker now or a big one tomorrow, he will take the small one now. He has not yet learned to endure the tensions of waiting. To mature, a child must learn how to restrain his desires for later fulfillment.

I recall how hard this was for my impetuous ten-year-old son. When he received his weekly allowance one Saturday, he told me that he was going to buy a pair of swimming goggles. I inquired as to the cost and found it to be his complete allowance. I told him that it would be up to him, but pointed out that if he bought the goggles he would have no money to go swimming at the pool. I recommended that he wait and save part of his money for the goggles, while using the rest for his swimming. After two or three weeks he would then have both.

"No, I'm going to buy them today," he said, and he did just that.

I don't think there has been a hotter July week in my experience. It was difficult to watch David sitting in the backyard wearing his swimming goggles while his friends went off to the pool. After many similar experiences over a number of years, David, now a father himself, learned not to sacrifice the future on the altar of the present.

Inability to wait damages lives. Young people can't wait until marriage to have sexual relations. A young man can't wait to have a car, so he quits school, jeopardizing his economic future. An immature married couple can't wait for luxuries, so they go deeply into debt.

These people have not learned to accept the tensions of waiting because their parents never denied them anything. How can Johnny be expected to wait for things if he has always had everything his little heart desired?

The Bible talks about the value of sowing a good harvest now and reaping later. It tells us to cast our bread upon the waters now and find it after many days, and to lay up treasure now and enjoy riches later.

Effort and reward

Some children are never given the thrill of putting forth effort and receiving the rewards of that effort—not only material reward but the deep satisfaction of accomplishment. Young people need to learn good work habits during childhood so that they will not expect rewards without effort.

Children also need to learn that certain kinds of actions bring bad consequences. Many times mothers whose sons have been convicted of a crime have tearfully asked, "Why would he do this when we have given him everything?"

Such mothers are answering their own question. A child who has been given everything has had no opportunity to develop responsible attitudes. Conversely, a youth who has never been allowed to reap the consequences of his own actions has had no opportunity to learn from his own mistakes.

At home mother protected him from father's discipline. At school she shielded him from his teachers and managed an "out" for him when he was about to reap the consequences of his insolence and laziness. Now that his impulsive behavior has finally brought him to the court, he is beyond his mother's protection and, for the first time in his life, must reap his own consequences. How much better for him to learn about such consequences at home.

Training a child socially involves teaching these all-important concepts of healthy social adjustment. They will be taught best by our living example.

THUNDERING DISOBEDIENCE

If the practice of obedience is at a low ebb these days, this may well be because far too many parents far too frequently set their children examples of disobedience.

Fathers who deliberately run red lights, exceed speed limits (and then announce that they'll "beat the rap" because they know the right people), ought not to be too surprised if a teenaged son or daughter of theirs someday lies crushed among a mass of twisted steel on some lonely rain-washed country road.

Mothers who lie for their children (Suzy was too sick to do the assignment!) in order to relieve them of a temporary inconvenience are setting a very poor example of obedience to God's commands.

Statistics prove that there is a direct proportion between the increase in school absenteeism and adult absenteeism from work. The employee who blithely calls in sick because he simply doesn't feel like working should not be horrified if his son or daughter stays away from school without any legitimate reason whatsoever.

Obedience, it needs to be said, is a virtue that is not restricted to any one age bracket. Parents would do well to consider—even as they rant and rave about the disobedience and waywardness of children and teenagers—that their examples thunder so loud that their children often can't really hear what they are saying. LEONARD J. FICK

Am I my child's crutch?
Marguerite and Willard Beecher

A child who makes a problem out of eating or any other natural function is a child who is emotionally dependent and is using his parents as a crutch. Most parents have been defeated in helping the whole child because they have tried to cure the symptom currently presented. There is no way for a parent to "cure" bed-wetting, night terrors, or sleepwalking, by concentrating on these symptoms. Parents need to see the many other ways in which a child expresses his dependency during the whole day and night.

When is a symptom not a symptom of emotional crippling? How shall we differentiate a legitimate physical symptom from a similar symptom that indicates emotional disaster on the horizon? A child may begin vomiting as the first sign of a real illness. Or he may vomit over the days or years with no physical findings evident at any time. And sometimes symptoms make their first appearance with an illness but persist long after the child has been cured.

The big factor in differentiation lies in the question of the child's using the symptoms to get special help, preferment, and undue consideration in relation to those around him. Many children are chronically phlegmatic and listless at home and at school but can run like a deer to catch a fly ball in a baseball game. Many vomit daily in winter as a protest against school, but are miraculously well in summer. The symptoms must be fitted into the whole picture in order to understand when they are genuinely physical and when they constitute an evasion.

Parents have to view with new eyes the whole day and night as a continuum. If they do this, they find that their so-called single-problem children are depending on them all day long and also feel entitled to use them as crutches at night. They will find that the child who seems to have only one problem has many. Perhaps he fails to pick up after himself, cannot decide what to wear, forgets his hat and overshoes, dawdles in dressing, cries easily when disappointed, will not allow his door to be shut, is generally clumsy, as well as dozens of other things. Each of these little things is a trick device to compel the parent to be a crutch. Each is a way of domination. The bedwetting, nightmare, or sleepwalking is only the nighttime continuation of the same daytime aggression.

The child tries a bit of everything at one time or another. If he finds his parents ticklish at any point, he simply makes a note of this and employs those things that made the most impression.

Many counselors become fascinated with the kind of symptom a child presents and try to find specific causes for the symptom. They try to find out whether the child was frightened by a lion when he visited the zoo years before, or whether he may have heard his parents making love in bed at night. There is no limit to which some counselors will not go in conjuring up probable causes for the various symptoms children employ in their fight for domination of their parents.

It is not the lion at the zoo that causes the nightmare, and it isn't the creaking of the springs in the next bed. If the child is using any symptom—this one or that one—we may be sure he is doing so because he has tested it and found it strikes fear in the heart of the parent. In our civilization, for instance, the fear of sexual exploits is one of the strongest taboos we know, and therefore it is an ideal weapon for a child. However, most of the so-called sexual delinquents are children who have always managed to dominate their parents in one way or another and have found in sex the strongest of all weapons to use in their fight for dominance. These are the children who have been allowed to use parents as crutches in many areas of life and have had no training in self-reliance or independence.

If a parent has not already begun to train a child for self-sufficiency, there is no better time to begin than today! In the beginning, only one maxim needs to be kept in mind: No parent should do for a child anything that the child is physically old enough and able to do for himself. Even with children who are ill or with those who have cerebral palsy and similar organic handicaps, we must do less each day so that they will be obliged to learn how to help themselves more each day. They need to feel somewhat deprived so that they have the incentive to grow up.

Any display of anxiety on a child's part is apt to make today's parent have heart failure. This is one of the neatest tricks a child may employ. A couple of nightmares and sweats is almost a guarantee for a child who intends to keep a parent from winning independence and who intends to keep himself infantile. In such outbreaks, of course, there may be a physiological process at work, but one should also consider that there may be a psychological factor involved. Anything as dramatic as nightmares and night sweats that is purely physical would probably be accompanied by a temperature and would develop shortly into a recognized illness. But such occurrences, when psychologically based, find the child essentially well the following day—especially if there is something he wants to do that day.

Unbridled anger is the same sort of device. If we cater to each and every anxiety and temper outburst of a child, we lead him to consider that every person is an instrument for his convenience. As he grows older he will not find people outside his home who are willing to serve him in any such fashion. They will resent his attempts to cast them in such roles and will reject him justly. He, in turn, will call the world unjust because it does not heed him.

It might be well to tell the story of Tommy's temper tantrum. It gives us a succinct picture of how a child tests the whole surrounding terrain to find soft spots he can use for goofing. Tommy was four and the only child of wise parents. His mother was not the kind of gal to feed anyone's neurosis, not even Tommy's—if he thought of starting one. One afternoon she was visiting on the lawn with a neighbor who had a son Tommy's age. The children were playing together while the parents visited with each other. Suddenly the neighbor's boy threw a temper tantrum. Tommy watched in amazement as the child kicked and beat his fists and as the mother petted and placated him. Tommy's mother noticed his entranced interest and suspected he was putting this display away in his file cabinet of not-to-be-forgotten items. She was prepared, therefore, for what followed.

That night Tommy and his parents were eating dinner. Tommy got down from his chair to go across the living room to the bathroom. In the middle of the living room—in full sight, of course—he threw himself down on his belly and started screaming, just as his little friend had done. His father was taken by surprise and was halfway out of his chair when he caught a high-sign from his wife that he should not bite on this one! He sat back, and husband and wife continued their conversation as if nothing were happening there on the living-room rug. Poor Tommy was stranded out on a limb with his blooming temper tantrum!

Anyone who can recall the last temper tantrum he had, remembers that it was hard work! And additionally, it is certainly unprofitable for any actor to play to an empty house. Poor Tommy was spending energy without appreciation. It did not take him long to realize that the jig was up. In a few moments he reared up on his elbow as a prelude to standing up again. His mother heard him remark to himself as he did so, "Well, this isn't getting me anywhere! " With that, he went off to the bathroom as he had intended to do before the temptation to entrap his parents occurred to him. And so this little Columbus failed to land on his parents' territory and had to sail back to his own resources!

The yardstick for parents to keep in mind in establishing minimum demands should be based on training children to be more self-sufficient and helpful rather than permitting them to make unnecessary trouble for others. Unless this is done, a home is not a home; it is just a battleground.

What marriage preparation is necessary? *Anthony Florio*

The more mature a person is, the more successful his marriage is likely to be. Just what do we mean by mature? Maturity in the sense that we are thinking of is a relative thing. We may be mature enough at age six to enter school and attend to some of our needs like eating, dressing, etc., but we are not mature enough at that age to understand the high-school curriculum or to exercise complete control over all of our needs. Maturing is a process involving growth and, except in the physical sense, few if any of us ever achieve complete maturity on all levels of our personality.

But we do recognize that marriage requires a level of maturity that includes willingness to assume responsibility for our own actions, for our own welfare, plus the welfare of a mate and children. It includes vocational readiness, the ability to earn a living that will provide adequately for one's family. In some circumstances the parents of college-student married couples agree to pay their expenses until graduation. This situation requires a level of maturity that will enable both young people to strike a fine balance in their attitudes toward their helping parents.

A young person contemplating marriage ought to be mature enough to recognize his or her reasons for wanting to marry and to judge correctly whether those reasons are adequate. A girl who rushes into marriage to escape an unhappy home life isn't acting responsibly. After marrying, the probability is that there will be two unhappy individuals. Or the couple who do not love each other, who have nothing in common, whose dispositions clash, who come from totally different backgrounds frequently marry when the girl finds she is pregnant. They marry "for the sake of the child" and condemn that child to emotional crippling. This is immature reasoning and irresponsible behavior.

A very young couple have not lived long enough to experience many of the situations that alone can teach them mature responses. So when parents, or pastors, or professional counselors advise against early marriage or teen marriage, the reason may not be merely because you are too young, but that you are not yet mature enough to handle all that is implied in the marriage relationship.

Marriage means responsibility

What do we mean by this phrase, "all that is implied in the marriage relationship"? In spite of the impression given by advertisers, TV, movies, and popular fiction, you won't spend most of your married life in bed or sitting on a couch holding hands. Your wife won't look great in a bathing suit forever. Your husband may go without a shave or leave his dirty socks on the floor. And there may be times when you'd like to give your children back.

Children? But you may be planning to marry in your teens, grow up together (there's no satisfactory way of doing this without putting enormous strain on the marriage), and avoid having a family until you've outgrown your immaturity and are ready for parenthood. In spite of the Pill and the best intentions, brides do get pregnant, and successful parenthood requires more than the ability to procreate, to prepare a formula, and to change diapers.

When you bring into the world another human being, he will also be a living soul, one who will have the opportunity to accept eternal life through his relationship with Jesus Christ, or who will forfeit that experience and be separated eternally from God, through his unwillingness to believe. If you aren't mature enough to assume the role of a parent, then you are not mature enough for marriage.

Qualities that help make a good marriage

The more alike people are intellectually, ethnically, socially, educationally, athletically, spiritually, etc., the easier their marital adjustment will be.

I'm thinking now in terms of positive qualities. The old saying that opposites attract may be true, but this need not be a barrier to a happy marriage so long as the opposite qualities are in those areas where they will function as complementary to each other, rather than promoting discord, or where the opposite negative quality in one partner is not in a crucial area and can be gradually modified with adequate motivation and understanding.

Danger signs. Blinking red lights mean STOP, then proceed with caution (if at all!). It is better to take this brief test before you become engaged so that if definite danger signs turn up you will have time to do something about them before committing yourself officially to marriage plans.

1. A general uneasy feeling about the relationship. Lack of inner peace. A nagging, aching, disturbing feeling inside that says, "Something is wrong."

2. Frequent arguments. Never sure how the date will end. More fighting than fun.

3. Avoiding discussing sensitive subjects because you're afraid of hurting your partner's feelings or starting an argument.

4. Getting more involved physically. You resolve to limit the acceleration of your physical intimacy, but find that on each new

date you start again at the place where you left off. Just one of the reasons for this being a danger sign is that your relationship may remain on the physical level only, throughout your courtship and marriage. After you're married you may not like the personality that goes along with the body.

5. If you find yourself always doing what your partner wants you to do. Constantly giving in, being accommodating. This could indicate a selfish, domineering partner and/or a serious insecurity on your part.

6. If you detect serious emotional disturbances such as extreme fears, extreme shyness, bizarre behavior, irrational anger, inflicting physical injury, inability to demonstrate affection.

7. If you feel you are staying in the relationship through fear. For example, if thoughts like these go through your mind: "I wish I could get out of dating him, but I'm afraid of what he might do to me. Or he might commit suicide."

8. If your partner is constantly complaining about apparently unreal aches and pains and going from doctor to doctor.

9. If your partner continually makes excuses for not finding a job, or borrows money from you frequently.

10. If your partner is overly jealous, suspicious, questions your word all the time, feels that everyone is against him.

11. If the one you date is a perfectionist and is constantly critical.

12. Treats you contemptuously. Uses biting sarcasm.

13. Parents and other significant people are strongly against your marriage. Consider their reasons before you make a final decision.

14. Lack of spiritual harmony.

15. Few areas of common interest.

16. Inability to accept constructive criticism. Doesn't apologize when he is wrong.

Visits. I hope that you and your partner have had opportunities to visit in each other's homes before your engagement. This is the time to see your intended mate in his or her home surroundings and within the family circle. Couples need to be aware that there are three families involved in this new relationship of marriage. Many of the parents' traits will be imbedded in your mate and he or she may be inclined to perpetuate the kind of home that has become familiar.

Your future. It is also important in premarital counseling for me to find out to what extent the couple have discussed housing, finances, and family planning. Will the wife continue to work after marriage and if so, how does the man feel about this? What are their mutual interests, their hobbies, their level of education, their attitudes toward sex, toward authority? How do they feel about each other's friends and relatives? Do I detect the possibility of a power struggle between them? If they are Christians, to what extent are they committed to Christ? Are they concerned about being controlled by the Holy Spirit? Or is one content to be merely a churchgoer? As a couple are they praying seriously about their coming marriage?

Last chance! If you haven't asked yourself the following questions prior to your engagement, the engagement period is your last chance to ask them.

1. Why am I going to get married to this person?

2. If this person had no sexual appeal to me, would I still feel that he or she would make a good friend whose companionship I would enjoy and whose conversation wouldn't bore me?

3. Will this person make a good parent for my children?

The only valid reason for anyone to get married is "because I believe God wants me to spend the rest of my life with this person whom I love and respect and these are his reasons also." This means exactly what it says —the rest of your life. Not "till misunderstandings do us part," or until he or she loses physical attractiveness, or until I find someone better, or until I'm tired of responsibility and decide to enjoy my freedom.

Marriage is both high privilege and solemn responsibility—and a call to an adventure in abundant living under the Lordship of Jesus Christ.

"I am come that they may have life, and that they might have it more abundantly" (John 10:10).

Many a marriage could be saved by humor—true humor, not the sadistic variety. Children's minds could be the storehouse of pleasant memories if their experiences within the family circle, and with friends and relatives, involved wholesome play, clever repartee, games on their level, the give-and-take of kidding around, and the prank that does not lower the other person's self-esteem.

If play takes its rightful place in family schedules, if unpredictable episodes of playfulness are permitted, and if aspects of humor which are misunderstood or cruel are screened out, the Christian family can be spontaneous in this manner as well as Christian in crusading against evil. R. LOFTON HUDSON

Should our teenager marry? from *Seventeen*

Dear Kit,

Your breathless letter arrived this morning, and to tell the truth, although it caused my coffee to get cold, I wasn't too surprised by it. Ever since you went back to boarding school, your mother and I have had the feeling that you and Bob might want to get married this summer, after graduation. And now you have told us.

You ask, a bit apprehensively, how I feel about it. Well, not as automatically negative as you probably expect. A lot of teenage marriages fail—one out of two, according to the gloomy statistics. But that means half of them make it, too. I don't think that age is the key factor. There's a lot of growing to be done in any marriage, whether you start at sixteen or sixty. The big question is whether or not circumstances exist that make such growth possible.

Let's take a long, cool look at the plusses and minuses of teenage marriages. The biggest plus is that marriage is the best solution to that most ancient and urgent of problems: sex. Marriage solves the thorny dilemma of will-we-or-won't-we, should-we-or-shouldn't-we. Nobody should underestimate this, because sex without fear or guilt is ten thousands times better than sex that is hung up in the brambles of lacerated consciences.

A second great advantage is flexibility. Your personalities aren't fixed; your attitudes aren't rigid; you can adapt—to each other, to new environments, to new problems. You have a kind of buoyancy, an optimism that assumes things are going to work out, or that even if they don't, the errors can be corrected. A lot of people lose this exuberance as they grow older; but while it lasts, it's worth its weight in diamonds.

Another plus is that when you marry young, you have tremendous physical energy, inexhaustible vitality.

And, finally, you have a superabundance of romantic love. Cynics are always pointing out that this isn't enough, in the long run, to make a marriage go—and maybe they're right. But nothing on earth is so exciting and mysterious and rewarding—nothing, really, is so encouraging about the human race—as this first, almost unbearably sweet desire to escape from the prison of self and become part of another person. And certainly most very young marriages have this quality to the highest degree, untarnished by any other motives whatsoever.

After all the good things have been said about teenage marriage, though, some other things must be said, too—about the pitfalls and hazards. Last year I talked with the presiding judge of a California Domestic Relations Court, and he listed the five factors —the five deadly factors, he called them— most likely to bring these marriages crashing down: 1) Money troubles; 2) immaturity; 3) cultural gap; 4) interfering in-laws; 5) premarital pregnancy.

I can see you scowling indignantly at No. 5. All right, we'll eliminate it. (We're lucky to be able to do so. Researchers tell us that more than half of the teenage brides are pregnant. With built-in resentment on both sides, and hostile pressures from society, the rate of failure for such more-or-less-forced unions is very high.)

But how do you and Bob stack up against the other hazards? Let me try to rate you on the basis of 100 points—twenty-five in each area.

Take money troubles, for instance. According to a University of Michigan study, half of all teenage married couples have a net worth of less than $250, a pitiful and frightening figure. Teenage husbands who work earn, on the average, less than $2500 a year. This means no margin for error, no margin for fun, for illness, or for a baby. It usually means living with one set of in-laws or the other. It all adds up to Trouble, with a great big menacing T.

You say that you could go to work and be the breadwinner while Bob continues his education. That may be more noble than wise: I'm pretty sure both of you couldn't survive on your earnings. Besides, one day you might wish you had gone on to college yourself.

If Bob gets a subsidy from his parents, or from us, it will mean that he isn't really the head of his household. He'll still be a dependent, subject to certain pressures and controls. So, where the hazard of money is concerned, I don't think that you and Bob would score higher than ten out of a possible twenty-five. Sorry 'bout that!

Now, how about immaturity? I suppose by that the judge meant self-centeredness, inability to compromise, to rise above hurt feelings, to postpone immediate pressures in favor of future benefits, or to do unpleasant chores when they need to be done—that sort of thing.

Well, my feeling is that none of us is ever fully mature. Trying to be is a lifetime job. We all start out more accustomed to getting than giving, to putting our own interests and desires first. To make the switch to a degree of selflessness—at any age—takes intelligence, patience, time. I think that you and Bob have the intelligence; I think that with time you can learn the patience. So here I'd award you twenty points of a possible twenty-five.

Cultural gap was next on the judge's list. If the marriage partners come from noticeably different cultural levels, problems are not just probable—they're inevitable. There may be differences in speech, food, customs, the kind of people you're comfortable with. In one family, people may enjoy discussing abstractions; in another, such matters never find expression.

These considerations are real, and the judge warns against letting a strong biological attraction blot them all out. Sometimes, he told me, when he has a chance to do premarital counseling, he advises the youngsters to try an experiment: spend twenty-four hours in each other's homes with no romancing or physical contact at all. If boy and girl can force themselves to be observant, and remain pleased with each other's family and way of life, then there's hope for the future.

How would you and Bob rate here? Very high, I'd say, except for one thing: difference of religion. He's Catholic; you're Protestant. No doubt you have discussed this, and feel that it offers no obstacle. But it might later on. Let's score you twenty out of twenty-five.

The fourth deadly factor is interfering in-laws. Where young marriages are concerned, all too often in-laws criticize, meddle, make demands. Well, I don't think your parents are much like that, or Bob's either. Oh, I'll admit that when I got your letter, something in me balked. A whole crowd of instincts shouted, "Hey, wait a minute!" But this reaction is just a form of protective affection. The father has been his daughter's protector for so long that he doesn't want to hand the role over to some semi-stranger who looks as unready to him as he once looked to his father-in-law. A wise daughter won't resent this; she'll just work her way around it with the patient determination that all women have when they really want something. So, where the in-law problem is concerned, take twenty of the possible twenty-five points.

That gives you a total score of seventy out of 100. A passing grade? Yes, but just barely. Which brings me to a question that you will not like, but which needs to be asked: Why don't you wait a while?

I can hear your anguished protest, see Bob's frown. I know in advance your reply: that you have found the perfect mate, that you haven't the slightest interest in anyone else, that in a year—or twenty years—you'll feel exactly the same.

Yet a year from now, inconceivable though it may seem to you, one of you may have had a change of heart. I'm not saying that this will happen; what I'm saying is that a waiting period would be a solid test of the durability of your affection, which hasn't been tested very thoroughly so far. Maybe you don't owe any such test to your parents. Perhaps, however, you owe it to each other.

Sometimes the growth of the durable, lasting kind of love can begin better outside the tensions and pressures of marriage than in them. Why don't you and Bob let yourselves grow a bit inside the framework of your love before making a final commitment to it? Waiting can be hard, I know. But a fairly long engagement can also be, especially for the girl, a wonderful time of romance, of dreams, of slowly unfolding intimacy. Such a time— without dishes to wash, bills to pay, or diapers to change—can ultimately be rewarding beyond measure. This is something our modern world seems to have forgotten in its clamor for all-of-everything-right-away.

Whether you take this advice or not, you may be sure of one thing: nothing is going to change the way I feel about you.

I remember very well the night you were born almost eighteen winters ago. It was the darkest pre-dawn hour, the hospital was very quiet, and suddenly I heard a baby's cry—one sharp, poignant, far-off sound. The delivery room was far down the corridor, through two or three sets of doors, and I should not have been able to hear anything at all. But something in me knew that that cry was you. And it was. Since then I've always liked to think that no matter what happened, or how much time flowed by, or how many doors came between, we'd always be able to hear each other. Sentimental maybe, but somehow I think it's true.

Love always,
Dad

Education must give much more attention to specific preparation for married life and parenthood. A good many people, and not all of them young, are insufficiently prepared for the shoals of married life. They are surprised by tensions and crises, and they do not know how to meet them. Some people do not realize that tensions and crises are necessary parts of married life, that they are inevitable in even the most harmonious marriage. They do not know that it is of the essence of a good marriage that crises arise and that they are overcome through the common effort of both parties to understand, to be patient, to endure, to stick together, and thus to grow to ever fuller understanding.

The development of the personality of a good citizen ought to be the principal aim of all education insofar as it concentrates on family problems. The task is twofold: to build up character and impart knowledge ... What is needed is a school curriculum in which education for family living constitutes an integral part of all teaching, from nursery school all the way up to college. DR. MAX RHEINSTEIN

3

Sensible
Sexuality

Is sex education necessary?
Letha Scanzoni

During the reign of the emperor Nero, a writer named Patronius composed a classic comedy—*The Satiricon*—satirizing the morals of Rome. One scene can provide a lesson for parents and all others who are entrusted with the sex education of children and teenagers.

A husband and wife were deeply concerned about their son and wanted to shield him from sexual temptation, especially homosexual ones. Thus they placed the boy in the care of a man who had impressed them with his evident aversion to homosexual practices. They felt the boy's best protection from both knowledge and experience in sexual matters would lie in having a constant chaperone.

But the tutor himself took advantage of the boy's innocence and introduced him to the very experiences from which the boy's parents had hoped to shield him.

There have been many parents who thought they could help their children best by sheltering them from knowledge of sex. I think of the father who took his children out of Sunday school when he heard that a lesson made mention of circumcision. I think of the mother who was shocked when her daughter excitedly told of a film she'd seen at school. It showed how a baby comes from a tiny ovum within the mother. "Just think, I was once a little egg like that," exclaimed the girl. But the mother's reaction was one of dismay, and she began phoning neighbors to start a campaign to take sex education classes out of the school. This child, who had been on her way to a positive, wholesome outlook on sex, ceased to share her feelings with her mother. During her high school years, the girl became pregnant and dropped out of school to get married.

When we try to shield youngsters from sexual knowledge, we are actually failing them —handing them over to other, often misleading, sources of information. How much better that we ourselves as Christian parents provide them with information and guidance given in the context of a vital faith in God and undergirded by the teachings of his word.

Back to Patronius' sexually explicit satire on the society of imperial Rome. It's important to see how mistaken are our notions that children in our day are exposed to the topic of sex to a greater degree than at any previous time in history. Patronius was writing his *Satiricon* at the very time many of the New Testament epistles were being written. In other words, this is what life was like in the long ago world of Bible times. And yet God expected his people to live up to his standards and to train their children likewise. "You must abstain from fornication; each one of you must learn to gain mastery over his body" (1 Thessalonians 4:3, 4, NEB).

Think of the world of the Old Testament. The ancient Israelites were surrounded by nations of idol worshipers whose worship centered around fertility cult practices. Ritualistic sexual orgies were held. Temples employed prostitutes, and sex acts were part of the religious ceremonies held therein. Images of the male and female genitals were publicly displayed for purposes of idol worship. Yet, in such a setting God said, "You shall love the Lord your God . . . And these words which I command you this day shall be upon your heart, and you shall teach them diligently to your children, and shall talk of them when you sit in your house, and when you walk by the way, and when you lie down, and when you rise . . . You shall not go after other gods, of the gods of the peoples who are round about you . . ." (Deuteronomy 6:5–7, 14, 15, RSV).

Children were to learn to reject the sexual idolatry and values of the people round about at the same time they were to learn obedience and loyalty to the Lord God in their midst. God is saying the same thing to us today. It is not a matter of shielding and protecting our children or trying to hide our heads in the sand or run away from the kind of emphasis on sex we sometimes see in today's world. We need to face life as it is, not with fear but with confidence, believing that God wants to answer the prayer of Jesus, "I do not pray that thou shouldst take them out of the world, but that thou shouldst keep them from the evil one" (John 17:15, RSV).

The world

If we are to give our children adequate sex education, we must know something of the world in which they are growing up. What are the sexual values being presented by the mass media? To what extent is sexual activity outside of marriage taking place? What kinds of questions about sex are being raised? We need to prepare ourselves to help our children develop discernment with regard to materials to which they are exposed in these times—to guide them so that they can learn to view matters from a distinctly Christian perspective.

We need to be aware of research findings. For example, a study by two social scientists from Johns Hopkins University. One of the most striking findings of this reseach was that sexual activity is beginning at younger ages. If premarital intercourse is increasing among teenagers, Christian parents have all the more reason to provide a good, sound sex education long before their youngsters reach the adolescent years.

We must also be aware of the rethinking that is going on about sexual attitudes and behaviors. For example, some young people feel that sexual intercourse should be reserved for marriage but any other sexual behavior is permissible beforehand. Thus, petting practices are widespread, including breast and genital contact and petting to orgasm. In my book *Sex Is a Parent Affair,* I tried to provide some guidelines for parents and teenagers in thinking through this subject in a Christian perspective, and that's the issue of "technical virginity."

We should also be aware of two principal outlooks on sex that are espoused by many today. One is the playboy view. Sex is fun and that should be all that matters. In the other view, if two persons are relating to each other as whole persons and are not exploiting each other but simply want to express their love, then sexual intercourse could be all right in their particular circumstances, even though they aren't married to each other.

Christian parents and leaders need to be prepared to answer the arguments of this second view in particular, because I'm finding in traveling around the country speaking to high school and college men and women that a significant number of Christian young people are taking it very seriously. We have to help young people understand what God's plan for marriage is and how sex fits into this plan.

Many sex education opportunities come our way simply through the television set, newspapers, and magazines. In our home over the years, the mass media presentations of sexual subjects have stimulated many fascinating discussions with our sons on such topics as transsexual surgery, prostitution, homosexuality, living together outside of marriage, abortion, venereal diseases, rape, childbirth, nude bathing, to mention just a few of the topics that have come up.

By taking advantage of the opportunities provided by what our children see and read and wonder about, we can prepare them for many of the questions and decisions about sex that they will face later.

The Word   The Bible was never squeamish about sex. It is frank and forthright, and has far more to say on the subject than most people realize. The foundation for sex education lies in the story of creation in Genesis 1, 2—that God made us and God loves us. Children can learn how wonderful God's design of the human body is, the way our eyes and ears work, the way babies grow, the way cuts heal, and so on. We can help our children see that God made two different kinds of bodies for people—male bodies and female bodies. Parents and children can talk about some of these differences. God has designed the bodies of women and men so that they can fit together in a special way. God planned that in this way husbands and wives could have babies.

Children can learn these things gradually— not all at once, but in building block fashion as parents are alert to questions and curiosity at different ages. Parents can talk about these matters in natural fashion all day long, while walking with their children, while observing animals and birds, or while reading Bible stories together. For example, try to get your children to talk about why God told Noah to put a male and a female of each animal in the ark. They can be helped to see that sex is beautiful and good as God intended it. It is not something to be ashamed of or afraid of. No parts of our bodies are dirty or bad. God made

our bodies, every part, and what he made is
very good.

As parents study Scripture and learn that
joyous sexuality is part of God's intention for
marriage, they can become comfortable with
their own feelings about sex and better able to
convey the scriptural sense of wonder to
children approaching adolescence. Passages
like the Song of Solomon and Proverbs 5:18,
19 emphasize the utter delight in one another
and the joy and playfulness of the marital
embrace as husband and wife express their
love physically. 1 Corinthians 7:3, 4 speaks of
the equality of the sexual relationship and
recognizes that both women and men have
sexual desires—and both partners in a
marriage have a responsibility to meet the
sexual needs of the other. These are topics
about which there is a great deal of discussion
today and parents can help their teenagers
especially to see that the Bible addresses itself
to these matters, including female sexuality,
quite clearly.

And then there are the warnings about
misusing God's good gift of sex. In Hebrews
13:4, we are told that marriage is something
good and honorable and that sex is a
wonderful, important part of marriage. But at
the same time, God will judge those who
engage in fornication and adultery. This
passage is a combination of the positive and
the negative, and we must keep the two in
balance. We must also make sure the children
don't get the idea that sex sins are the worst
kinds of sins, and emphasize God's forgiveness
of those who have not obeyed his
commandments, who are sorry and tell him so.

What we must convey to our children is that
Christian sex ethics are Christ-centered. We
belong to our Lord and want to please him in
our sex life as well as in all other areas of life.

Only then can we experience life at its best, life abundant, and true sexual freedom.

The works   And now a look at the works of God. The design of the human body is marvelous. No wonder the psalmist cried, "O Lord, how manifold are thy works! In wisdom hast thou made them all" (Psalm 104:24). If parents are going to do a good job of sex education in the home, they should be studying the male and female reproductive systems and preparing in advance for their children's questions—including knowing the correct names for the various parts of the body and being able to explain how they work.

I'd like to close with an excerpt from *Sex Is a Parent Affair:*

Many parents are able to answer the earliest questions about reproduction without embarrassment. But it's the big question, "How does the daddy put the sperm cell in the mommy?" that makes parents nervous, flustered and tongue-tied. Such fears and nervousness should not be necessary. Simply explain that God has designed the father's body so that sperm cells are made in a little bag of skin that hangs between his legs. God has also designed the father's penis so that it will fit into a special opening in the mother's body, the vagina. Because a husband and wife love each other, they want to be as close together as possible. God designed their bodies to fit together just perfectly. At special times as they lie together in bed, husband and wife show their love for each other by joining together. The father places his penis into the mother's vagina, and sperm cells pass through his penis into the vagina and then swim up into the uterus and tubes where they may meet a tiny egg cell. If a sperm joins with an egg, a baby begins to grow inside the wife.

When a husband and wife show their love in this special way, it's called sexual intercourse, or sex relations. God's design of male and female bodies to fit together this way is really very marvelous and nothing to be ashamed of. Of course, sexual intercourse is more than fitting together and it's also more than procreation. At the appropriate time, you can explain that husbands and wives like to show their love in this special way. Perhaps you can say, "You know how you like that happy, warm feeling of being cuddled and told we love you. Look how many times you say, 'Hug me, Mommy,' or 'Squeeze me real tight, Daddy.' Well, it's something like that with a husband and wife. They love each other very, very much. They like to hug and kiss and be real close to each other. God made their bodies a special way so that they can be so close, it's like being one person—because that's what God said being married is supposed to be like. Although married couples show their love in lots of other ways, God planned sexual intercourse as a very special way of showing their oneness."

This then is one way that we can handle sex questions in the light of our Christian faith. It is a way of helping our youngsters know that the Lord is good. Sex education in the home is a privilege and a challenge. May God help us to creatively take hold of that privilege and respond to that challenge because we love him and because we love our children.

Can sex really be taught at home? *Dr. Kenneth Gangel*

One of the features which makes the home such a viable context for sex education is the frequent happening of events which provide a significant stimulus for good sex education.

A new baby in the home or neighborhood. As a pregnancy becomes obvious, it is natural for children in the family to ask questions. How foolish are the answers given by many Christian parents in their attempts to avoid the subject, when all they need to say is, "God is making a baby grow inside mother." The enthusiasm with which mom and dad await the arrival of the new baby, and their verbalizations of what is happening, provide at least a six month course in sex education with attitudes being formed every day.

Common terminology such as "labor pains" may even prejudice a little girl negatively toward the experience she anticipates in the future. Some Christian psychologists suggest that children be allowed to observe breast-feeding while having explained to them precisely how God ordained this form of physical nurture.

Observing parents or other children bathing, toileting, etc. If junior takes a shower with dad he will very quickly ask the meaning of parts of the male body and how they are different from the bodily parts of little sister and mommy. There are perfectly good answers for such questions and no Christian father should be embarrassed to give them, and give them accurately.

Care of pets. Why does the dog need to be penned up when she is in heat? What about the process of the delivery of that calf? Why do rabbits have so many babies? Every question is a beautiful opportunity for the explanation of not only animal biological fact, but the parallel explanation of the growth of the family in love.

When children use sex words. Sometimes such a word may have no meaning at all for the child. He just heard the boys on the street use it, and so he used it at home. Rather than rushing for the soap to administer just punishment for such "dirty talk," the parent should view this as a golden opportunity to explain the word and the proper context for its use. The administration of the soap may extinguish all further uses of the word, but it also might extinguish any willingness to discuss words and concepts of a similar nature with parents.

After attending a wedding. Christian weddings are full of symbolism. Just like many of the feasts in the Old Testament, the symbolism can be used as an educational catalyst. Why is white always used in a wedding? Why does the groom kiss the bride only once in the ceremony, and why does he do it in front of all those people? Why do brides and grooms exchange rings at the wedding? Why did the bride carry a Bible? Why do people give gifts? How much more significant a motivator for education is the wedding than the classroom!

Observing his own body. Totally apart from seeing the anatomy of other persons, the child will soon raise questions about his own body. Sometimes his observation is physical rather than verbal as parents notice him playing with parts of his body. Rather than slapping hands and building in a negative disposition toward sex organs, the parents can explain why it is improper to engage in that sort of behavior, and how God has ordained a significant use for the sex organs.

Mass media and books. Almost all children

watch television. Even in Christian homes where the controls on what is watched may be carefully exercised, there will be ample opportunity in the most innocent and wholesome of programs for children to observe behavior and incidents which can and will trigger questions about sex. There is no point in trying to keep the child away from all such influences. Parents should recognize in them what professional educators call "teachable moments" and be ready to capture them for the purposes of Christian nurture.

Formal instructional times. Probably 90 percent of all the child learns about sex will take place in informal questions and situations such as those described above. There ought to be, however, a definite effort on the part of the parents to program into the life of the home periods of sex education which are deliberately constructed for that purpose. These need not be classroom sessions in which a child sits and listens to a lecture nervously delivered by one of the parents. Perhaps they will consist of deliberately planned conversations between father and son or mother and daughter; the showing of filmstrips such as those produced in conjunction with the Concordia Sex Education Series; the reading and discussion of literature written for children and young people on the subject of Christian education; and attending formal sex education classes in church or Christian school.

Principles for Christian sex education

There is no principle more significant than that biblical love must be the cradle for sex education if the baby is going to grow up healthy and normal. Christian love is a clearly defined biblical attitude and not an emotion. Once that context has been clearly formulated, then the rest of the task becomes relatively easy, providing the Christian keeps himself informed and observes some guidelines for sex education in the home.

Always encourage open communication in the home. Don't slap mouths, don't censure statements, don't inhibit the child's natural expression of his thoughts to his parents. Obviously we are not advocating here a continual receptivity to the behavior of children when that behavior has been expressly condemned over a period of time. The focus here is on spontaneous outbursts of sexual words, phrases, or ideas which children will emit from time to time.

Answer all questions directly, honestly, and simply. Do not provide more information than that for which the child has asked. One of the myths of sex education is that fathers should always answer the questions that boys ask and mothers should always answer the questions that girls ask. Actually both parents should be willing to answer either child, because each parent is the parent of all his children. As the children grow older they will tend to gravitate toward the parent of the same sex with their questions. In the early days, however, the children should get the impression that sex is an open subject in the family and that either parent can speak with authority on the issues.

Always exercise positive parental example. Rather than shouting at each other, affection should be seen between parents, the enjoyment of being close, embracing frequently— impressing the observing children that tenderness and warmth go hand in hand in the relationship between husband and wife. Children who observe this normal behavior frequently in the home will not be embarrassed when they see it and will tend to accept it and emulate it as the natural course of events in the Christian home, which of course, it should be.

Teach sex positively, not negatively.
Children and young people should look
forward with pleasure to marriage, child-
bearing, and the other sexual aspects of
parenthood. The mother whose unhappy
marital experience causes her to say to her
daughter, "You can never trust a man," is
leading her daughter to the very unfortunate
experiences she would like her to avoid. The
dad who is observed by his young son reading
Playboy may discover that his son develops a
philosophy in which he thinks of women as
property rather than people.

Be spiritual and biblical throughout.
Children should understand the why of
Christian marriage, not only the what and the
how. Sex education is meaningless unless it is
based on the principle that marriage exists
primarily for fellowship between the husband
and the wife which is parallel to the
communion between Christ and His church.

Be casual and informal. Sex is a natural
and common part of living. It only takes on
grotesque and unnatural forms when we
superimpose those forms upon it. Sex
education should not be stimulating to older
children and teens, but rather just as normal
as learning other kinds of behavior patterns
essential to life. Furthermore, the proper
response of the sexes to each other is a genuine
pleasure and it doesn't have to be treated in a
sanctimonious, hyper-Puritanism which locks
its secrets in a golden box. Such an attitude
too often discovers that the box turns out to be
Pandora's.

*Use scientific terms for the parts of the
body.* Parents who propagate myths about
childbirth or make up strange and
meaningless names for parts of the body will
soon discover that a credibility gap develops
with respect to sex education and the

confidence which children have in the parent's authority to speak on the subject. Only perverted people say that sex is basically wrong. How foolish to adopt this strange nomenclature for parts of the body when accurate terminology does exist. By what strange contortion of truth are these words thought to be spiritual?

Base your biology on sound Christian theology. Any education which does not recognize the fact that all men are the creation of the sovereign self-revealed God must eventually distort a truthful view of sex education at best, and turn it into nothing more than animal biology at worst. Such errors should never be propagated in the Christian home and do not have to be if the evangelical church will shoulder its responsibility in ministering to the whole man and therefore provide programs in biblical sex education for its people.

Numerous studies over the past quarter century have shown that persons who have had no sexual experience prior to marriage have had happiest marriages. A new study made at Pennsylvania State University confirms these findings by a different approach, using an extensive and well-validated test that predicts marital happiness. David F. Shope and Carlfred B. Broderick studied eighty girls who were contemplating marriage and who were virgin. They were compared with eighty girls who had been sexually active. Both in the qualities found by the test to be associated with marital happiness, and those associated with good sexual adjustment, the virgins made definitely higher scores.

How do I answer those sex questions? *W. Cleon Skousen*

When a child asks, "Where do babies come from?" his folks must not assume that this is merely morbid curiosity. Questions about babies are normal at four; often they come even earlier, so a parent needs to be prepared. It helps to keep in mind that such questions are desirable and wholesome at this age. It is an excellent opportunity to begin cultivating sensible attitudes in little people.

A child's education involves two fronts. First, he wants to know the plain, simple facts. Secondly, he wants to know the meaning or interpretation of those facts.

These are some of the questions which most children ask while learning about sex. The suggested answers follow each question:

1. *Where do babies come from?* They come from their mothers. They grow in a special place in the mother's body which is called the uterus. The baby starts out as a tiny cell and then gradually grows until it is ready to eat food and breathe air; then it is born.

2. *How does the little cell which grows into a baby get into the mother?* A baby grows from a cell which was already in the mother's body. It is called an egg cell or an ovum. Egg cells are produced in the mother's body by two small glands called ovaries.

3. *How does the baby get out?* Babies are born through a special passageway in the mother's body called the vagina.

4. *How does the egg cell know when to start growing into a baby? Can a mother just start making a baby any time she wants to?* No, a mother has to wait until a sperm cell is given

to her by the father. It is the sperm cell from the father which joins with the egg cell to start the baby growing.

5. *How does the mother know when the baby is ready to be born?* She can tell by the movement of the muscles in her body which are getting ready to push the baby out into the world through the special passageway.

6. *Does it hurt to have a baby?* Yes, all of the muscles have to stretch and push to help with the baby's birth. The stretching and pushing is painful, but when it is all over and the mother gets to see her baby, she feels it was worth all the trouble and pain.

7. *When a baby is growing inside its mother, how does it breathe?* A baby doesn't have to breathe air until after it is born. Before birth it is able to get all the oxygen it needs through its mother.

8. *When a baby is growing inside its mother, how does it eat?* It doesn't have to eat because there is a little tube which connects the baby to its mother. When she eats, the food gives strength to her body and the nourishment which she has received passes through the little tube into the baby. This little tube is called the umbilical cord. It is attached to the baby's stomach at the navel or belly button.

9. *Why don't I have a tube attached to my belly button any more?* Because now that you have been born you can eat with your mouth, so you don't need to be fed through the tube any more. That is why the doctor took it away after you were born. Anyway, you couldn't eat ice cream and lots of good things through the little tube and enjoy it as you can when you eat it through your mouth. It is lots better this way now that you have been born.

10. *If the mothers have the babies, what are fathers for?* The mother can't start growing a baby unless the father gives her a sperm cell

from his own body. The mother can't grow a baby by herself. That's why fathers are so important. And anyway, while the mother is growing the baby she has to depend upon the father to go out and earn the living so the family will have a house to live in and food to eat. Fathers are very important.

The above questions usually come during the earlier stages of childhood. They are the questions children usually ask between four and eight. Beginning around eight or nine a child will ask these questions:

11. *Where do fathers grow sperm cells?* These are made in the testicles. However, boys do not grow sperm cells until they begin to grow up and are getting ready to be fathers.
12. *How does the father give the sperm cell to the mother and start the baby growing?* This is done during mating. The sperm passes from the testicles and up through the penis. It enters the vagina of the mother and then makes its way up through the uterus to the Fallopian tube, where it meets the egg cell or ovum and joins with it. This is called conception. (If you have a family doctor book, this process can be traced on the sketch of the female reproductive organs.)
13. *Where is the place where the baby grows?* A few days after the egg cell has been met by the sperm in the Fallopian tube, it slips down into the uterus or womb and attaches itself to the soft wall. That's where it grows into a baby—in the womb.
14. *How long does it take to grow a baby?* It takes nine months for the baby to develop fully. Kittens and puppies can be grown by their mothers in a lot less time.

Is our child a homosexual?
Barbara Wyden

When Tom Sandler came home from work,
his six-year-old son, Sandy, was sitting in the
middle of the living-room floor playing with
his sister's dolls. Mr. Sandler gave Sandy a big
coming-home hug and said, "Boys don't play
with dolls. Dolls are for girls."

After the children had gone to bed, Mr.
Sandler told his wife, "I'm worried about
Sandy. He shouldn't be playing with dolls. Do
you suppose he's going to grow up to be—you
know, queer?"

Mr. Sandler was needlessly worried. His
Sandy could not have been more "real boy."
Lots of little boys play with dolls at one time
or another, and parents needn't be upset about
this unless a youngster exhibits other, more
disturbing behavior.

Not so long ago, no father would have
dreamed of openly raising such a question.
But today—when the past Broadway season
produced four successful plays with
homosexual themes, when homosexuality is a
commonplace at the neighborhood movie
house, when *Time* magazine devotes a cover
story to the emergence of the homosexual into
our daily lives—Mr. Sandler's question is not
alarmist; it is pertinent. Young parents are as
concerned about a son's sexual development as
they are about his mental or physical
development.

A former president of the Association for
the Advancement of Psychoanalysis warned,
"The ideal of a healthy masculinity, which
combines strength and tenderness, is being
replaced by the image of an aggressive
supermale whose arrogant vindictiveness is
glorified as masculine. Today there is a taboo
not only on tenderness but on sensitivity and

creativity, and the man who is interested in art, music, and writing automatically decreases in value as a male."

No mother or father sets out to bring up a boy to be a homosexual, but sometimes parents, because of their own unresolved sexual or emotional problems, unwittingly push a boy toward homosexuality.

The stories of Herbert and Albert, two boys whose lives were strikingly similar in some aspects—and significantly different in others—illustrate many of our misconceptions about true masculinity and some of the ways parents may divert a son from a normal heterosexual future as a husband and father.

Herbert Bonsall was born while his father was overseas in the Army, and he was two-and-a-half years old when Mr. Bonsall saw him for the first time. Mr. Bonsall had a hard time readjusting to civilian life. He criticized his wife for the way she dressed, handled her budget, and brought up Herbert. He told her she was "making a sissy out of the boy" and that he, as his father, was going to "toughen him up."

For example, he taught Herbert to swim by tossing him into a pool. After such treatment, some boys would never have learned even how to float, but Herbert became a proficient swimmer. When the boy was old enough, his father enrolled him in the Little League and would work out with him in the backyard every night after supper. It meant a lot to Mr. Bonsall when his son pitched a winning game. And Herbert soon learned to play to win. He desperately wanted his father's approval and did everything to win it.

In high school Herbert was the outstanding pitcher on the baseball team. He was a handsome, well-developed boy, and his ability to win games made him the hero of the school

every spring. But he was a strangely lonely
hero. The other boys on the team resented his
drive to win and complained that he was not
sportsmanlike. He had no close friends.

He was happiest at home. His mother never
criticized or pushed him, and she sympathized
with the rough time his father gave him on
weekends. Whenever she did things for
Herbert, whether it was baking his favorite
chocolate cake or buying him an expensive
sweater, she would always say, "Now, don't
tell your father. You don't want him to get
after us."

Now let's look at Albert's story. He was six
when his father died of hepatitis. The little
boy had adored his father and he took a long
time to adjust to the loss. From the time
Albert was in third grade, he had more
domestic responsibilities than most girls have
in their teens. He was a quiet boy and never
fussed about these tasks. In fact, he seemed to
enjoy cooking.

Albert's mother taught him to play the
piano and supervised his practice after supper.
He showed considerable talent. On weekends
his uncles took him bowling or fishing or
sometimes to a movie, but when Albert was
given a choice, he always asked to go to a
concert.

In high school Albert played in the school
orchestra and formed a rock-'n'-roll group
with two other boys. By playing at parties, he
made pocket money and a bit extra to put
aside for college.

Though names and details have been
disguised, these accounts contain the essence
of the atmosphere in which the two boys grew
up. A psychiatrist would have no trouble in
identifying the youngster who became a
homosexual. He was not quiet, artistic Albert,
but Herbert, the rugged, good-looking athlete.

The summer before Herbert went to college, he had his first homosexual experience with a young man he met while working as a lifeguard. At college he immediately formed another homosexual relationship. He has now dropped out of college and is living with an older man. He is now seeing a doctor regularly, but insists he is happy as he is and does not want to change.

"Herbert's is a typical case," the doctor explained. In the first place, his father was not much of a father. He resented his son and bullied him. He inspired fear in the boy—not love and admiration. The last thing in the world Herbert wanted to do was to grow up to be like his father.

"In the second place," the doctor continued, "Herbert had no friends. His father's insistence on winning made the boy so compulsive and ruthless about athletics that he alienated his teammates. So here again, he had no masculine models to identify with.

"Third, Herbert's mother treated him more as an ally and protector against her husband than as a son. Herbert was the only man in her life, and they were so isolated that the boy never had a chance to learn what normal family life is like. In fact, he met no male after whom he might have patterned himself.

"All these factors worked together to push Herbert over the brink."

What are parents to do? Happily, the most important factor in assuring that a boy will grow up to be heterosexual is the easiest to arrange, because it is so natural: Fathers should love their sons. A team of medical psychoanalysts, in reporting on their long-term landmark study of homosexuality, concluded, "A constructive, supportive father precludes the possibility of a homosexual son."

Fathers can take heart from the fact that

experts agree it is not the amount of time a man spends with his son that counts but the quality of that time. When a father is warmly concerned about his boy's welfare and enjoys doing things with him, he has the strongest possible guarantee that the boy will grow up feeling comfortable in his role as a male. And, by extension, the boy will feel comfortable with the opposite sex.

The child who grows up in an emotionally secure family will not be confused by what seems to be a blurring of sex roles. It will not seem contradictory if Father occasionally puts on an apron and tackles a mountain of dirty dishes, or if Mother gets out the stepladder and starts painting the living room—provided the work is done in a spirit of happy cooperation. But if Mother is domineering and orders her Milquetoast husband to do the dishes or else, or if Mother feels she is the only competent person in the household—that nobody will paint the walls or do anything if she doesn't do it herself—then a boy may find himself at sea.

A few guidelines may help to reassure anxious mothers and fathers.

—Children are tough. There is no need to weigh every word and action lest it damage a child's healthy sexual development. In this connection, parents should understand that a "seduction" attempt by an older man or boy will not turn a youngster into a homosexual.

—Parents should enjoy themselves. There will rarely be a problem involving sexual identification if Mother delights in her role as woman, wife, and mother; if Father shows his love for Mother and takes pride in his children.

Here are suggestions that will help parents move cautiously.

—Push, but not too hard. If a boy seems

reluctant, it is important to encourage activities that will involve him with other boys. These activities must be within his capabilities so that his self-esteem will be bolstered, not weakened.

—Go easy on the sex and venereal-disease lectures. Of course, these problems should be discussed, but not in a frightening manner.

—If you think your son has a sex problem, don't pry. Make yourself available and receptive so he can talk about any fears that inhibit him.

—If you think your son has a potential homosexual problem, go slow. The experts warn, "Don't lecture, don't investigate." An attempt to help may simply convince a boy that his parents think he really is a homosexual. Parents should try to figure out just what in the family situation may be causing his troubles. If possible, the boy might be encouraged to talk to a friendly outsider about his social life—not about his intimate emotional problems—so that he may reveal some of his worries. If these explorations indicate the possibility of deep problems, professional help should be made available.

Above all, parents should not get the idea that they are in danger of turning their sons into homosexuals just because they made some mistakes along the line. Dr. Irving Bieber says, "It's not easy to produce a homosexual. You've got to work at it."

Is masturbation sinful?
David A. Seamands

Although Menninger states that the taboo against masturbation vanished almost overnight at the turn of this century, the taboo about discussing it certainly did not. In spite of the fact that it is perhaps the most widely engaged in sexual activity, it is rarely talked about. It is a case where nearly everybody does it, but nobody talks about it. It has only been in the past few decades that even secular sources began to write about it, while up-to-date Christian discussion has been limited to recent years. Secular psychologists and psychiatrists tend to confuse the issue by making the term too inclusive, so a simple definition is in order.

Masturbation is deliberate and conscious self-stimulation so as to produce sexual excitement with the goal of orgasm. Whether or not the goal is achieved depends upon age and other factors, but it is certainly the ultimate aim of the sexual arousal. Masturbation can be observed in small children, but the chief period for it is during adolescence and early young adulthood. Without doubt it is the major sexual activity of teenagers.

Hulme quotes the old joke, "Ninety-nine out of a hundred teenage boys and girls masturbate and the other one's a liar." Just how widespread is it? For obvious reasons it is not possible to state with complete accuracy, but data derived from questioning thousands of people in clinical survey leaves no doubt that it is an extremely common practice among both males and females of all ages. The Sex Information and Education Council of the United States (SIECUS) says that about 90 percent for males and above 60 percent for females, over a period of time, is a realistic figure. Most experienced counselors would confirm similarly high percentages on the basis of their own records.

What should be the Christian attitude toward such a common practice? In the past it has been totally, almost violently, condemned without any open and adequate reasons given. Jack Wyrtzen's book on youth's purity problems is typical: ". . . secret sins. You know what I'm talking about—I don't have to spell it out; those vile, dirty, personal pollutions." One writer states he has seen a large roomful of university men praying for forgiveness and strength to resist this sin. With such a high percentage of active incidence among youth, how can any evangelist fail to fill the counseling room or altar when he cries out against "secret sins" or "lust in solitude"?

Modern evangelical Christian writers and counselors vary greatly in their attitude toward masturbation. Adams, in a chapter entitled "Masturbation Is Sin," condemns it *en toto* because of its enslaving nature and lustful thoughts, and says it is a perversion of the sexual act which is not presented as an option in the Bible. Bingham declares that it is an evil, but not wholly evil since it is a sin without the social consequences of other sexual sins. Miles has a detailed, thorough, and excellent examination of the subject, discussing when masturbation is sinful and when it is not. Vincent points out it is one of those gray areas for Christians and that each incident has to be treated individually. He comes out fairly close to Miles's conclusion. Hulme takes a similar position and seems to treat it as more immature than sinful. Shedd takes some of the above arguments and carries them further, saying that there are times when masturbation can be regarded as a gift from

God and a wise provision for growing up.

Let me now try to set forth my own conclusions on the subject, which are based on counseling uncountable numbers of people.

1. *There is no clear and direct word on masturbation anywhere in Scripture.* The two passages used in ancient times, Genesis 38: 8–11 and 1 Corinthians 6:9,10, have nothing to do with it. Onan's sin was his failure to obey the ancient Hebrew law by practicing *coitus interruptus,* and was not masturbation. The King James Version term "abusers of themselves," in the Corinthian list, was a mistranslation and is now correctly rendered "homosexuals" in all modern versions.

When we know how almost universal and ancient masturbation is (it is mentioned in the *Egyptian Book of the Dead,* circa 1550–950 B.C.), and when every other sexual sin such as fornication, adultery, homosexuality, bestiality are listed and clearly condemned, why is it—if it is always a sin—nowhere mentioned in the Bible? I realize the argument from silence is dangerous, but in the case of something so widespread and well-known it would seem to be conspicuous by its absence.

2. *From a scientific and medical standpoint we now know that there is no mental or physical harm in masturbating;* so there are no moral arguments for health reasons. All this means that we will have to use other related Christian principles in determining its rightness or wrongness.

3. *Therefore, I believe that the act of masturbation in itself is neither good nor evil.* What, then, determines this? Two basic Christian principles. First, *the thought-life.* When masturbation is accompanied by sexual fantasies, it clearly comes under the condemnation of Christ's words about

"mental adultery" in Matthew 5:27, 28, and is a sin. According to SIECUS, it is usually accompanied by such fantasies in three-fourths of males and half of females. However, I agree with Miles that the experience is possible without fantasy or lust, so that it cannot simply be taken for granted that it is always a lustful and thus a sinful act.

Second, *the social and relational life.* When masturbation, with or without lust, becomes an emotional substitute for proper interpersonal relationships, when it is used as a means of escaping from the pressures of loneliness, frustration, and depression, then there is no question that it is harmful to the person and therefore wrong from a Christian viewpoint.

Years of counseling has forced me to distinguish between masturbation as a temporary and occasional means of relieving normal sexual buildup (almost an inevitable part of normal growing up, particularly for teenage boys) and masturbation as a compulsive, enslaving habit which feeds, and is in turn fed by, deeper emotional hang-ups. Some of these would include an inability to relate to any person—especially those of the opposite sex—depression, deep-seated resentments, and the inability to find normal ways of coping with frustration and anxiety. In this case masturbation is really only a symptom for deeper problems which are far more serious and damaging than it is. In my experience some of the worst cases of the latter kind are among married persons. It can, in a Christian, unfortunately become the peg upon which he hangs his guilts and anxieties that keep him from actually getting to the real problem. Parents, pastors, and Christian counselors must learn to discern the difference between the various types.

May I suggest what I have discovered to be some practical ways of dealing with masturbation:

1. *Do not try a direct, frontal spiritual attack.* My main quarrel against this is that instead of lessening the problem, it usually makes it worse. Nothing provokes masturbation more than to create anxiety about it. Try to get the person's mind off his guilt and anxiety by explaining to him that it is one of those gray areas where rightness or wrongness depends on other factors. Usually he has already tried prayer and Scripture reading with the only result that he feels worse than ever for breaking his promises to God. His prayers are often doing more harm than good, for they are totally negative. Words of reassurance about God's accepting love, his faithfulness even when we fail, and teaching the person how to pray positively ("Thank you, Lord, for loving me and healing me and helping me with all my problems") will break the vicious circle of guilt and despair.

2. *Get his mind onto his social life and his interpersonal relationships.* Often he is a lone wolf and needs to break out of himself. "Socialize, don't fantasize" is another good suggestion. Persons who do this find within a matter of a few months that the compulsive nature of masturbation has been broken, reduced to a minor and only occasional means of relieving sexual tensions which finally may be abandoned altogether. The true joys of making friends, finding companionship, or of a dating relationship have filled the need formerly filled by a poor substitute. He no longer masturbates because he doesn't need to. He has grown up, matured, and "put away childish things."

My wife and I brought up our three children on the basis of this attitude towards masturbation. Where there is openness of communication on the subject of sex, including masturbation, we can testify that it will be simply an incidental part of growing up and not become a major problem. As one of my teenagers said to me one day when we were talking about it, "Don't worry, Dad; it's sure no big deal with me!" I think that sums up my view. It's high time we stop making such a "big deal" out of masturbation and give it the well-deserved unimportance it merits.

Our daughters have known for a long time just how babies are born, and have accepted, we hope, their theoretical knowledge of sex gravely and sweetly. But the tides of spring run strong. Home ties are breaking off and to the confusion of new voices and circumstances and the competition for popularity will be added the pulse of their own blood.

. . . What memorable word can we teach them that they can repeat like an incantation if the tide should become a threatening flood? . . . I shall remind my daughters simply that there is such a thing as right and wrong. I shall commit the dreadful heresy of talking about sin. . . .

Some writers . . . have set down superbly reasoned appeals for chastity. But how strong is reason against a tidal wave? I think conscience proves a superior shelter. My daughters shall be told there exists a moral law and an ancient commandment and they do wrong to flout them . . . I should like to argue the wholesomeness of treating extramarital relations as sinful . . . to begin with, sin implies goodness, and the young love goodness with all their hearts. We all know what idealists they are, how fiercely they react against injustice and cruelty, how they hate hypocrisy and cant.

. . . So what in the end shall I tell my daughters about chastity before marriage? Of course, I shall be sensible and point out the ordinary social penalties attached to any other conduct. I shall touch on the possible pregnancy, the untidiness, the heartbreak. But I shall also say that love is never merely a biological act, but one of the few miracles left on earth, and that to use it cheaply is a sin. PHYLLIS MC GINLEY

Should I give my daughter the pill? *Herbert J. Miles, M.D.*

In recent years medical science has developed an oral contraceptive—a small pill that can be taken by mouth that will prevent pregnancy. When taken carefully according to a physician's instructions, it is almost 100 percent effective.

The question before us is this: Is it within the scope of Christian morals for single girls to take the pill in order to avoid pregnancy from premarital sex relations? The following letter from a prominent clergyman illustrates the problem.

Recently a mother, Mrs. X, came to me, her pastor, with the following problem. She said, "Pastor, my daughter is, I believe, a good girl. We have tried to give her religious training. But we cannot be with her all the time and are aware that, as any young person, she is under influences other than the home and the church that make severe demands upon her. Recently I have been wondering if I should introduce my daughter to 'the pill'; I hope she will not engage in premarital sex, but just in case, would not a controlled situation be better than an unwanted pregnancy? Now, pastor, I know what the Bible says about sex. But I also know I must relate to my daughter in today's world. What should I and what can I do?" What can the mother do? And how can a pastor help both the mother and the daughter?

This question is complex and involved. Yet it is crucial to many mothers and daughters in our day, thanks to the immoral cultural drift promoted by vested interests, social climbers, and the philosophy of materialistic humanism.

Many parents have a feeling of helplessness. The time for this drift to be met head-on by moral and religious forces is long overdue. We must stop ducking this question. Today's world, as bad as it is, is not as bad as the world in which Christianity was born. In that world, woman was something to be used and sex was something to be associated with religious worship. Yet today the birth of babies out of wedlock is one of the most sad and destructive social burdens in our society. God forbid that any clergyman, or any Christian mother, should encourage it in any form.

Let us examine the question "What can and should Mrs. X do?" She needs to very carefully think through the temptation to give her single daughter the pill to avoid a pregnancy. Some observations are in order.

1. The question seems to assume that her daughter (let's call her Jane) must either use the pill or have an unwanted pregnancy. Is there not a third alternative, namely, morality and sexual self-control until marriage?

2. If Mrs. X introduces Jane to the pill, what is she saying about her daughter's moral stability? Assuming Jane is, as she says, "a good girl" with "religious training," what will she think about the way her own mother trusts her?

3. Mrs. X says she "knows what the Bible says about sex." As a Christian, why doesn't she take the Bible more seriously? In the Bible, the word "fornication" means sex relations by a person who has never been married. "Adultery" means sex relations of a married person with someone other than his or her married companion. In several biblical lists of evils, both fornication and adultery are given and made to be equal with each other. Also, fornication is said to be equal with drunkenness, stealing, murder, and idolatry.

The Bible says that people guilty of these actions (1) are not led by the Spirit of God, (2) are directed by motives that come out of evil hearts, (3) are spiritually unclean because of these actions, and (4) cannot inherit the Kingdom of God. Fornication, with or without the pill, is not a Christian option.

4. If Mrs. X introduces Jane to the pill, is she not encouraging her to be immoral? If Jane should be guilty of premarital sex, hiding behind the protection of the pill, does this not make Mrs. X share in the responsibility for her immoral actions?

5. When word gets out that Jane is on the pill, and it will, can we not expect Jane to be less resistant to young men's advances? Is not giving Jane insurance against pregnancy equal to inviting a test? Is this the way for a mother to build strength of character in the life of her daughter?

6. Mrs. X seems to be placing second things first. Is she not more concerned about what society thinks about a premarital pregnancy than what God thinks about immoral behavior? Is she not more interested in self and present expediency than in what is right or what is long-range social and moral progress? Has she not allowed her personal fears to overcome her rationality?

7. When Mrs. X says, "I must relate my daughter to this present world," what does she mean? Is she not saying that our culture approves and practices premarital sex— therefore, Christians should bend with the times and follow the immoral way of culture? I cannot buy this reasoning. It is humanistic relativism; that is, it is right for the individual to follow what everybody else is doing. The truth is that not every youth is guilty of practicing premarital sex, and it is not right for those who do.

Mrs. X must understand that I am not arguing against the use of contraceptives, nor am I trying to promote the birth of babies out of wedlock. And yes, it is difficult to draw a line between the social problems involved in babies being born out of wedlock and premarital sex. Both present major social problems. However, it is immorality that causes babies to be born out of wedlock and not vice versa. Babies born out of wedlock are the result and not the cause. Why don't we change the cause rather than promote sinful and unsocial results? To get rid of moral and spiritual standards will erode and destroy our organized family life upon which effective society and civilization rests.

OUR CHURCH OFFERED SEX EDUCATION—TO MOTHERS

Several years ago our pastor asked my husband, who is an obstetrician, and me to help him in premarital counseling of young people in our church. Married women began to approach me asking, "When are you going to teach a class for us? We would like to do a better job of instructing our children." Classes were formed, and I began teaching sex education to mothers.

One of the purposes of the class is to provide mothers with the necessary facts. Basic information is presented regarding anatomy, physiology, the sexual development of a child, Christian attitudes towards sex, marriage relationships, conception and pregnancy, and venereal disease. I use charts, films, and other visual aids.

Communication of sexual information to the child is the other area stressed in the classes. Knowing the facts isn't enough. Many mothers confess, "I know what to say; I just don't know when, where, or how to say it." Others worry about knowing how much to tell a child.

Role playing in the class helps in this area. One mother takes the part of a child asking questions, and another mother attempts to answer. Often just going through this "practice time" makes it easier for the mother the next time she is asked a similar question by her own child. One woman, mother of two daughters, says, "After twenty-four years of married life, I was able to rid myself of many 'old wives' tales' and as a result, my husband and I have found new meaning in our own marriage relationship." Another woman says, "As our marriage was strengthened, much of the tension and pressure subsided, and we were much more able to communicate with our children about sex." MARY KEHLE

4

Teen
Problems

How about an abortion?
C. Everett Koop, M.D.

I could have a telephone call any day from an outlying hospital saying that they had just delivered a baby who has no rectum, whose bladder is inside out, whose abdominal organs are out in his umbilical cord, and who has a cleft spine with an opening in his back so that you can see his spinal cord. In addition, his legs are in such a position that his feet lie most comfortably next to his ears. Now the dilemma that is presented to some people in such a situation is this: "Should we operate or should we not? Should we let this baby die, unattended, or should we do the things that we know how to do best and let him live?"

Dilemma is defined as "a perplexing predicament, a necessary choice between two equally undesirable alternatives." I am not sure that everyone would agree that the two alternatives I have mentioned are equally undesirable. Yet, everyone talks about rights these days and I would like you to consider whether you think this baby has the right to live. Does this family have the right of a choice? Do I, as the baby's surgeon, have a right of choice? Do I have the right or the privilege to try to influence the family to think the way I do?

The liberalization of abortion laws has brought the whole problem of the sanctity of life into focus. My reasons against abortion are logical as well as theological.

First, the logic. It is impossible for anyone to say when a developing fetus or embryo or baby becomes viable, that is, has the ability to exist on its own. The logical approach is to go back to the sperm and the egg. A sperm has twenty-three chromosomes and no matter what, even though it is alive and can fertilize an egg, it can never make another sperm. An egg also has twenty-three chromosomes and it can never make another egg. So, we have eggs that cannot reproduce and we have sperm that cannot reproduce unless they get together. Once there is the union of sperm and egg, and the twenty-three chromosomes of each are brought together into one cell that has forty-six chromosomes, we have an entirely different story. That one cell will, if not interrupted, make a human being just like you, with the potential for God-consciousness. I do not know anyone among my medical confreres, no matter how pro-abortion he might be, who would kill a newborn baby the minute he was born. My question to my pro-abortion friend who will not kill a newborn baby is this: "Would you kill this infant a minute before he was born, or a minute before that, or a minute before that, or a minute before that?" You see what I am getting at. At what minute can one consider life to be worthless and the next minute consider that same life to be precious?

Also, most anti-abortion individuals lean heavily upon religious convictions in coming to their pro-life position, and the Scriptures seem to say from cover to cover that life is precious to God.

In the 139th Psalm, David writing about himself says, "Thou hast covered me in my mother's womb. I will praise thee, for I am fearfully and wonderfully made; marvellous are thy works, and that my soul knoweth right well. My substance was not hid from thee, when I was made in secret, and curiously wrought in the lowest parts of the earth. Thine eyes did see my substance, yet being unperfect; and in thy book all my members were written, which in continuance were fashioned, when as yet there was none of them." When God called Jeremiah to be a prophet, he said this: "Before I formed thee in the belly I knew thee; before thou camest forth out of the womb, I sanctified thee...."

I believe this refutes any question about a later viability of the fetus and it certainly supports the New Testament doctrine that God knew us from before the foundation of the world.

Development before birth

By the time a baby is eighteen to twenty-five days old, long before the mother is sure that she is pregnant, the heart is already beating. At forty-five days after conception, you can pick up electroencephalographic waves from the baby's developing brain. At eight weeks, there is not only a brain, but the fingerprints on the hands have already formed and except for size, will never change. By the ninth and tenth weeks, the thyroid and the adrenal glands are functioning. The baby can squint, swallow, move his tongue, and the sex hormones are already present. By twelve and thirteen weeks, he has fingernails, he sucks his thumb, and he can recoil from pain. In the fourth month the growing baby is eight to ten inches in height. In the fifth month there is a time of lengthening and strengthening of the developing infant. Skin, hair, and nails grow. Sweat glands arise. Oil glands excrete. This is the month in which the movements of the infant are felt by his mother. In the sixth month the developing baby responds to light and to sound. He can sleep and awake. He gets hiccups and can hear the beat of his mother's heart. Survival outside the womb is now possible. In the seventh month the nervous system becomes much more complex, the infant is sixteen inches long and weighs about three pounds. In the final two months there is a time of fattening and continued growth.

Techniques of abortion

There are three commonly used techniques of abortion; each may have its variations. The technique that is used most commonly for early pregnancies is called the D & C, or dilation and currettage. The cervix is stretched to permit the insertion of instruments. The surgeon then scrapes the wall of the uterus, cutting the baby's body to pieces and scraping the placenta from its attachments on the uterine wall. Bleeding is considerable. An alternate method to be used at the same time is called suction abortion. The principle is the same as the D & C. A powerful suction tube is inserted through the open cervix. This tears apart the body of the developing baby and his placenta, sucking them into a jar. These smaller parts of the body are recognizable as arms, legs, head, etc.

The second most common type is called the salt poisoning abortion, or "salting out." This method is carried out after sixteen weeks of pregnancy. A rather long needle is inserted through the mother's abdomen directly into the sac surrounding the baby and a solution of concentrated salt is injected into it. The baby breathes in and swallows the salt and is poisoned by it. The outer layer of skin is burned off by the high concentration of the salt; brain hemorrhages are frequent. It takes about an hour to slowly kill the baby by this method. The mother usually goes into labor about a day later and delivers a dead, shriveled baby.

A final technique is hysterotomy. A hysterotomy is exactly the same as a cesarean section with the one difference, namely, that in a cesarean section the operation is being done to save the life of the baby whereas in the hysterotomy the operation is being done to kill the baby. These babies look very much like other babies except that they are small, weighing, for example, about two pounds at the end of a twenty-four-week pregnancy. These babies are truly alive and they are allowed to die through neglect or are deliberately killed by a variety of methods.

Semantics and brainwashing

Five years ago, everybody agreed that abortion was killing an unborn baby. Now we have been brainwashed so that words do not mean the same things that they used to mean. For example, you find that the abortionists do not talk about babies in the womb except when they have a slip of the tongue. They prefer to call these "fetuses," but even better, when they call the developing baby "the product of conception" it ceases to have a personality and its destruction could not possibly mean killing. As recently as 1967, at the first international conference on abortion, a purely secular group of people said, "We can find no point in time between the union of sperm and egg and the birth of an infant at which point we can say that this is not a human life."

In this war of semantics, somehow or other liberal thinking has switched the truth that the unborn child is the victim of the abortion to the fact that the mother not wanting a pregnancy somehow or other is the victim of pregnancy.

Contraception vs. abortion

Contraception is something that prevents the union of sperm and egg; it is not abortion. Contraception and family planning in the larger sense come under the heading of sexual ethics, while abortion has to do with human rights. If this is true, and I believe most firmly that it is, what one does in the matter of birth control or contraception is up to the individual to decide on the basis of his own conscience. However, once conception has taken place, then the consideration of abortion moves out of the field of sexual ethics and directly into the field of human rights.

I can think of no better thought to leave with you than that expressed by Malcolm Muggeridge, widely acclaimed British author for the past forty-five years. "Can it be seriously contended that the mere circumstance of being delivered transforms the developing embryo from a lump of jelly with no rights of any kind, and deserving of no consideration of any kind, into a human being with all the legal rights that go therewith?

"Our western way of life has come to a parting of the ways. Either we go on with the process of shaping our own destiny without reference to any higher being than man, deciding ourselves how many children should be born, when and what varieties, which lives are worth continuing and which should be put out, from whom spare parts—kidneys, hearts, genitals, brain boxes even—shall be taken and to whom allotted.

"Or we can draw back, seeking to understand and fall in with our Creator's purpose for us rather than to pursue our own; in true humility praying, as the founder of our religion and civilization taught us, Thy will be done.

"We can survive energy crises, inflation, wars, revolutions and insurrections, as they have been survived in the past, but if we transgress against the very basis of our mortal existence, becoming our own gods and our own universe, then we shall surely and deservedly perish from the earth."

Should I keep my baby?
Carroll H. Lee

"First I thought I would keep my baby when it was born. Then I thought of the baby and what it would miss by not having a father or a proper home, and I decided that I would let it go for adoption. Now that I've seen the baby, I want to keep it again. I'm so confused, I don't know what to do, really, or what is the right thing to do!"

The concern and anxiety expressed by this girl is perhaps typical of many like her who struggle with the question, Should an unwed mother keep her baby?

Actually, there never has been an official agency policy on this subject. The decision of whether to keep an illegitimate child or whether to give it up for adoption has been left to the individual mother. It is her child and she has the reponsibility to make her own decision regarding its future. On the other hand, there have been and still are social pressures that influence her decision.

Parents often put considerable pressure on a girl to go into a hasty marriage with the baby's father (assuming that he can be identified, is willing, or can be coerced into the union) to "give the baby a name," or else they slip their daughter away to some distant relative or friend to have the baby secretly and subsequently give it up for adoption.

It is sometimes difficult to tell whether some of these parents are more concerned about their daughter and her child, or about the family image.

It would be foolish to doubt the sincerity of many others, perhaps the majority of parents, who find themselves in such a position. There is an impressive volume of data to show, however, that the young couple hustled into an

unplanned marriage, primarily because of the
girl's pregnancy, is facing heavy odds against
forming a stable home.

Community pressures are always present
too: What will the neighbors think? Will a girl
face difficulty in finding friends, in being
accepted by her peer groups? Will she be able
to find a suitable husband if a prospective
mate must also take on the responsibility of a
child?

There are questions of economics and
career. If she keeps her baby, will she be able
to finish school, find employment, be self-
supporting? Who will care and pay support
for herself and the baby while she carries on
with those activities so normal to her age
group, yet so perplexing when complicated by
a fatherless child?

It is not suprising that over the past several
decades it has become an accepted practice for
young unmarried mothers to give up their
babies for adoption. Through the careful
auspices of adoption agencies, the child is
assured a good home, and the mother can go
about her life, sadder, but hopefully wiser
than before.

More recently, however, there has been
some change both in official thinking and in
social practice. There seems to be greater
public understanding and tolerance for the girl
who does decide to raise her own child. It is
also much easier for her to get assistance to
finish school, take vocational training, or
otherwise prepare herself for economic
maturity.

Perhaps the greatest factor, however, is the
example given by girls who are courageous
enough to accept the additional responsibility
of raising their children, and are making a
success of it. It can be done. Consider these
two examples:

Lori is an attractive young woman who was twenty-one when her baby was born. When asked what made her keep her baby, Lori considered the question thoughtfully for several minutes before she answered.

"I suppose that girls give up their babies because they don't see how they can raise them," she answered finally. "Perhaps they think the baby will interfere too much with their lives—you know, keep them from getting a husband later on."

Gerry, a chubby little fellow a year old, pulled himself up beside her and coaxed to be picked up. Lori paused to give him an affectionate hug before she continued.

"I thought about letting him be adopted, I suppose all girls do, but I knew I couldn't. It's hard to explain. I guess the simplest answer is that I kept him because he was mine. I'm glad I did—I've never regretted it!"

Lori had been a university junior when she met Gerry's father, who was a year older than she. For a while they went steady, but then his interest waned.

"Tom wasn't ready to be serious about anything but his degree. When I told him I was pregnant, he became angry, said I wasn't going to trick him into marriage! I was angry too, and hurt. I told him I never wanted to see him again—I never have either, and I still don't want to!"

Lori went home at the end of the semester. She had always enjoyed a good relationship with her parents and did not hide her condition from them. At first they were shocked, but they stood behind her. Later she went to stay with an aunt in another city until the baby was born, and then returned to her home.

The parents paid the costs of confinement and later, when Gerry was a few months old, her mother looked after the baby while Lori took a job as a receptionist in a medical clinic.

At first she stayed close to home, not wanting to go out with former friends. She wonders yet if this was because of how her friends felt about her, or whether she was worried over how they might accept her. She feels now that the friends who really mattered didn't change their attitude toward her.

Gerry occupied much of her time, but gradually she began to take part in social life around her. She particularly enjoys the fellowship of a young adult group in her church, and is now engaged to marry a Christian laboratory technician she met there.

"Of course I've told George all about the baby," she added. "He thinks the world of Gerry and is going to adopt him as soon as we are married."

Lori had the advantage of a good home and understanding parents to help her recover from the mistake she had made.

Marie had no such good fortune. She had spent much of her childhood in various foster homes and had never formed a close tie with her foster parents.

With grade ten education and little experience to help her, she started out on her own at seventeen, working as a waitress and sharing an apartment with another girl. She dated a number of boys who frequented the cafe where she worked, never going steady with any of them. They offered a bit of excitement in a monotonous life, and seemed to fill some of her longing for affection.

She was not sure herself which of two boys was the father of her child, and neither would own up to his responsibility.

When Marie could no longer keep her job as a waitress, she contacted a worker from the Children's Aid Society who arranged for her to enter a church-sponsored home for unwed mothers. Her counselor there helped her to look at both sides of the question of keeping her baby or giving it up for adoption placement, but left the decision wholly to Marie. She feels that it was perhaps her own disappointment about not having a mother that made her decide to keep her baby.

After Marie left the home, the welfare authorities helped her to get settled and gave her financial assistance to care for herself and the baby girl. She did not return to her former town, but stayed in the city, sharing an apartment with a mother of two small children who was deserted by her husband. This arrangement proved to be helpful for both.

When the baby was older, Marie's social worker helped her enroll in an adult education course. She hopes that in a year she will be qualified to take a stenographer's job. The other young mother in the apartment looks after the baby while Marie is at school, and Marie cares for the other's two children while their mother takes a hairdressing course.

Marie will have several difficult years ahead of her without the support of parents or other close relatives, and under circumstances that present a number of problems and little time for relaxation.

The church should present the Christian message in such a relevant way that young people would look forward to marriage and the formation of a family as a goal of such importance that casual sexual experimentation would be avoided, and the worth of the individual respected.

In the context of the Sunday school and youth programs of the church there is a golden opportunity to show love, the "more excellent way," as well as for giving a Christian interpretation of moral values.

There is an opportunity to show understanding and to give support for the girl who finds herself, for whatever reason, in the role of an unwed mother. This can give reassurance to those like Lori, who have the good fortune to have understanding parents and considerable opportunity, but who need a continuing fellowship and wholesome activities. It can be invaluable, perhaps the difference between success and failure, for those like Marie who have so much against them from the start.

One can hear the echo of the Master's words, "Inasmuch as ye have done it unto the least of these . . . ye have done it unto me!"

 *What influence does the father have in helping his daughter to grow up to be a good specimen of femininity? The evidence is strong that a girl does not develop feminine personality merely by imitating her mother. The father's particular relationship with his daughter seems very important in her sex-role development. He may foster the establishment of a positive feminine identity by treating her as a female and encouraging her to behave in ways which are considered to be feminine by her society.*

The father's relationship with the mother is very important. The wife's emotional health, self-regard, and capacity for appropriately nurturing her children (are) influenced by her husband's attitudes and behavior. The father has this double responsibility! But the direct identification with the father seems to be very far-reaching. BILLER & WEISS

Is a marriage license or wedding ceremony necessary? *Herbert J. Miles, M.D.*

Dora wrote me the following letter, inquiring about the wisdom of a "common-law marriage," that is, a marriage in which a man and woman begin living together as husband and wife without buying a wedding license or having any kind of wedding ceremony, either public or private.

I have been dating this boy for several months. We have talked about by-passing a marriage license and any type of marriage ceremony and just simply begin to live together as husband and wife. He will be transferred from the factory here to another state in a few months. We could begin living together at that time. We are church members, and we have our own religious ideas. We want our marriage to be successful. We want some children, but we like to be independent and do our own thinking. Why should everybody go through the silly routines of buying a license and the equally silly and expensive wedding ceremony?

I like to be objective and give other people the right to do independent thinking, but I cannot approve of common-law marriage. It is basically antisocial; that is, one who advocates it is announcing, "I'll live my own life the way I want to and everybody else can go 'jump in the lake.'" Suppose for a moment that we universalized Dora's idea and abolished all marriage licenses, marriage records, and marriage ceremonies; what would this mean? It would mean chaos, total social chaos. In order to have civilization, society must know who is married to whom. Even early primitive peoples recognized this. They did not have strict legal regulations with permanent marriage records in a county courthouse. But they required a marriage ceremony, and all the community was invited. These were major social occasions. Their real purpose was the need for making a marriage known by establishing it before witnesses so that through the years they would know who is married to whom. No society, past or present, has ever existed without some controls over human behavior. Controls over marriage and the family are basic to proper control of human behavior.

In spite of these facts, common-law marriages have been tolerated in our society, but they are now illegal in thirty-six states.

I note that Dora identifies herself with Christianity. The Scriptures call for followers of Christ to cooperate with community social organization, so long as it is not in conflict with basic Christian teachings. The last six of the Ten Commandments are social commandments.

Why does Dora want to keep her marriage so secret? Is she ashamed of her fiancé? Is she afraid of his values and lack of social and moral stability? Is she afraid that her marriage won't last? Is she looking for an easy way out if it doesn't work? Suppose she has children? Would she feel as responsible for caring for them as she would if she were legally married? Will she not be dependent on society (its schools, courts, churches, community youth organizations, etc.) to help her socialize her children? Suppose her husband gets tired of her, leaves, and claims that the relationship was never agreed upon as marriage; what could she do? It would be his word against hers. Suppose her husband became wealthy and then died; would she be able to inherit from him as his wife? And what about the legitimacy of their children? Would their children have inheritance rights? What will Dora do when her children grow up and ask about her marriage? How will they feel when they learn that all other children's parents are legally married and theirs are not?

I will never forget a distraught mother, age forty-five, who came to me privately with her problem. She was living in a common-law marriage. Everyone in the family was now an active church member. Her eighteen-year-old daughter had suspected the problem and was demanding to see her parents' marriage license. The burden of the mother's conversation was, "We regret that we did not have a legal marriage. It was a miserable mistake. What should we do now?" In the conversation she decided, in tears, that she had no alternative but to (1) ask God's forgiveness, (2) tell her daughter all, (3) ask her daughter's forgiveness, and (4) see her pastor and a lawyer about the wisdom of planning a legal marriage immediately.

Is it possible that the real reason Dora objects to a marriage license and ceremony is that she is unsure of herself, unsure of her fiancé, radically self-centered, or really looks upon marriage as a tentative relationship?

Formal weddings can be expensive—too expensive. But would it not be wiser for a person who objects to the expense and formality of a wedding ceremony to buy a marriage license and have a small, inexpensive home wedding? The legal trend in our society is to do away with common-law marriages.

In life and in marriage, we must live in society. Any couple will live to rue the day that they enter a marriage that is not accepted by society.

What if our boy is arrested?
Donald Robinson

An interview with Milton G. Rector,
President, National Council on Crime and
Delinquency.

Q. Mr. Rector, when one's child is arrested,
how soon does a parent find out about it?

A. In a well-run police department, parents
are notified as soon as an arrested child is
brought into the station house. Or the
child is allowed to phone home himself.
Unfortunately, in the majority of the
nation's 40,000 police departments,
officers sometimes hold a child for four or
five hours without notifying his parents
that they have him in custody. Poorly
trained police may ask him to make a
sworn statement to them without his
lawyer or his parents being present. They
may offer to let him go home if he
"cooperates" with them—an absolutely
illegal practice which any youngster
should refuse to go along with.

Q. Say my thirteen-year-old boy telephones
me from a police station that he has been
arrested for burglarizing a vacant house.
What advice should I give him?

A. I'd tell him, "Don't answer any questions,
son. I'll be right down with a lawyer." This
is not a permissive parent taking a child's
side against the police. If my child has
done something wrong, I think he should
be held accountable. At the same time, I
don't want him to say things to the police
in his fright and excitement that might
damage his case. Some children are so
scared that they confess to crimes they
never committed.

At the police station, follow the same

advice yourself. Wait until your lawyer arrives before you give information about your child to the police. And, whatever you do, don't participate with the police in questioning your child. It can make things worse. I recall a case in which a young girl was picked up for stealing. Her horrified parents joined the police in questioning her, and the girl blurted out to them that she'd stolen before. Suddenly the child was involved in two offenses, not one.

Q. Who should go to the police station following notification of arrest—the father, or the mother, or both?

A. Both, if possible. A youngster will do better if concern for him in a crisis is shared by both his parents.

Q. What are the procedural steps after a juvenile has been brought to the station house?

A. Ordinarily, the police will release the child in the custody of the parents until the initial hearing in juvenile court the next morning. However, the police may lock him in a detention center overnight if it is a serious crime and if they're afraid that the parents won't produce him in court.

At the initial hearing, a juvenile court judge will decide whether there is sufficient cause for the court to act in the case. If there is, he will release the child to the parents or order that he be held in detention. Strangely, in most states, children can be locked up without the right to post bail—a constitutional right for an adult criminal. Nor does a child have the right to a trial by jury. However, he does have the right to counsel, the right to remain silent under interrogation, the right to cross-examine witnesses.

Q. What is the best way to get the child

released in one's custody until the case
comes up in court?

A. Most police officers are sympathetic to
children and happy to release them until
the arraignment unless the child is a
menace to society or a real smart aleck.
Impress upon the police that you, his
parents, are concerned about your child's
welfare, that one of you will stay at home
with him, that you will deliver him to court
in time for the arraignment.

I can tell you two things not to do. Don't
yell at the cops, "You framed my child!"
And don't grab your child and shout, "Just
wait until I get you home!" The police may
think it's safer for the youngster behind
bars.

Q. Can you teach a child a lesson by letting
him stay in jail a couple of nights?

A. No child deserves that kind of lesson.
Being in jail is a traumatizing experience
for youngsters. Some are brutalized. Some
hurt themselves. All are further alienated
from their parents. Just recently a case
came across my desk of a seventeen-year-
old college freshman who was arrested
because the police found marijuana in his
dormitory room. The boy's father let the
police keep him in jail overnight. When he
got there in the morning, the boy's nose
was broken and both his eyes blackened—
the result of a fight begun when older,
tougher prisoners tried to gang-rape the
younger boys.

Q. What attitude ought a parent to take
toward a youngster when the police release
him to his home prior to the court
hearing?

A. A parent has a right to disappointment,
even anger. But the time to take it out on
the youngster is not when he is in deep

trouble. It's then that a child most needs his parents' understanding. So, sit down and talk calmly. Assume that your child is innocent until he is proved guilty. If he admits the charges against him, find out why the misdeed happened. Don't excuse the youngster's behavior. Let him know that what he did was wrong. But don't reject him because of it. Remember that the child has a future, and this is not the end of it.

Q. How can the right lawyer for one's child be found?

A. Ask your family lawyer for the name of an attorney with juvenile court experience. Don't, whatever you do, let your family lawyer represent the child unless he has done juvenile court work himself. Procedures are quite different from an ordinary criminal case, or a civil case; you need someone who understands them. Once you've found a good lawyer, urge your child to level with him completely. "Whether you've told me the truth or not," I'd say to my child, "tell the lawyer everything."

If you can't afford a private attorney, the Public Defender or a Legal Aid lawyer will represent the child, or the judge will appoint a lawyer to defend him at the court's expense. A problem is that these lawyers are appallingly overworked. If you can possibly raise the money, engage a private lawyer.

Q. Is it wise for parents to offer to make financial restitution for the damage a child is accused of having done, or could this be construed as an attempt to buy off justice?

A. It's a fine idea to propose restitution provided it is the child who pays, not his affluent family. The child can wash the paint off the building he has smeared, or help the neighbor whose house he has vandalized make repairs. But he should also do more than just make restitution; he should volunteer to make amends. He can take on a regular obligation to mow the neighbor's lawn, for instance, or he can do community service of some sort.

Police are favorably impressed when a youngster recognizes that he has done wrong and is willing to work it off, and they often let such individuals go free with a reprimand instead of booking them. This can be vital to a child's future. For when he applies for admission to college, for a civil service job, for a bank loan, for credit, he may be asked, "Have you ever been arrested or convicted of a crime?" If he answers "Yes" to either question, he probably will be rejected. If he is convicted of a felony—possession of drugs, for example—his answer may bar him from entering any profession.

A juvenile arrest record is, of course, supposed to be confidential. But most police departments do not keep them separate from those of adult offenders. Many don't record the final disposition. So, a juvenile arrest record, even one that's incorrect, can follow a person all his life.

Q. If one's child is guilty of the crime he's accused of, should his lawyer advise him to plead guilty?

A. Let me say frankly that the average juvenile court lawyer disagrees with me on this. Most advise their young clients against a guilty plea unless the case for the prosecution looks absolutely unbeatable. Even then, they'll tell you that plea bargaining—in which a youngster pleads guilty to a lesser offense in return for a lighter sentence—is possible. For example, I know of a fifteen-year-old boy in Washington, D.C., who was charged with pulling a gun on a police officer. His lawyer arranged with the prosecutor's office to plead him guilty only on possession of a dangerous weapon, and the boy got off with probation.

I'm not sure that this was good for the boy, though. It seems to me that a youngster who has broken the law should go to court and tell the whole truth: "I did it, Your Honor. I'm ready to take the consequences." An understanding judge and understanding parents can help him work the problem out and make sure that it never happens again. That's what a child needs to grow up into a decent, self-respecting adult.

Wise parents should demonstrate to the judge that they will do everything in their power to help their child rehabilitate himself. They should have a plan ready, providing for psychiatric care, tutoring, a job—whatever the child needs to get over his problems. They should show the judge that incarceration is not necessary, that their home has more to offer the child than any institution.

What works with a child on drugs? *Tom Watson*

"We got a phone call last night that shattered our world."

The person on the other end of the line was middle-aged, middle-class, an active church member, a good wife, a loving mother. I could almost see her in the kitchen baking cookies.

"Can you come down to the station, Mrs. Mitchell?" the sergeant had said. "Your son has been arrested on a charge of selling drugs."

"Robert's always been a good boy!" She started crying. "We've worked hard—tried to give him the things we didn't have." Now she was sobbing.

"We go to church regularly. Robert did, too, until he started running around with that crowd. I teach a Sunday school class. How can I ever face them again? The Bible says to train up a child in the way he should go, and when he is old, he won't depart from it. We've tried—really done our best—"

I knew she was right. Some of the most mixed-up kids I have seen come from beautiful Christian families. To be sure, broken homes and rotten parents are turning out drug addicts by the thousands, but we have to face the fact that some of the worst kids come from some of the "best" families.

"Let's take Johnny to a psychiatrist and get him straightened out," a parent says.

Unfortunately, it doesn't work that way. I have attended seminars with psychiatrists who quite frankly admitted they were at a loss to deal with the drug problem. In five years of ministry to troubled youth, I have never seen a drug addict cured by a psychiatrist or psychiatric clinic.

Drug programs

A key man on the staff of Yale University's Drug Dependence Institute told us once in a seminar that their research indicated that a 12 to 15 percent effectiveness ratio was good, and that most governmental programs operated in the range of a 5 to 10 percent cure rate for drug addiction.

Methadone and the drug antagonist programs are the greatest farces of all. I say this as one who has tried. For seven months we operated a federally funded methadone detoxification program. Usually, before they even completed the program, the addicts we treated were back on the streets.

Christian rehabilitation facilities

A number of Christian rehabilitation facilities are in operation and are doing a good job of reclaiming drug addicts—Teen Challenge, Nicky Cruz Outreach, Inc., and several others. If you can get your child into such a center, he may receive the love and nurture he needs to fight his way back from addiction.

Charity begins at home

You can probably do more than anyone else to supply the help your youngster needs. With the right attitude and actions, you can achieve a great deal. Before we examine your role, let's take a look at what your role is *not*.

A doormat. One thing your son or daughter needs to hear from you right away is that although you love him, you are not going to permit him to walk all over you and the other members of the family. People who get into drugs often develop an exaggerated view of themselves, and their ego demands the restructuring of all the lives they touch.

Not only does the doormat approach create a hell on earth for the family, it is terribly damaging and disorienting to the teenager.

One father I know handled this problem quite well when his sixteen-year-old daughter called him from a distant city after running away the day before.

"Last night mother and I were pretty upset —we were heartbroken. We miss you and are concerned about you," he said. "But this morning I went to work, mother went to her Bible study, and your brother went on to school. We want you to be a part of our lives, but if you choose not to, then we will have to go on without you. Our world is not going to end just because you walk out of it."

A teenager needs to know that he is loved and needed, but it is a dangerous thing for him to get the impression that he is the center of your world. Once he feels that, he will seek to manipulate you, resulting in misery for you and destruction for him.

"We'd love for you to come back—we'll even send you airplane fare," the father continued, "but in order to rejoin the family, you'll have to agree to some ground rules. When you get home we will sit down and talk about it, and if you think we are unfair or arbitrary, you always have the option to leave again." The girl agreed to return home and to give the rules a try.

On this foundation, the stage was set for her recovery. During the next two years, the daughter pushed at her restraints, often just to test the limits, but recently she has started doing much better.

A preacher. The teenager who is into dope lives with terrible feelings of guilt. He is not about to sit still and listen to a parent preach to him about his sins.

He is also living with so much fear that he has to have defense mechanisms to survive. The more you try to talk about the harmful effects of drugs, the more he is likely to tune you out. At this stage in his life, he is convinced you don't know much. He may even be proud of the fact that he already knows more about drugs than you'll ever know— however erroneous his information.

"Should I just stand silently by and watch him kill himself?" I almost hear you exclaim. Indeed not, but preaching is not the effective way to deal with his needs. The young person is in rebellion against God, and you are a part of what he is rebelling against. When he makes his peace with God, he will submit to you.

Savior. Much as you want to, you cannot save your child from the grip of Satan. This is a work of the Holy Spirit. It is a work only he can do. In fact, your efforts to rescue him may only delay, or possibly even prevent, his encounter with the only real Savior—Jesus Christ.

If your youngster does not need you to be a doormat, a preacher, or a savior, what does he need from you?

Your role

Tower of strength. As hard as it may be to believe, with all his pronouncements to the contrary, your child is lost, frightened, guilt-ridden, lonely. Can he turn to you for help?

To be a parent, especially in a drug crisis, requires a great deal of poise and strength— more strength, in fact, than you can probably muster on your own.

One father told me, "I'm not going to let this situation with my daughter defeat me. I have found a lot of comfort in the Holy Spirit, and I'm convinced there is even more there for me."

His daughter's reaction to his faith was, "My daddy's faith through all of this has amazed me. I know I have put him through hell, but he has never lost his serenity. In fact, it seems to be growing." Her conclusion was beautiful. "I hope some day I can come to know God like that."

Acceptance. People who do dope are looking for acceptance. It is very important that you accept your child as he is, to avoid chasing him further into rebellion, but it is equally important that you maintain your own values.

With God's help, it is possible to accept a person while rejecting his actions. A good example is the way Jesus handled the situation of the woman taken in adultery. He said to her, "Nor do I condemn you. You may go; do not sin again" (John 8:11, NEB).

The story is told of three boys in the nineteenth century who were kicked out of an ivy league college for having a big drinking party. Their parents were notified by telegraph, and all responded immediately.

"You have disgraced us. Don't come home," said the first message to arrive from home.

"How could you, after all we have done for you?" said the wire from the parents of the second boy.

The third boy's father sent a wire which said simply, "Steady, boy, steady."

Isn't this what real love is all about?

Confidence. In one of the most turbulent periods of my life, a friend looked at me and said softly, "Tom, I believe in you."

I don't think I shall ever be able to express what that meant to me at the time and many times since then.

Many kids who are into drugs tell me, "Everybody is down on me."

"I know you're going to make it," a friend told his son, even though the boy was shooting heroin. An even more beautiful thing is that he told me privately, "And, you know, I believe he will."

Every teenager on drugs feels that it is a temporary state of affairs and that someday he is going to shake it. Your expression of confidence in your child and in the power of God may help more than you will ever know.

The best way for you to bring life to the situation of death in which you now find yourself is to let God give you his new life. He can and will give you the power to face anything—not just with a negative kind of resignation, but with adequacy. This is not some utopian dream; it is reality in the lives of thousands of people. If you are not experiencing it, you are living beneath your privileges and robbing those around you of the strength and life they so desperately need.

CORRECTING WITHOUT PROVOKING

"And, ye fathers, provoke not your children to wrath," Ephesians 6:4. Fathers are not to be related to their children in such a way that a word of correction leads to resentment or anger. The responsibility for correction without antagonism lies squarely upon the father.

"Don't provoke" does not mean "Don't correct." The trick is to carry out this responsibility without alienating the child.

Parents who have lost or forfeited a meaningful relationship with their children are on thin ice when they begin to correct. Absentee parents discover after it is too late that what they have sown (disinterest and lack of attention), they are now reaping. Their children often become disinterested in the parents' values, life-styles, and God. Discipline becomes virtually impossible because children who are emotionally rejected have little interest in establishing relations with parents who have neglected them.

I know a boy of twelve who, when chided over his unwillingness to join his friends in a wrong course of action, answered the taunt, "You're afraid your Dad will hurt you" with the beautiful words, "No, I am afraid I will hurt my Dad." Here was a father who had learned how to encourage, correct, and admonish without provoking.

Disciplinary overkill is an open acknowledgement of parental failure. It is not firmer discipline which is needed but parents whose very lives draw their children toward the right path. ROBERT MOUNCE

You say you're not going to church today? *Eugene H. Peterson*

When the young teen in your house first says, "I'm not going to church today," what will your reaction be?

Panic? Anger? Exasperation? Dismay?

Maybe he has already said it.

The Christian parent has a lot at stake in the response that his child makes to God. He has invested a lot of prayer, a lot of concern, a lot of training, a lot of love, and he doesn't want to see it wiped out.

The task was clearer when the child was younger. A young child must be raised in "the nurture and admonition of the Lord." He must be taught "line upon line and precept upon precept." He must be provided with faithful church associations. He must know what is in the Bible, that God loves him, and that he lives in a moral universe where things count eternally.

But when this child arrives at the teen years, things begin to fog up a little. No longer is he primarily a "learner" (although he is still learning). Now he becomes more and more a "decider." He begins to practice making decisions, so that he will be able to live responsibly in an adult world a little later on.

The parent is in a dilemma. He wants the youth to learn to make adult decisions and get practice doing it with as little interference as possible. But is he being responsible in allowing this freedom to extend to the areas of church and God?

Some parents think not. "As long as you live under my roof, you will go to church with the rest of the family. We'll not discuss it any more."

Other parents take essentially the same position but use pressure tactics to enforce it. "If you don't go to church and Sunday school today, you're not going bowling tomorrow night." Or, "If you maintain a perfect attendance at church and Sunday school for the rest of the year, I'll buy you a stereo for your room." The variations on these items are infinite.

Of course, some parents give up the struggle. They give in to the persistent complaining and heel-dragging that makes every Sunday morning a scrimmage. They go to church minus a teen but with a little more peace. But if they have left him at home, they have picked up some feelings of guilt and failure which go along in his place. They have difficulty enjoying their peace.

Still other parents think that when a teen begins questioning the faith of his fathers (or father!), it is a signal to the parent to begin to develop and make more explicit a new relationship—a relationship between two Christians. In addition to the responsibility of being a Christian parent, there is a call now to be a Christian person, sharing the meaning of a personal faith.

Your own sense of failure and your own discoveries of forgiveness need to be shared. Your sense of pilgrimage, of not having arrived, your gratitude for grace—all these need now to be talked over. If you insist on keeping up a front of religious success and total commitment and absolute assurance, all you will do is widen the credibility gap.

It is a serious Christian mistake to think that when questions arise and doubts and rebellions begin to be expressed, the strategy called for is an intensified publicity campaign: "Families that pray together stay together . . . if you leave the church, you are leaving the richest heritage of mankind . . . how do you expect God to bless you if you turn your back on him like this . . . etc." The Christian parent is not called to mount an advertising campaign on behalf of the Deity.

One father said something like this: "I remember having those feelings myself; in fact, I still have them from time to time. You're beginning to think and feel as an adult. Many of the things that you are finding distasteful are what you experienced as a child in the church. If you stay home, you don't have anybody to argue with or test yourself against—except your childhood memories. You are having an argument with the church; in very few arguments is one person right and the other wrong. Nobody would want you to uncritically swallow everything that is going on in the church; but if you walk out of the room, the possibilities for adult, responsible debate are eliminated.

"Let me give you an example. If you told me today that you hated girls and never wanted to associate with them again, I think I would respect your feeling. But on the basis of that feeling, I wouldn't permit you to enter some celibate order in which you would never be able to have any contact with women again. There are still hang-ups to get over. It would be better if you kept learning about girls and had some responsible relationships with them as you grow up so that you develop some depth experience in the nature of the man-woman interaction.

"That's kind of the way it is with you and the church too. Part of my responsibility as a parent is to try to keep you in the mainstream of experience as long as possible so that you know as much and experience as much as possible so you will be equipped to make good, adult decisions.

"Right now you have a fresh vision of the whole operation that adults long involved in its structure lack. It is important to have the benefit of your fresh insight. You ought to know that part of the reason that you have this insight is that you don't have the long-range responsibilities and vested interests in things as they are. Those who have these responsibilities and interests, including me, don't find it easy to express some feelings and ideas. Consequently your objectivity is valuable. As a fellow Christian I need you, and I think there are a lot of others in my place."

The young teen, deep within, is beginning to say, "God can no longer be taken for granted. It is not enough for me to assume my parents' attitudes toward God or slip into my parents' practices in the church. What happens from now on must be mine."

This may not take place perfectly smoothly.

What the parent must know (regardless of how he chooses to respond to it) is that this doubt and questioning and rebellion is evidence that something deeply significant is taking place in the personality of his offspring. There is a changed perception toward his own deepest commitment. He is wondering what it is going to be like to maintain adult relationships with God. He is making the preparatory moves in coming to his own adult, personal faith in Christ. It should be counted a good time because the parent can now share the struggles and achievements of his own Christian faith with this emerging person. Resistance to the church is no disaster!

Parents who prefer the kind of person who has never examined the meaning of his life against the call of God are bound to believe that when that examination does begin to take place there is a youth problem, or a religious problem. But others will know that the

Christian gospel has at its core a plea for personal decisions and fresh starts. "No inherited religion," it says; "your faith has to be your own, not your father's."

So what do you do when your teen begins to resist the church and the religious practices of the home? You first of all give thanks to God that another person is beginning to sense the personal dimensions of what it means to be in relation to God. What you do not want is to raise a child who blandly and impersonally continues in a stream of traditional religion, inheriting his faith from others.

And then you ask God for the grace to be an honest, open, faithful person to this youth; that you have the resilience, the strength, and the grace to engage in frank conversation about your own life in Christ; that you be kept from bluffing; that you be prevented from letting your own pride interfere in the development of this new person in Christ; and that your life will be deepened by sharing Christ with this newly emerging person in your home.

Make your Sabbath distinctive. Scholars of ancient Hebrew tell us that the word "holy" in the Commandment literally means "different," and also that it derives from the same Hebrew root as "healthy." Thus the Commandment could be read: "Remember the Lord's Day to make it different and keep it healthy"—a day for imparting fresh vigor to body, mind, and spirit.

Make your Sabbath a family affair. Sunday should be a day of joy. Besides attending church as a family, we sought to do things that day that we didn't do on other days of the week. We played Bible games, discussed family problems and plans, visited relatives, had a brief period of Bible study and prayer, sang lively gospel hymns. There was no ban on healthful recreation, either. We enjoyed playing ball or going swimming.

I felt that we had at least partly succeeded in making Sunday a warm family day when one of our girls, now married, said recently, "Daddy, the thing I miss most of all is our Sundays." REV. BILLY GRAHAM

5

*School
Review*

Can parents help a failing child? *Ada Breise Cromer*

It was shortly after our son, Gary, started junior high that I was forced to admit he had serious learning problems.

His teachers told me he refused to try to do his work. As one of them said, "All he does is sit there and dream."

But though Gary's teachers had reported that he was a slow learner, especially in reading and writing, they also said he had a perfectly good mind, if only he'd apply himself to his studies.

But this wasn't all the evidence I had that he was bright—even gifted. Right from the beginning it was clear that Gary had a rare talent mechanically, especially along lines dealing with electricity.

All through elementary school, Gary's electrical creations monopolized his time. His grasp of electrical principles was remarkable, as was his intuitive knowledge of the fundamental mathematical relationships involved in making his various gadgets. He had been working with radios and crystal sets since he was seven, and he often brought his creations to school to share with his classmates. As for the rest of the work, year by year he squeezed through, so I didn't realize how handicapped he was, scholastically.

Now, toward the end of the first semester of junior high, I was told that Gary's work was far below satisfactory. If he didn't show marked improvement, he would have to repeat seventh grade. I knew that such a setback would make Gary bitterly ashamed and unhappy. Who knows what far-reaching consequences such failure might have.

I knew Gary was reserved, shy, and

sensitive; in his experiments he sometimes seemed to live in a small world of his own.

Something must have happened to my son along the way, the school counselor told me, something that caused him to lose confidence in his ability as a student. Believing that he couldn't keep up with his classmates, he sought refuge in the one thing he knew he could do well—the construction of all things electrical.

Couldn't the school personnel help Gary? Perhaps they hadn't sufficient staff, or didn't know him well enough. In any event, they hadn't helped, and I realized it was up to me. In spite of a guilty feeling that parents aren't supposed to be teachers, I decided that, trained in education or not, I was going to help Gary by whatever methods seemed right to me. So with a mixture of guilt, compassion, faith, and determination, I started to help my son study at home, with the resolve to get him up to grade level before it was too late.

Gary's immediate response was negative. He hated reading. Spelling, too, was a terrific ordeal. Each homework session started with grim protest. Sitting him down to a lesson required patience, persistence, and ingenuity on my part.

We followed the teacher's assignments. I presented the work as interestingly as possible, using reference books with pictures and relating amusing experiences from my own school days to lighten his mood.

During our homework hours each evening, Gary did his arithmetic problems only because of my persuasion—let's face it, insistence. Since he was unable to make much sense of the reference books, I read them to him. I actually coaxed him word by word through the written work of English and geography, spelling the words, correcting his mistakes, explaining over and over. And all the time I tried not to show the worry and irritation I felt. I determined that I would not explode with anger when I saw his eyes haze over, as thoughts of wires, resistors, and radio tubes, no doubt, entered his mind.

On his rare occasions of concentration, Gary responded with quick, accurate answers that amazed me. His eyes would light up with pleasure at his achievement. These glimpses of ability encouraged me to continue when my instincts told me to quit while we both still had our sanity. It seemed, at times, as if Gary were deliberately trying to make me give up.

He had methods. Such as breaking the lead of his pencil. Or dropping the pencil on the floor and taking a long, long time to find it. He teetered on his chair or lounged across it in ungainly positions. He doodled on everything within reach, including my fingernails. There is a deep groove in our desk several inches long, worn from months of Gary's digging at it.

"You're helping him too much," my husband warned me. "He'll never learn to read well if you do it all for him."

I knew this was true. But Gary read at a discouragingly slow pace while time ebbed away. When someone is drowning, I reasoned, first you plunge in and rescue him. Then you teach him how to swim.

All during this period, in the hours allowed for his electrical work, Gary made his usual wholehearted and rapid progress. His creations continued to amaze me. I was certain he was gifted, and I remembered that Thomas Edison was a poor student whose mother had taught him at home. I knew I had to keep on helping Gary. I couldn't give up.

To add to our problems, Gary kept "forgetting" to write out his assignments and bring home his books. Not really sure that I was doing the right thing, I walked to school daily to get the assignments and to catch Gary as he came flying from his last class, so we could get his books from his locker.

After several weeks of this, Gary began voluntarily to copy his assignments and bring home his books. I almost wept with relief. Something told me I had made a chink in the wall my son had erected against studying. Also, his teachers were beginning to see improvement. And I used this to prop up Gary's confidence in himself and to encourage him to continue his efforts.

By the end of six weeks Gary was consenting to do his homework without protest, but his interest in electricity still took precedence over all else.

Time passed and Gary's report cards showed no better grades. He still failed almost every examination he took.

Nevertheless, at home he was completing his lessons in one-third of the former time. Also, he was now able to read the written directions for arithmetic problems, and his spelling had improved. Best of all, his attitude toward study had changed so that mostly he worked steadily, even cheerfully.

One day Gary returned from school with a noticeable spring in his step. "We were watching a good movie in social studies," he said, grinning. "Something went wrong with the projector, and the kids were groaning because we were going to have to go back to the classroom. But I fixed it with the teacher's bobby pin."

"You did?" I said. "Then what happened?"

"They all clapped and cheered. My social studies teacher couldn't believe it."

Although Gary was now getting passing grades in other subjects, he continued to fail in social studies. Could we link his talent with his studies, his teacher wondered. She asked him to build an electrical question board, wired so the correct answer flashed a red light. It brought an A and high praise from Gary's teacher as well as admiration from his classmates. This seemed to increase his confidence. His classwork improved rapidly.

Gary was asked to make another board, this time based on the map of Africa, so that the location of central points would ring a bell. This earned him another A, and its construction brought praise from the faculty as well as the students.

A new light shone in Gary's eyes during those last days of the term, and when I was informed that he was to pass the seventh grade, my gratitude knew no bounds.

But unlike the school term, lessons did not end. Gary still needed to study throughout the summer. We continued with his reading. "Don't tell me," he'd say when a word stopped him. "I can do it." He was no longer floundering in deep water. He had learned to take his first strokes alone.

I sensed a new exhilaration in my son. I also felt something else in his attitude toward me. Respect? Perhaps. But surely a deeper understanding and a closer relationship than we'd ever had before.

Gary will continue to need help in the years to come. But I know for sure, now, what I always believed—a mother should never give up. Whether or not it is considered pedagogically sound, if your child is in school trouble and you think you can help, you've got the right to give it the best try you can. No matter what the difficulties, I'm certain that a parent can be of genuine, unique assistance to a child in the lifelong process of learning.

What if Johnny can't make the grade? *Iona Raney*

Mike's accomplishments in school fall just below his parents' expectations, although he tries hard. He's a model boy, has only a slight tendency to stumble running the bases in a ball game.

Paul, clumsy and awkward, moves constantly. He disturbs his class, interrupts his fellow students, disrupts organized play. Faced with an arithmetic assignment, he works a couple of problems, chews his pencil, finally eats his paper.

Suzie, a clean, pretty girl with a ready smile, daydreams. She doesn't know whether to add or subtract, or what page to read. She never disturbs others, never joins a lesson.

All these children have normal intelligence, loving parents, and no apparent physical defects. Yet all are underachievers in school.

In ten years of elementary school teaching, I found one to three children like these in my class every year. Their learning disabilities were not severe enough to qualify them for remedial reading or the school psychologist's services. They were too good to get help, but not good enough to keep up with the class. Their parents lived in a special kind of agony, with little hope of normalcy for their children. The children suffered guilty feelings about themselves when rigid teachers inferred the children were willfully lazy.

Medical help Recent medical advances offer help for at least some underachievers.

The youngster may have *too little or too much thyroid function.* For many years, doctors have prescribed oral thyroid for the listless youngster with an underfunctioning thyroid. Treated youngsters perk up and generate enthusiasm.

Quite recently, Johns Hopkins Hospital in Baltimore found that hyperthyroidism (overfunctioning of the gland) caused difficulty with school work. The overactive thyroid caused restless, wiggly youngsters who couldn't work methodically. With thyroid treatment, they settled down and schoolwork improved.

Cross laterality or mixed dominance hampers a great many children.

When Joe lurched across the room alone at eight months, his parents were elated. They knew he showed superior intelligence by skipping the creeping and crawling stage. In school, five years later, Joe's superior intelligence didn't manifest itself. He read badly in first grade, called "s-a-w" was, and "o-n" no. He wrote and threw a ball with either hand.

Since he never crawled, the motor pathways of his brain didn't develop sufficiently. The electrical impulse which travels almost instantaneously between the lobes of the brain was slowed. Neither lobe truly dominated. Joe was right-handed, left-eyed, and used both feet equally well. Had the motor pathways developed—through crawling, oddly enough— one side would dominate.

Motor pathways develop when children go through the physical motions of creeping and crawling. Even ten- or fifteen-year-old youngsters profit from creeping and crawling on the floor.

Joe worked with a skilled therapist a half hour a day for six weeks. Exercises pitted the right hand against the left foot and the left hand against the right foot. Joe became a better than average student.

Allergies severely hamper some children's schoolwork.

Jan suddenly began blinking furiously. Her schoolwork slipped seriously and dramatically. She gave up her violin, unable to keep her place in the music. Her parents, frantic over a seemingly sudden onset of neurosis, ignored the symptoms, hoping they'd go away.

Finally, they faced the prospects of psychiatry. But first, a medical exam. Doctors discovered that an allergy made her eyes red and itchy. The symptoms were treated, and the schoolwork returned to normal.

Another child's continual sniffling kept him from performing at his best. Still another's stomach ached after certain foods. Any of these could indicate need for psychiatry. A simple blood test at the doctor's office exposes cells indicating allergy, if that is present.

Peter displayed symptoms of *minimal brain dysfunction*—a medical name covering many types and kinds of disorder.

In more severe forms, these children suffer cerebral palsy, epilepsy, autism, and aphasia, highly recognizable tragedies in a family's life. In mild forms, the youngster is labeled lazy or is called a problem child, and his true ailment goes untreated.

Because Peter regularly disrupted his fourth grade class with emotional outbursts, his teacher and principal decided he needed outside help. His parents, shocked, sought a psychiatrist, under threat of Peter's expulsion from school. Assured he wasn't emotionally crippled, the doctor ordered a neurological exam.

Abnormal brain waves showed on the electroencephalogram. His brain literally clicked on and off in spasms. When this happened, Peter lost the place in his book, forgot what he was saying, didn't hear the last syllable of a spelling word, or didn't remember if he'd multiplied four by six yet. Frustrated, he acted out his displeasure.

At four he'd whacked his head on a concrete floor, and two years earlier convulsed with a high fever. No one can tell which event caused the damage.

Giving a nervous child a nervous system stimulant would seem like heaping gasoline on a brush fire. But the stimulant lets the youngster perceive more clearly, encompass more fully, and understand better what goes on around him, doctors learned. With greater understanding, the need for hyperactivity and acting out diminishes, and about two-thirds of these children succeed with drugs.

Hyperactivity stops after puberty. Drug therapy, helping the child through the frustrations of being turned off spasmodically, prevents personality problems from the hyperactivity. It makes him more lovable.

In addition to drugs, doctors recommend special handling and an enlightened school and home environment for the mildly brain-damaged hyperactive child.

The symptoms of brain damage are so obscure, and the method of determining brain damage so complicated and expensive that doctors and teachers often settle on some other cause. Peter's teacher mistook his symptoms for emotional damage, for instance. Overt physical symptoms, such as hesitancy in speech or rolling of the eyes, may or may not be severe enough to see. Even an electroencephalogram doesn't prove conclusively whether there is minimal brain dysfunction. A complete medical, neurological, and psychological study may tell if this is at the root of the child's academic and behavior problems.

Four steps   If your underachiever is to profit from recent medical advances, there are four steps to take:

1. Compare the youngster's progress at school with everything you know about him. If you are certain his achievement in reading or spelling or arithmetic or several subjects is really under his ability, then—

2. Inquire at school. Ask the principal, teacher, nurse, and coach to check the consistency of intelligence and achievement or behavior. Their test results and observations combine to give them a complete picture of your child. Test results are not usually revealed to parents, but most teachers will tell you if there is a gross disparity between tested intelligence and achievement.*

Make an appointment for a week or so after your first call to let them concentrate on this study. Their report will be more pertinent and penetrating than if you go in without warning them. State your concern about your youngster very bluntly. If there is indeed an inconsistency, then—

3. Tell your doctor frankly of your worry. Ask his help in tracking down the source of it. It may take a while. Allergies, brain damage, thyroid, and mixed dominance are not all easy to diagnose.

The doctor may order electro-encephalograms to study brain waves, electrocardiograms to study heart action, allergy tests, metabolism tests, blood and urine samplings, and other lab work.

4. Should medical disorders be ruled out, then psychiatric help is the next step. Although difficult to accept, this is the only hope some children have of achieving a full, satisfying life. Many communities offer child guidance clinics, lessening the financial burden.

*Editor's note: *National legislation has now been passed requiring school districts to reveal students' test scores to their parents.*

Every underachiever need not continue in that frustrating role. The very term "underachiever" signifies greater potential. Four simple steps may let a child break out of apathy and disappointment, and gain contentment.

Half of a child's development of intelligence and personality is completed by the age of five, and growth after that is slow and much less easily influenced.

It is now recognized that the IQ is not absolutely constant, and it is also recognized that it is basically determined by the child's inheritance. The long-term effect of extreme environments, abundant or deprived, may in exceptional cases amount to as much as twenty IQ points; but such extreme environments must be felt early in life. If they exist during the first four years, they can have far greater consequences than if they were felt through ten later years, from age eight to seventeen. In short, there is a decreasing effect of improved environment with increasing age; or stating it in another way, there is increased stability with age. But after age seventeen, "powerful forces" in the environment will be required to produce much change.

By the average age of about two, it seems evident that at least one-third of the variance at adolescence on intellectual interest, dependency, and aggression is predictable.

The most important period in a child's life is the period before he enters school or even enters kindergarten. The production of a better society depends largely on the production of better parents.
DR. B. S. BLOOM

Can we prevent a dropout?
Pearl Gibbs

Eddie, in suburban Atlanta, dropped out of high school six months before graduation in order to join the Navy. Beth Ann quit school to marry Benny. June dropped out to get a job and help out at home. Kenny left to work and buy a car. Paul was expelled for rebellious behavior. And so it goes. Not one of these teenagers really needed to leave school. But they did.

Will your child quit school this year? According to a thirteen-year follow-up study reviewed in the American School Board Journal, dropouts do not materialize overnight. Regardless of the suddenness of their decisions to quit school, they are many years in the making.

"Dropoutism" is by no means a total indication of lack of ability to do acceptable schoolwork. This is true no matter how many poor grades and uncompleted school assignments may seem to force the issue.

"School-quitting" is merely a symptom of unsolved problems in the life of a young person. In other words, when your youngster suddenly announces he is dropping out of school because he hates it, wants to join the service, plans to get married or find some job, you can be fairly certain that there is a buildup of emotional experience behind it all. These include personal heartaches, fears, frustrations, insecurity, little money, as well as a possible rebellion against authority and some loneliness.

Parents, of course, view "dropoutism" with mixed emotions. No matter how long the problem has existed, it still comes as a shock in many cases.

Sometimes, however, a dropout is met with

complacency. Bill R. was brought up in a Youngstown, Ohio, home where the emphasis was on making a dollar in preference to anything else. Consequently, his paper route and lawn-mowing jobs were given approval. His schoolwork was relegated to insignificance. So the day Bill quit school to take a full-time job at the corner gas station, his folks gave him a pat on the back.

On the other hand, many youngsters are victims of social or pressure-conscious parents who want to live their lives through their children. Such parents feel like failures when the child chooses a life of his own.

"John has to go to college!" an irate, midwestern bank president father informed his son's school principal. "I went to Yale. My father was a Harvard man. All my brothers are college men."

At home, the father pounded away at his boy with everything he could think of to persuade the boy to make a try for higher education. Finally, he resorted to taunts and threats.

"If you don't go to college, you'll be drafted and be a common foot soldier in the Army!" he said. "Maybe you'll even get hurt. Then how will you feel, knowing you've broken your mother's heart?"

Parental response often runs the gamut of rebukes, threats, violence, and complacency. Can any of this bring about answers to the problem? No, of course not. There is an urgency about it, though. Guidance experts agree that once a young person has really made up his mind to leave school, there is very little that anyone can do to change his mind.

The solution to the problem lies in preventing a child from wanting to be a dropout in the first place. And the home is the ideal place to do the job.

How can this be done?

Below are suggestions to prevent "dropoutism" in your child's life. They are a summation of helps offered by teachers, parents, and youth leaders I have known through the years. Some are firsthand tips from my own experience as a parent and as a director of religious education in a large Ohio church. I have also included a few tips for the parent with a teenager who has already made up his mind to quit school before he graduates.

1. *Take an interest in your child as a person!* The experiences your child may have in his elementary school years will have a significant influence on his success or failure in high school.

Danny became a potential dropout while he was still in kindergarten. You might say it began when he wanted to exhibit his twin turtles in the Children's Animal Fair. His mother wouldn't give permission to Danny to take them. Other children brought their pets. Danny couldn't take part.

Another year Danny begged his parents to come to his classroom during open house. His folks were too busy to go. When he needed help with his arithmetic, he was told that was his teacher's job. When his report card showed he was an underachiever, the Morrows brushed it aside as unimportant. Soon Danny got the idea that schoolwork was something you put up with until you could do the things you really liked doing.

But besides encouraging a youngster to take part in his school endeavors, and to do them well, parents should also stimulate him to do a little thinking on his own, to reason things out. Then when problems enter his life, he can tackle them one by one instead of letting them mount until he has to run away from them.

Here is what the Coopers did: Although only five years old, Mae Ellen Cooper was a child with an amazing curiosity. Most of it came from the interesting places her parents took her to visit. Sometimes they would go to a park, a zoo, or to an art or history museum. Once they attended services in a very beautiful church. It was special and had numerous lovely multicolored stained-glass windows. But each place they went, Mae Ellen was encouraged to remember all that she saw.

Before long, Mae Ellen could retell the story of all her adventures. When she mispronounced a name or a word, her parents gently corrected her. All this was a help to Mae Ellen in her school years.

Today Mae Ellen is a teenager and still tackling problems as they come her way. In her growing-up years, she was included in family discussions about social problems, morals, values, and even politics. Consequently, Mae Ellen confidently takes part in conversations and discussions in school. She knows what she believes. She knows how to express herself. She thinks things through, accepts responsibility for her thoughts, and is satisfied with her achievements. Few dropouts can say as much.

2. *Take an interest in your child's achievements.* There is much that a parent can do to encourage a child to make good grades in school.

Probably one of the best ways to induce a child to do homework is to give him a nice table or desk with a good light. Here he can tackle his studies in much the same way a businessman would his sales report. But it also pays to offer help if the child feels confused about his work.

Setting aside a time in the home for homework can include the whole family. Why can't Mother do her sewing and mending during that time? Why can't Dad work on the family budget? The idea is to provide a study atmosphere in the home where every member in the family is trying to accomplish something.

When your child enters junior high school, he will begin selecting courses to study. Take time to go over them carefully with him. Be sure he is enjoying what he is doing. Stay tuned in with the youngster so you will know when something is upsetting him. Make your child proud of himself. Don't put him in the position of trying to do things just to please you. This is very important.

Letting your child make choices will help develop his independence. Don't push him. Allow for a few mistakes. Stand by to help him back on his feet. Be a parent. But also be a good friend and confidant. This kind of relationship takes building. You don't erect it in the teenage years. You put it together piece by piece from the cradle on.

Keep in mind that all children will not materialize into white-collar workers. They have dreams and ideals buried inside of them which need to be explored. In the process of helping your child accept the responsibilities of schoolwork and life itself, also help him to find himself and like what he finds.

3. *Stay reachable when his world falls apart.* The child who can grow up in an atmosphere where both his weaknesses and strengths are tolerated is indeed most fortunate. Few dropouts come from these homes. But every dropout needs this kind of attention.

Psychologists list self-confidence and self-esteem as the two main ingredients every person needs for emotional stability in life. With them your child can lick the world.

Without them he can only run away and hide. That's what "dropoutism" is all about.

If your child has announced that he is quitting school, are you willing to help him find what he wants in life? Will you try to reestablish your communication lines? If it turns out that he was wrong and you were right, will you stoop to pick up the pieces of his life without censure?

It is not too late for your teenager to make a comeback. He just needs a chance to find himself. Let him have it. Life stretches out long and beautiful before him. Let him push on through, picking and choosing, and learning what is best.

The Christian parent has a partnership with God in training children to take their place in life. No matter where your child is in the lineup according to age, pray daily for him. Ask the Lord to give you wisdom, to place his hand upon him, and to lead you in the way you should go. Rest upon the promise that he will.

Fathers, don't scold your children so much that they become discouraged and quit trying. COLOSSIANS 3:21, TLB

Don't keep on scolding and nagging your children, making them angry and resentful. Rather, bring them up with the loving discipline the Lord himself approves, with suggestions and godly advice. EPHESIANS 6:4, TLB

Should our child go to college? *Elizabeth McCullough*

Is a college education valuable for young people today? Is it worth the expense and the time? I know a family that has had almost daily arguments over these questions for over a year. Seventeen-year-old Bill wants to go to a trade school instead of college after he graduates from high school next year. His parents, however, have had other plans for him. Their two older children went to a local university, and they have just assumed that Bill would go too. Bill's father is convinced that going to college is the only way to "get ahead." Bill's mother works part-time, and the money she earns has always gone into an education fund for her children—to be used for one purpose, Bill found out, or not at all. "Bill can have the money for college," she says, "but not for trade school."

Other young people are having the opposite problem. Susan, for instance, has wanted to go to college for as long as she can remember, and until recently her parents didn't feel strongly about it, one way or the other. Now they are definitely against it, and if Susan goes to college, she will have to meet all her expenses alone. Susan's father thinks a degree is a luxury he can't afford, and he points to all the college-educated people who are having a hard time finding jobs. "Susan needs to learn some skills that will always help her get a steady job" is his attitude.

The uncertainty of the economy is no doubt one of the reasons many skim over the merits of higher education. It is true that college graduates are unemployed and underemployed in large numbers. Many young people know what it feels like to be just one more in the crowd of graduates—English, history, psychology, or sociology majors—out looking for a job. (Not to mention certified teachers, engineers, and business majors.)

But the economy is only one of the reasons the debate over the worth of a degree has come up at this time. Isn't it also true that we are beginning to examine the values that have developed with regard to higher education? And when we look closely at why young people have been encouraged to go to college, we can see that some of the reasons have no connection with the philosophy or goals of a liberal arts education.

Bill's father talks about "getting ahead," and to him that means making money. It also means getting out of the so-called blue-collar jobs and into a profession, which commands more respect. Some people call having a high status in a community and making a good income being a "success"; others call it "making something of yourself." Regardless of what it is called, for the past thirty years going to college has been seen as the accepted way to achieve a better life.

After World War II the country was in a period of prosperity and optimism. Getting a degree became not only a desirable goal, but a possible one for many people who couldn't have even thought of it before. The message to the taxpayer was "insure a place for your child."

In most school systems, college preparation became the order of the day. High schools became so much geared to preparing young people for college that vocational education fell behind. High school graduates who did not want to go on to college were seldom prepared to do anything else. (Typing and shorthand skills are the only exceptions that come to

mind.) In her book *The Case Against College,*
Caroline Bird tells of the interviews she
conducted with several hundred college
students to find out how they feel about their
educations and their futures. When students
were asked why they were attending college in
the first place, one of the most common
responses was "because my parents wanted me
to go."

Still others said that going to college was a
graceful way to leave home—they could ease
out from under their parents' control without
confronting any issues or hurting any feelings.

I know more than one woman who was told,
either directly or in more subtle ways, that
college was a good place to catch a worthy
man. But going to college is an expensive way
to catch mates, or leave home, or live out a
parent's dream. If college classes are filled
with young people who are there for the wrong
reasons (according to Ms. Bird only about 25
percent are actually interested in the course
work), then it is natural that they come to feel
it is a waste of time and money. For many
parents, paying the costs of higher education
means scrimping, saving, and much sacrifice.
If they are sending their children to college to
insure their getting a good job or making a lot
of money, then the parents are bound to be
disappointed too.

So now we are seeing the pendulum swing
away from traditional college educations.
Liberal arts degrees are being abandoned as a
waste of time almost as quickly as they were
espoused as a suitable goal for everyone a
generation ago. While looking critically at our
values about education is necessary and
healthy, we should be careful not to blame the
universities or liberal arts programs for the
disappointments of students and parents. I
have never seen one word in a college catalog

that promised students anything more than a chance to learn. There are no guarantees for status, money, or permanent job security.

We should also make sure we don't abandon the idea that college should be made available to anyone who wants it and is capable of the work.

Limiting the number of places in universities, making it difficult to get into college, or restricting financial aid would be socially regressive actions. Universal access to higher education was one of the good things that came out of the emphasis on college after World War II. We can be sure that the 25 percent interested students come from all economic groups.

Perhaps Susan's father is being realistic when he says Susan needs to learn practical skills that will fit into a specific job slot. But does that mean she has to give up college? I don't think it does if she can find a way to combine vocational training with liberal arts studies.

We can help our children in their dilemmas over their educations and their futures if we get rid of some of our own preconceived ideas about careers and youth. We've become used to thinking of the years between ages eighteen and twenty-two as the time when definite, and usually final, career decisions are made. Yet who ever said that a college education or a vocational program had to be completed during those years? I don't know who, but somehow the idea stuck. In recent years, we've seen one group of people contradict this completely. Thousands of women have returned to school, in many different programs, after spending years at home raising their children.

The image of "Joe College" and "Betty Coed" spending four carefree years at college and coming home with a degree hasn't ever been true for large numbers of people. Students who finance their own educations have often had to take time out to work and save money. Others become undecided about what they want to study, and they drop out and try other things. Some return later, but others find suitable occupations and don't go back at all.

While she was doing research for her book, Ms. Bird talked to many young people who had decided to leave college in order to travel. She points out that while many adults still think young people who backpack across the country are shiftless and irresponsible, this image is largely untrue. Young travelers work at subsistence or seasonal jobs to support themselves, and most of them are not a burden either on their parents or society. And who is to say that they aren't maturing and learning?

We also do our children a disservice by making snobbish judgments about different kinds of work. Bill's parents still have the idea that being a plumber or an auto mechanic isn't quite as good as being an engineer or a lawyer. Behind the attitude is the idea that "brain work" is superior to manual labor. (As if plumbers and mechanics didn't use their heads!) A friend of mine recently told me to "get back into the real world." The "real world" is the one where a teacher is still more respected than a carpenter, and a doctor is respected more than a nurse. But just because that attitude is still the prevailing one doesn't make it right. Why should we go on perpetuating a hierarchy of respect for occupations in our own children?

Bill's vocational education is important to him, and it seems foolish for his parents to hold back money saved for him just because his plans are different from their own.

(Thousands of parents would be happy if their teenagers had a goal at all.) If Bill were to give in to his parents and go to college, he would be one of the many students in college today who do not want to be there.

So we get back to the original question. Is a college education valuable, and is it worth the time and the money? The answer is really very simple. A college education, or any education for that matter, is only valuable and worth the effort if the student chooses it for himself.

In recent years we have seen an increase in the demand for what is usually called "adult education" or "continuing education." In the area where I live, the state university and community schools offer night classes in a variety of subjects, from woodworking to creative writing. Similar programs have been started all over the country. The people who attend these classes come from all age groups and occupations. These people have not put an age limit on their educations. Isn't this the attitude we want to instill in our children?

Certainly we want our children to know that whether they choose to go to college or to vocational school, or to travel and take seasonal jobs, their educations can continue all their lives.

Is a secular college dangerous? *Milton K. Reimer*

The decision to enroll in the secular college or university has far-reaching implications for the Christian young person and his parents. Education always leaves a lasting impression on a person and molds him for the future. But the influences of higher education cause a young person to adopt ideas more quickly and fully than in lower levels of education.

In many instances going away to college is the first time the young Christian is away from home. The secular influences are no longer modified or countered by the Christian home environment and restrictions. The student must now decide for himself whether or not he will maintain his Christian standards and hold to his Christian beliefs. He must either develop his own defenses against agnostic world views or be swallowed up by them. For many young people from Christian homes, attending secular colleges has been a fatal experience; they have succumbed to the life-style of the world.

It becomes the legitimate concern of every Christian parent—and every Christian youth —to try to prevent such spiritual tragedy. One of the steps in that direction is to understand the college environment and to be aware of the nature of the forces which will affect the student. An old adage says, "To be forewarned is to be forearmed." And when the Christian youth knows about these forces and realizes there are intelligent Christian answers to them, he can maintain a confidence that otherwise might be shaken.

However, it is important to understand that knowledge alone will not prevent disaster.

Many people, young and old, often go against better judgment to accept Socrates' argument that all a man needs to do right is to know right. In contemplating attending a secular college, the Christian young person must first ask: Does God want me at this school this year? If he does, then he will give the strength and grace to meet the difficulties, whatever they may be. Like Daniel, the Christian student must be determined not to defile himself with the ungodly opportunities that will surround him.

One trend on campus is a growing interest in religion. Colleges and universities are establishing departments of religion. Religion courses attract large enrollments of students. In the field of education, there is frequent reference to the role of religion in the schools. A growing percentage of students are interested in discussing religion and moral values, both individually and in classes.

At first glance, these facts might appear encouraging—and in some ways they are. But in reality, the kind of religion that the majority of students and professors are interested in is far removed from biblical Christianity. They reject the idea that absolute truth was communicated to man by a personal God, which is the biblical position. They propose a subjective view of religion— the view that one person's personal ideas about religion are just as good as the next person's views.

It is important for the Christian student in the secular university to be aware of this paradoxical phenomenon. The presently apparent condition of tolerance in the university culture is no more a friend to biblical Christianity than was the skepticism of the past. There may be less overt resistance to the gospel, but to view this as a growing kinship with evangelical Christianity could be a fatal mistake.

A positive result of the new interest in religion is a growing awareness of the evangelical viewpoint on university campuses. Organizations such as Inter-Varsity Christian Fellowship and Campus Crusade for Christ are attracting students and faculty alike.

Related to the growing interest in religion is a growing interest in the occult among college students. Some universities are even offering courses for college credit in witchcraft and black magic. In the educational journal *Phi Delta Kappan,* Walter R. Coppendage discussed the rise of the occult among college students. He stated, "Free universities across the nation sponsor classes in Eastern thought; the ancient Chinese book of fortune telling, I-Ching, has become a best seller on progressive college campuses. Psychedelic paraphernalia —black light posters, incense, Oriental art— are obvious household equipment throughout student apartments. The intense interest in astrology epitomizes the fascination with the occult!"

Another area for concern for Christian parents and students is the increasing sexual freedom on secular college campuses. There has always been more sexual freedom on the college campus than clsewhere, but the general moral laxity on campus has removed almost all restrictions. It is almost impossible for a young student, in his own strength, to maintain moral purity in this environment.

In this area, pressure comes from all sides. Professors in the classrooms often seem obsessed with the topic of sex and use it as illustrations to make points and as humor to obtain student interest. Colleges are also pressured to loosen social regulations by eliminating visiting rules and providing coeducational dorms. This does not mean that the elimination of restrictions always leads to moral promiscuity, but it does remove many of the social barriers and puts an almost impossible strain on an individual's willpower. In order to maintain his Christian standards, a young person will need to keep constant watch over his thoughts, desires, and habits, as well as his devotional life. He must continually claim victory through Christ.

A third danger zone is a current tendency to emphasize the present—the here-and-now. The "in" cliché is relevancy. Being relevant in itself is not wrong. The Christian needs to be concerned about his current experiences with the Lord, about the present problems of society and his responsibility toward them and about his dynamic witness to contemporary society. However, the current thinking is an abuse of the necessary emphasis. There is a tendency to reject all of history and its lessons as irrelevant. The past has nothing to teach us, the future is irrelevant, and all that matters is the present—this is the common philosophy of life.

It is easy for a student to get all wrapped up in this "relevancy" movement, but it is essential that the Christian youth recognize the fatal pitfall. His whole Christian faith is based on an actual historical event. The Apostle Paul says, "If Christ be not raised, your faith is in vain; ye are yet in your sins" (1 Corinthians 15:17). Biblical Christianity demands that one never lose sight or appreciation of events that occurred in time and space. Some sincere students have said, "It doesn't really matter if Christ actually rose from the dead or not. The important thing is what the idea of the resurrection means to me here and now." That is the attractive but fatal argument that Christian students need to guard against.

Finally, there is an almost universal rejection of authority of all kinds. This may be expressed in outward rebellion against the university administration. But more likely it will be a subtle attitude toward all knowledge. The concept of an absolute is no longer considered valid and has been replaced with relativism. In this view, there is no authority outside of the individual—no absolute right or absolute wrong, only personal choices based on the present situation.

This prevailing attitude is perhaps the most disastrous of all dangers that the young Christian will face. It undermines his resistance to moral laxity, and it weakens and dilutes biblical Christianity and doctrine. It also removes the necessity for basing his Christian beliefs squarely on the historical events of Christ's life, death, and resurrection. According to this view the individual sets his own standards; he decides what is right or wrong. There is no outside measure by which a person's moral standards can be established; there is no possible way for one person to tell another that his conduct is either good or bad; one's conduct is totally subjective, or based solely on one's personal opinions. This moral subjectivity is comparable to a sailor trying to cast his anchor inside his ship or trying to guide his ship by a star attached to the top of the mast.

Once the Christian has been infected with this subtle subjectivity, the devil has essentially disarmed him, for he can no longer speak with the authoritative voice of "Thus saith the Lord." Young people from kindergarten to college, as well as older people in society at large, are constantly bombarded with this point of view. The real problem for our youth in public education is that even valuable information is taught within this subjective context.

These trends and influences are only a sample of the conditions existing on secular college and university campuses today. But they do represent some of the most significant areas of concern for the Christian student. To remain constant in his faith, the Christian student must constantly assess his position in relation to the areas stated above and make sure he maintains a proper relationship to the truth of God's Word.

Children who have an easy life, free from troubles, may not be prepared for "real life" later on, according to a forty-year follow-up of youngsters in a survey at the Institute of Human Development, University of California at Berkeley. "Many of the youngsters who came from very stable homes failed to develop an immunity to different kinds of stress and at age thirty were, for the most part, not mature," say psychologists Jean MacFarlane and R. D. Tuddenham. When the study was begun, so long ago, they had supposed that children brought up with great security and a trouble-free childhood would also grow up secure enough to cope with whatever life might hold and that "children whose early lives were shadowed by economic uncertainty, emotional tensions, or illness in the home would have a burden to carry that would be hard to overcome as they grew older." It didn't work out that way. Many of the children who had a tough time at home were found, as adults, "to possess an extra strength and adaptability which must certainly have been developed through the extra efforts they had to put forth in coping with their problems in early life . . . At thirty, they were more mature, self-confident, and more able to cope with life than many of their contemporaries who had had everything going their way."

Is a Christian college preferable? *Robert Webber*

Recently, during a discussion on the values of a Christian education, a woman said with a note of despair in her voice, "Oh, I hope I can persuade my son to go to a Christian college. I'm sure if he can just get into the atmosphere of a Christian school he'll turn out all right."

This assumption, which is characteristic of many well-intentioned parents, is false. There can be no guarantee that Christian college graduates will become strong Christians or leaders in the church. There is always a minority that goes the other way and becomes either apathetic or antagonistic toward Christianity. Usually this happens despite the love, interest, and many hours of counseling offered by dedicated faculty members.

It's only natural to ask why a student runs into a spiritual dead-end street in a Christian atmosphere. There is no easy answer. There are many factors: the student's background, influence of friends, church association or lack of it, and response to campus experience. But also, it must be admitted that spiritual default is sometimes related to the cultural milieu of the Christian campus itself. Because that is the subject of my concern, I will mention three conditions which occasionally provoke an adverse response.

First, there is the danger of the spiritual atmosphere of a Christian college. It is ironic that the very thing a Christian college seeks to perpetuate may become its own worst enemy for some students. Specifically, I speak of a spirituality that is structured rather than spontaneous. Most Christian colleges seek to create a climate of spirituality by daily chapel, prayer before classes, dormitory prayer meetings, Christian Service Council projects, and spiritual emphasis weeks. As one student put it, "It's too much of a good thing. After a while it becomes so commonplace."

"That's the problem," said a junior, "you just get to the place where you take everything for granted. For me there's no more reality; it's all perfunctory. It's really scary." In my own opinion, some Christian colleges provide too much spiritual mothering. Sometimes this overprotectiveness backfires. Some students, resting in the security of the situation, become apathetic. Others, feeling that this kind of Christianity offers no challenge to life, react by becoming antagonistic.

Also, this business about an external Christianity produces a certain amount of phoniness. Let's face it—there's a lot of pressure to conform on a Christian campus. Students who don't conform find themselves unacceptable to the administration as well as to some of their peers. The weaker student tends to play the spiritual game and go along with the formalities just to be accepted. This kind of hypocrisy destroys the potential for real, honest, gut-level faith. Its ultimate end is a retardation of Christian growth and character.

Another very serious problem is the legalistic attitude toward behavior. Many colleges have long lists of rules which regulate the whole life of the student. Almost every rule, especially those having to do with dating, dress, and general conduct, find their rationale in the argument, "We do it this way because it's the Christian way to do it."

I am not arguing against rules. I am arguing against the idea that the peculiar rules of a Christian college are part and parcel of the Christian faith. To say that it is Christian to keep your hair short, wear long skirts, and abstain from movies is to confuse the issue. It makes nonessential rules essential. The essentials appear less significant by contrast.

I don't know how many students have said something like this to me: "If legalism is what Christianity is all about, then forget it."

These students understand something important. They are not going to allow themselves to become party to a dogmatic, closed-mind, and ill-defined subculture. After all, Paul described legalism as a gospel which is "another." Legalistic Christianity runs the risk of becoming "another." The danger is that the student who gives it up may think he's giving up Christianity. He misses the point. The accent of true Christianity is the freedom to be a responsible person, the freedom to model life after the real Jesus, not the plastic do-gooder of legalism.

A third problem centers on a pietistic anti-intellectualism. This attitude is reflected in the downgrading of such subjects as philosophy, science, psychology, anthropology, and sociology. It is built on the assumption that Christians should study only the Bible, everything else being secular and of less value. I have seen intelligent students damaged by this kind of obscurantism. As one said to me, "If the Christian faith is just a narrow sectarian view of life, then I can do without it." The tragedy is that many students who give up anti-intellectual Christianity do not realize that they are only giving up someone else's notion of the Christian faith.

Often anti-intellectualism reaps what it has sown after the student has graduated. This was the case, for example, with a friend of mine who said, "In graduate school I realized I had no adequate base for my beliefs. Dogmatism and emotional piety don't hold up under scrutiny." Fortunately, he came under the tutelage of intelligent Christians who showed him that base. But this doesn't always happen.

These three adverse conditions do not exist with the same degree of intensity at every Christian college. There is a great deal of difference among colleges which may appear, on the surface, to be similar. The problem of anti-intellectualism, for example, is almost nonexistent among the better-known institutions.

Also, we should not overlook the possibility that there are positive aspects to a strong spiritual atmosphere and a framework of regulations. Many students have found God's will for their lives through chapel and learned the importance of self-discipline through campus regulations. It is rigid, inflexible severity in these areas that lead some students into a spiritual dead-end street.

Well-balanced climate

In choosing a Christian college, then, I would encourage you and your daughter or son to find a school that provides a well-balanced, spiritually sensitive, and intelligent social, spiritual, and educational climate. In this situation a Christian student has the best chance to grow into a sensitive, mature, and responsible Christian adult.

So let me make a few suggestions on how to investigate colleges. The best thing to do is to visit the campus, attend classes, talk to the students, question the administrators and faculty. Also, read the literature. Look for a thoroughly thought-out educational philosophy. Does the school seek to integrate faith and learning? Is there an appreciation for a Christian world view? Do the course offerings show a concern for contemporary issues? Don't forget to read the student handbook. What attitude does the school take toward its rules? Are they conceived legalistically? And what about the academic qualifications of the faculty? Do they represent a wide variety of backgrounds?

These four years of college are most important. It's worth the time and effort it takes to think through the alternatives as you move toward an intelligent decision.

A young man was to be sentenced to the penitentiary for committing forgery. The judge had known him from childhood, for he was well acquainted with his father, a famous legal scholar and the author of an exhaustive study entitled The Law of Trusts. *"Do you remember your father?" asked the magistrate. "I remember him well, your honor," came the reply. Then trying to probe the offender's conscience, the judge said, "As you are about to be sentenced, and as you think of your wonderful dad, what do you remember most clearly about him?" There was a pause; then the judge received an answer he had not expected. "I remember, sir, when I went to him for advice, he looked up at me from the book he was writing and said, 'Run along, boy, I'm busy!' When I went to him for companionship, he turned me away, saying, 'Run along, son; this book must be finished!' Your honor, you remember him as a great lawyer; I remember him as a lost friend." The magistrate muttered to himself, "Alas! Finished the book, but lost the boy!"* —AUTHOR UNKNOWN

6

Critical Issues

Why do I overpunish my child? *Maggie Hempel*

I'm going to make some confessions here that I don't relish making. They're bound to cause ill feeling and I'm certain I'll be poorly judged by friends and relatives. But I think what I have to say may be of some service to other young mothers and to their children. I'm willing to suffer the repercussions.

When the doctor told me I was pregnant, I was happy. More than happy—I was ecstatic; and so was my husband, John. I had been trying to conceive for over two years, and both John and I were eager to start a family.

I immediately donned maternity clothes, even though I wouldn't need them for several months. They were my announcement to the world that I was carrying a child, that I was a woman who would soon become a mother. I was proud. When I think back now, I realize that there had always been a subconscious hint of wanting to become pregnant simply to prove to myself and to others that I could—to prove that I was a woman.

My pregnancy went well. The minor aches and pains were welcomed as a reminder that I was indeed pregnant and on my way to becoming a more "fulfilled" woman.

John and I waited eagerly for the baby, but we did very little together, as though our lives had to stand still for a while. All our energies and interests, especially mine, were directed toward that one end—my child, my motherhood.

My sister and her husband also lived in our city. She was the mother of three and expecting her fourth. I remember her repeated warnings to us: "Get out and do things! Soon your lives will change. Your freedom will be gone. Make use of this time you have together!" John and I laughed. I thought to myself, "But don't you see? We want our lives to change. We can't wait until they do!"

Our son was born in April, later than he was expected. We had succeeded. But my labor was long, seemingly endless—twenty-four hours. I was too worn out at first to enjoy the victory.

The four days in the hospital were pleasant. There were no large worries or anxieties except the usual insecurity of an inexperienced mother who is nursing for the first time. But John III was a healthy eater who soon taught me that he knew what he was doing, even if I didn't. He cried a lot those four days. We smiled and thought how cute he looked, screaming his head off behind the nursery windows.

My spirits remained high throughout the hospital stay, but I was eager to go home and begin my new role. On the fifth day the three of us left the hospital as a family.

The first few hours were calm enough. John III went to bed for a nap and slept peacefully. We had to stop ourselves from waking him to hold him and play with him. When he did wake up, screaming, I fed him. He stopped crying long enough to eat, but began to cry again as soon as the feeding was over. We tried everything, to no avail. It was an uncomfortable and frustrating feeling—we could not make our new child happy. We put him back to bed, but he cried for forty-five minutes until, finally exhausted, he fell asleep.

The days went by slowly with the same routine. There were very few minutes that he was awake and not screaming. The constant noise was beginning to get on our nerves— mine more than my husband's—and I tried desperately to find the cause of the crying. Although I knew I had enough milk to nurse him successfully, I decided to bottle-feed Johnnie, hoping this might make some difference. It didn't.

We asked our pediatrician what was wrong, but he said simply that some babies have to cry more than others. I felt too unsure of myself to push the point or explain just how much Johnnie was crying. I assured myself that if anything was physically wrong, the doctor would know.

John and I could go nowhere. We didn't want to disturb others with our baby's behavior, and we didn't dare submit a baby-sitter to such an ordeal. We were trapped in our home by the very dream of our lives. Our only periods of freedom were when we split up and took turns going out for an hour or so. I began to go shopping more often, spending more money—money we didn't have—and thus financial worry was piled on top of our other problems.

Soon I began to feel resentment toward Johnnie. After all, I thought, he was the one who had made me suffer so painfully and so long during my labor. He had caused fights between his father and me, arguments that were outgrowths of our worry and tension over him. He had taken away my freedom to come and go as I pleased, even to be comfortable in my own home.

Several months passed and my nerves became more jagged. I began to slap Johnnie and to spank him, even though I knew he couldn't understand why he was being hurt. But I needed to punish him for what, to my mind, he was doing to us. I was rough with him, shoving him around, showing him I was angry and disappointed. Of course, this only made his crying worse. I didn't hit him hard enough to injure him—it was just an emotional release for me.

But instead of helping, it only made me feel guilty, inhuman. After losing my temper and seeing the surprised, hurt look in his big eyes, I'd feel terrible. I'd pick him up and tell him I was sorry and hold him, only to repeat my actions later.

I talked to other mothers, trying to find someone who would understand but never admitting to anyone how much I loathed taking care of Johnnie. I tried to laugh and make jokes about it. I did learn one important thing—that every baby gets on his parents' nerves sooner or later. And ultimately I had to admit to myself that the problem was not with the baby, but with the way I was handling the situation. I came to realize that I hadn't wanted a baby at all—at least, not for the right reasons.

It was then that I told myself that if I couldn't change my behavior, I would have to admit that I needed help and see a psychiatrist. I was a danger to my child. I knew I would never injure him intentionally, but I could hurt him accidentally. Wasn't this how child beating began?

I made myself sit down and think out the problem seriously and—more important—honestly. I talked to my husband about it. Until this time he hadn't suspected how distressed I was or how I was taking it out on Johnnie. He was shocked, but he also was sympathetic. He tried to reassure me, to calm me.

And the more I thought about it, the more clearly I began to see. I had been behaving immaturely because I had been ignorant of what to expect, unprepared for the less-pleasant truths of motherhood. Certainly Johnnie couldn't be expected to know that his behavior affected others. He knew only his problems and was fighting instinctively for happiness and survival. Realizing all these things, I still became upset with him, but less frequently. And then I would force myself to walk away from him until I could get my temper under control.

At this point, I went back to our doctor and described the seriousness and the frequency of Johnnie's crying. He told me that nothing could be done for the time being, but that within a few months the problem would clear up by itself as the baby became more active and able to rid himself of gas (which, the doctor said, was usually the reason for his discomfort). Almost immediately I felt more relaxed, now that I realized Johnnie's problems weren't caused by my inadequacy as a mother. I felt secure again, even confident.

My relationship with Johnnie began to change. He wasn't challenging me or testing me; he was merely telling me that he had pain, that he was hungry or uncomfortable. My frustration at not being able to help him remained, but no longer did I blame myself. John and I began going out together, leaving Johnnie with a sitter. To our surprise, sitters could handle the situation as well as, or even better than, we could because they weren't so involved and didn't feel the sharp pangs we felt so often.

By the time Johnnie was five months old he was a different baby—happy and content, though still very active. That brought a flood of relief. Then I fully realized how foolish I had been in not seeking the doctor's opinion sooner, in feeling personally and constantly attacked by Johnnie, in being unfair to my husband and myself by not hiring a baby-sitter so that we could have time together to renew our relationship. I also know now that I had never understood what it takes to be a parent—the trials, the sacrifices, and the joys.

I started out as an immature, selfish, egocentric girl, and Johnnie taught me patience, understanding, and a degree of maturity. It worked out well for Johnnie and for me. But it could have been different—it could have been a disaster. And this still frightens me at times.

If I had educated myself on child behavior and infant disorders, if I had read about similar cases and been introduced to the problems faced by many young parents, if only I had understood the responsibilities I would face as a mother, this problem would not have reached such huge proportions. The more I talk with other young mothers now, the more I learn that most of us face the same problem to some degree. Talking together, we've reached even better answers about how to cope.

It is for this reason that I've written this story. It is extremely important that other young, inexperienced mothers not feel freakish because they resent or overreact to the problems a child creates. It is necessary that they feel secure in talking about these problems without fear of being rashly judged or condemned. Only then will child beating and other sufferings brought upon children be eliminated. We must tackle the problems together, for the safety of our children.

The fool who provokes his family to anger and resentment will finally have nothing worthwhile left. PROVERBS 11:29, TLB

If you are angry, don't sin by nursing your grudge. Don't let the sun go down with you still angry—get over it quickly; for when you are angry you give a mighty foothold to the devil. EPHESIANS 4:26, 27, TLB

How can children cope with a parent's death? *Gladys Kooiman*

Daddy came back—almost, anyway.

It started at Grandma's. My little four-year-old was standing before the television set, studying our family picture as if it were the first time he had seen it. Possibly because Grandma's picture was placed at his eye level, he took notice of it. (Ours, in a much larger frame, hung high on our living room wall.) I was listening to him as he was pointing out each member of the group with a chubby little finger and announcing, "Look, Mama, there is me, and there is Linda, and Judy and me and you and Howie and me and—"

Suddenly he paused at the figure of Daddy, and stumbling, as if for want of words, he continued, "and there is, and there is—" Then looking almost fearfully at me, in a hushed voice he whispered, "There's my Daddy."

All through the day and the long, lonely night the words, "and there is, and there's, and there's," kept echoing and reechoing in my consciousness. Each time I heard them I kept seeing his half-fearful face. Why had my little one been so reluctant to say "my Daddy"? Did it hurt so much? Was he perhaps sparing me? When was the last time he had mentioned Daddy? Or for that matter, when was the last time anyone at our house had mentioned him?

Among the hundreds of sympathy cards and letters I had received at the time of my husband's death, there was one letter which contained this message: "As time goes on you will want to speak of him often to your children." These words now rang in my consciousness as I probed for an answer.

When had I last mentioned Dad to the children? The past weeks had been such dark and difficult ones, and the very thought of my husband had brought such pain and loneliness. Could it be, I wondered, that to ease the way for me my children consciously or unconsciously were avoiding talk of Daddy in my presence? I must make sure.

The occasion to find out came more quickly than I had anticipated. We were having dinner the following evening, when my kindergartener began telling us the story of Peter Rabbit. Is there a child who does not get excited over and over again about Peter's escapades in the garden? But it was the mention of bunnies which brought a very funny incident to mind, with Daddy as the hero.

"Children," I began, "have I ever told you about the time that Daddy decided to rid our orchard of bunnies? Once when you older children were very small, we had a lovely new orchard started, with several young trees. In the fall Dad had carefully wound each little tree with fencing in order to protect them from hungry, nibbling bunnies. But that winter was no ordinary winter. The snow fell and the wind blew, and some more snow fell and the wind blew even harder, until the little apple trees were surrounded by snow drifts much higher than their wire collars. And the bunnies soon discovered the tender bark made good gnawing. Well, whenever Dad decided to take action, he never took half-way measures."

I proceeded to tell the rest of the hilarious incident. I tried to recapture for them the picture of their dad chasing through the snow in bare feet, with his shirttails flying. The children responded with a good laugh, and then the questions began: "Mom, did this really happen?" "How old was I then?" "Did Dad really go out in bare feet?"

It wasn't long before a new kind of remembering began. "Say, Mom, do you still remember when. . . ?" and, "I can still see how funny Dad looked that time we. . . ."

Yes, we were long at dinner that night. I doubt if any of us remembered what we ate though. I realized that for far too long I had been responsible for keeping a door locked, a door which should never have been closed in the first place. In a very real sense I had handed their dad back to them through the avenue of memories.

How unfair I had been. How much there was to learn in my new role—I seemed to learn so slowly. We speak often of Dad now and what a lot of joy it brings! Memories have a way of healing. Children have a right to these and should be encouraged to remember their departed father. I learned the hard way.

There are ways in which we do not speak of Dad. I have never tried to manage the children by reminding them of the punishment they might be receiving if Dad were here, nor do I feel it is right ever to curb their behavior by reminding them that Dad might be watching from up in heaven. Dad was the most devoted dad a child ever had, and we keep him that way.

Can I make it as both father and mother? *Katie F. Wiebe*

"I want you at home! I don't want to be baby-sitted!"

I tried to erase these words and the vision of my little boy's tear-stained face from my mind as I drove away from the baby-sitter's home to go to work. But what could I do?

A good, responsible person was taking care of him, but four-year-old Jamie wanted things to be the way they were before. A few months ago, when his mother was at home each day taking care of him, there had been time for games and stores and walks together.

Any time a home is broken, pain is present. I was overwhelmed at times by the painful reality. My husband's place at the table was empty. I was now the breadwinner and sole parent of four lively children.

Now, however, we were experiencing another loss as a family, much more subtle in its invasion of our home than death had been. Touch, sight, hearing, smell—all were useless to indicate to me what had left us. Yet each evening as I entered the door to face the evening's schedule of housework, I knew something was missing.

It wasn't the food; the girls were becoming fairly good cooks. The little dining area where we ate was crowded by five people, but it felt empty. At that moment God made me aware of what was missing. The family feeling was gone, that feeling of contented oneness and belonging. Death had robbed us of one parent, and now it was threatening to break up the whole family. We were becoming a group of five people living together in one house, one very busy woman and four children of assorted ages coming together to eat and to sleep. In trying so hard to earn shoes and bread for five, I had forgotten that life is more than a new dress for the spring concert or fried chicken for Sunday dinner.

When the family feeling is gone, how does one bring it back? I knew that something had to be done. I sat down at my desk to identify my biggest problems. My list looked something like this:

1. How to keep the morning exodus from being a free-for-all rat race.

2. How to keep that family feeling in the confusion of the evening return.

3. How to find more time for making meals, laundry, and housekeeping jobs.

4. How to help the children feel more secure.

5. How to keep the masculine element in the children's lives.

Just holding each problem at arm's length helped me tremendously, and I felt vastly better when I went to bed that evening. I now had a goal and a plan.

Part of my new plan was to start the morning preparations the night before by helping the children get their clothes ready, having breakfast partly laid out, and meals planned for the day. I also pinned up lists telling each child her tasks for the day. A little black-covered notebook became our daily log. I've noticed how even now the older girls sometimes return to this little book for recipes one doesn't find in cookbooks, for in it I gave instructions about exact times to put various foods on the stove and what kinds of saucepans to use.

The other part of my plan was to get to bed earlier and to get up earlier, for most tensions can be greatly eased by getting more sleep.

The evening return was harder to unkink.

Usually the moment I entered the door, at least one was waiting to nab my attention to tell me about a grade, the need for 75 cents for a book, or a party at church. I was tired from a day's work; we were all hungry, and sometimes someone had to run to the store to get something needed for our evening meal. The child who dared to move in and ask, when angels fear to tread, usually had little success. Even now we joke about five o'clock not being the right psychological moment to make requests of Mother to use the car or similar matters. Wait until Mother has taken her shoes off.

The secret of success for any family is a tie of some kind which holds the individual members together even when the family is apart.

My parents were never able to give us much money or many clothes, but in many ways they gave us more important things—a sense of personal worth before God and man, courage, hope, and love for one another. Our feelings of oneness was usually centered in some joint activity of all members of the family.

Now as a single parent, I realized that my own children needed more joint activities to bond us together. We found one in the family devotional period we tried to hold after the evening meal. Daddy was no longer a physical presence. By continuing our "family altar" as we had done before he left us, we discovered what God, our heavenly Father, might mean for a fatherless family.

Most working mothers have only limited time with their children; if they want that time to count, they have to make wise use of those few hours. Letting nonessentials in housework go was difficult for me at first, for I had always been a neat, fastidious housekeeper.

Yet I realized that time spent talking with the older girls or playing with the younger children was more important. Whereas I had hated toy-strewn rooms, now I learned to step over blocks, trikes, and trucks. Talking after the supper meal sometimes stretched out longer than we planned.

Shopping for groceries became a once-a-week affair. I had no scruples about TV dinners, pot pies, cake mixes, or other kinds of ready-to-eat foods. I thanked God for every convenience food. I limited ironing strictly to items of clothing like shirts and blouses, and streamlined other housekeeping tasks to meet only the basic requirements of health, comfort, and convenience. I saw no point in trying to be a Superwoman who did everything like the lady on the hill with a maid and butler.

Trying to keep a masculine element in the children's lives is, of course, very difficult. On Father's Day, when the other children made gifts for their fathers, my son made one for his mother. Other little boys and girls couldn't understand why he didn't have a daddy.

Again and again he came home with questions. Hard ones, too. Why don't I have a daddy anymore? Where is Daddy now? Why didn't God make him well? Will we see him again? If he's in heaven, why doesn't he need his bones in the grave? How will we know him in heaven without his bones and his clothes?

One of my biggest challenges is transferring the hope of the resurrection in Christ Jesus to the children. I pray that they may have the confidence to believe that even in death there is hope and that in life there must always be courage.

A family is also built into a strong unit by the members working cooperatively together. When one member is missing, the others have to do a little extra. It hurt me to see my youngsters struggling with adult-sized jobs and problems, but I was encouraged when I recognized in the older ones a growing sense of responsibility and care for the younger children.

I was sometimes tempted to take advantage of a conscientious child's sense of duty and overburden her before she was ready for so much responsibility.

During one difficult period when we pinched pennies harder than usual, the children became too conscious of financial pressure. I sensed it bearing down on them. Spirits were heavy. "We can't do anything. We can't buy anything. We can't afford anything." Mother had become a Scrooge.

Widows who must manage family finances alone for the first time without the security of a husband's income will find themselves being overly cautious. I was. I feared pauperdom as much as illness. As I learned to trust God in such matters, the children also came through with a more cheerful outlook. "Maybe we can't take that trip this summer, but we can do some other things."

On the other hand, a widow's love for her children may tempt her to shield them from hard experiences in life. "I had a hard struggle," said one parent, "and I don't want my children to go through such experiences if I can help it." So her child never learned to make his own bed or polish his own shoes. In later years every decision, regardless of how small, upset him.

Children need the experience of deciding certain crucial issues for themselves. This is hard for any parents, but especially for a widow. She may think the child has enough to bear not having a father, without adding other problems to his life. So she takes over for him.

With the father gone there may also be a temptation to let things go: house, car, lawn. The sense of pride in ownership is gone because the one who found joy in keeping the house and yard in good repair is no longer there. It's important to wash and wax the car, to clip the hedges, to keep the house tidy, to keep oneself neatly groomed and attractive, and to keep the children happy.

Fear of inanimate things bothers many women who live alone as much as giant problems in the spiritual realm. We believe that God answers prayers for courage, for strength, and for joy, but what can he do for leaky faucets and broken bicycles? I've shed many tears of frustration and agony over my children's behavior and my own lack of courage and peace of mind. I've shed even more over doors that won't close, drains that won't drain, and furnaces that refuse to heat.

I've learned since that most things that are broken can be fixed. Skilled mechanics and craftsmen are available for such tasks if I can't tackle them alone. Further, most men are considerate of such problems. As women, we waste too much nervous energy on inanimate objects. A short course in mechanics or plumbing might dry up many tears.

As the children moved through grade school, high school, and now college, I believe we managed to hang onto the idea that we are a family. Something holds us together.

The fall leaves had been dropping for several weeks, heavily covering the lawn. One day I laid down an ultimatum that that evening everyone would rake leaves. No one would get an exemption from work for any reason.

Shortly after supper the rakes came out and the work began. One child grumbled because she couldn't stay in and read her library book. Another didn't see why we couldn't just let the wind get rid of the leaves. But I persisted, and we worked together.

When the big pile of leaves was burning, the children warmed to the situation. They brought out foil-wrapped apples and buried them in the fire.

Late that evening as the fire embers flickered in the darkness, we sat together on the back step, tired and dirty, eating ice cream and discussing the merits of half-baked apples. A hush fell on us as we huddled together and enjoyed the gradually encroaching night. The grumbling was gone. In its place were a happy silence and the good feeling that "we're still a family."

I knew then that we were winning.

There are several million stepparents in North America, all of whom need some help in filling a difficult role. These problems are more difficult nowadays, when 80 percent of the stepfamilies exist because of divorce, than they were three-quarters of a century ago when 80 percent of the stepfamilies existed as a result of death. Nobody can replace a child's biological mother or his biological father, and nobody should try. This fact has obvious implications for the stepparent's role in his stepfamily. A wise and sensitive parent does not deny his stepchild's heritage. He does not deny the fact that the step-relationship is different from a relationship rooted in blood ties and legal obligations. By his (or her) very acceptance of these differences, the stepparent takes a major step forward toward helping his stepchildren live in the world they were born into, a world of all-pervading change, change embodied in the existence of the stepfamily itself. For life in twentieth century America is an experience in adaptation. To live successfully is to accept that change. To deny it is fatal.
FROM: THE SUCCESSFUL STEPPARENT, BY HELEN THOMSON

Can we be happy with a live-in mother-in-law?
Thelma White

"Well, that's that, she can't live there alone any longer, and that's final."

When my husband spoke in those terms, I knew further discussion was unnecessary. He was right, of course. His 68-year-old mother had fallen and broken her arm and was simply unable to manage for herself. She must come live with us. There seemed to be no alternative.

My mind scrambled around the problems entailed by her permanent visit. I simply didn't know how we could manage sharing a room and doubling up the children. If we were having problems finding a place for her to sleep, how could we ever solve the problems that would arise when she became a permanent member of the family?

That first evening after my mother-in-law came to live with us, we gathered into the living room to talk about the changes in all of our lives. Fortunately my mother-in-law is a very practical woman, a trait I found in her son and love him for. She got to the heart of the problem immediately.

"I know my staying with you will cause a certain amount of upheaval in your lives, but my son is right. I am too old to cope with that large house, and sometimes I did worry about having a serious accident and not being able to get help. I have been thinking about how we could all manage here comfortably and happily, and I have a suggestion to make. Since I plan to sell my home and most of my furniture, I could use part of the money to build a small apartment for myself here in your home."

My husband and I were both a bit startled by her proposal, but the more we discussed it, the more realistic it sounded. After careful consideration, we decided to add a bedroom and bath at one end of the house. This would enable her to have her own entrance and would afford her some privacy.

Our solution was fairly easy, but there are thousands of couples faced with the same decision who find their problems aren't as easily solved.

The first thing everyone in the home should understand is that the older parent is not a guest. A pleasant and straightforward discussion about how the household functions —who has what chores to do, when they are expected to do them, who should discipline the children and who should not, when the meals are generally served—will help the grandparent fit into the family scene smoothly and save a lot of hurt feelings in the future.

Even if the older parent in your home is the most accommodating person in the world, it isn't easy to have three generations under one roof. Long-established habits and patterns aren't easily broken, or for that matter even bent. A wife and mother has a pretty full day; often she rushes from place to place, then hurls herself about the house frantically trying to fix dinner while cleaning up the living room while making out tomorrow's shopping list while settling a sibling squabble. She may find the slow-paced life-style of the older parent setting her teeth on edge, and sometimes this can prompt a harsh comment. Often the older parent is critical of the apparently haphazard manner in which the home is run and will say so, with the prerogative of years, quite bluntly.

The harassed mother can learn a valuable lesson from the older parent. Slow down a bit. Nature does it for you when you start getting

older, but why wait till then? Try getting up
just a bit earlier in the morning to get the
laundry started; then it won't be sitting there
in a baleful bundle at three when the kids get
home and the confusion begins. Figure out a
more efficient way to accomplish the daily
tasks so you can walk instead of run.

I watched my mother-in-law over a period
of time and really began to admire the way
she managed her day, with quiet calm getting
everything done: a good lesson for me and a
definite plus factor for our home.

Privacy is essential for the older parent
grown accustomed to living alone. It really
works both ways: they want to get away from
you and you want to get away from them. If
the older parent in the home has a room to go
to in order to write letters, watch a favorite
TV show, or just have a quiet moment, he or
she won't be disturbed by the rest of the
family. By the same token, they may want to
lend a hand at a time when their presence
would be more of a problem than a solution.
Privacy is not a luxury; it is a necessity.

Just about the nicest contribution the older
parent in the home makes is to the children in
the family. When the grandmother or
grandfather moves into the family, the
children adjust to this relationship more easily
than anyone. Grandparents, of course, are
notoriously indulgent with their grandchildren
and sometimes this can present difficulties.
But these can be solved quite simply by
allocating a certain time of day for a visit to
the grandparent's room. This is a wonderful
arrangement for all concerned. In my case, I
decided the hour just before dinner was
perfect for these rather "formal" visits. The
kids looked forward to it, and I was delighted
to have them out from underfoot at the busiest
time of the day. As a result, we would all come

to the table happy and relaxed. In addition, the grandparent really appreciates the fact that the children have a specific time allotted for visiting instead of running in and out whenever they want. Our children regard this time of the day as a privilege, and always seem to put on their best manners.

Another unexpected dividend many families receive is a feeling of continuity in the family. A friend of mine, for example, was angry with her husband and was trying very hard to keep her mother-in-law from finding out there had been a quarrel. But when people live together it is impossible not to know when someone is angry. The mother-in-law began to relate a story from her son's childhood which my friend barely paid attention to until suddenly through the anger, like a shaft of sunlight through an ominous sky, the words began to make sense. The mother was telling of some incident in which her son had been unbendingly stubborn, and how she had handled the situation without arousing any more hostility. My friend immediately grasped the wit and wisdom behind the words. Her husband wasn't being mean or selfish; he was just reacting to a situation the way he had since childhood. The seemingly aimless story had a definite point. With a silent thanks to her mother-in-law for this new and welcome insight into her husband, my friend was able to defuse the explosive situation and learn a valuable lesson for the future. The kids, observant as ever, saw how effective Grandma had been in helping solve a family problem and the bond between them was strengthened.

One of the most obvious advantages of having an older parent in the home is the actual help they can provide. Many young women leading productive lives in the business world would not have that opportunity if it weren't for an older member of the family living in their home and helping with the children and housework. Everyone wants to feel needed, and what better way for the older parent to make a positive contribution than by helping with the younger children.

When the older parent moves in, what sort of financial arrangements should be made to keep things running smoothly? A straightforward discussion of the family budget is the best way to get the matter settled. Don't leave it to chance or hope that things will take care of themselves. They rarely do.

With encouragement, the older parent can soon find a very satisfactory social life among contemporaries. Church, of course, is a wonderful source for new friends. Select an activity that you think would be of interest to older parents and go along to that first meeting or activity. If they enjoy it the first time, suggest going back and plan to go along this time too. Once the pattern is established and they start to make friends in the group, you can ease your way out and leave them to their fun. It is really imperative that they make some friends of their own age group and outside the family.

My mother-in-law takes a daily walk and in a surprisingly short time made several friends along her route. One day I asked if I could go with her and enjoyed meeting her new pals. One was a dear old fellow who had the most luxuriant garden I've ever seen. I stood there for half an hour while they discussed the relative merits of various fertilizers, the best time to prune certain shrubs, and all manner of things relating to gardening. Further down the block we spent a little time with another friend, a scruffy, long-haired teenager who worked endlessly on an aged car. The way those two kidded back and forth, I knew they'd had many such conversations. As we walked on, he promised to give her that long-postponed ride in his car as soon as he got it running.

That's the way it went all afternoon. She'd made many friends right in our neighborhood, people I didn't know at all but should have. The pleasures of walking should never be underrated. Encourage the daily walk, good for the spirits as well as the health.

Life in a three-generation household can be very trying, but it balances out when you consider the advantages. Most of the problems can be avoided by establishing good communication right at the outset. If you are always ready to talk and be open in those talks, misunderstandings with the older parent can be avoided. Love them, enjoy them, and learn from them. Be tolerant with them. With some effort you'll find rewards in your three-generation household that you may not have expected.

A New England woman took her mother-in-law into her home. The old lady's continued questioning got on her nerves. But she kept the peace while she thought up an antidote. "From now on," she announced to her in-law, "whenever you ask me about our private affairs, I will either lie to you or give you a nonsensical answer. Which would you prefer?" Luckily, the old lady had a sense of humor, so nonsense won. The daughter-in-law recently reported, "The sillier my answer is, the more fun we get out of it—both of us." ALEX OSBORN

7

Neighbor Relations

What marks us as a Christian family? *Francis D. Breisch*

How can a Christian family influence the people around it for Jesus Christ? It cannot be done simply through words. The things we do and those we don't do, the way we relate to other members of the family and to our neighbors, the set of our jaws and the pace of our lives—all these are constantly telling people about us.

Surely love should be the cornerstone of a family that calls itself Christian. First of all, love should control the relationships between the members of the family. This is not to say that brothers and sisters will never fight, or that parents and children will always understand each other, or that husband and wife will always be in perfect agreement. That sort of perfection is unattainable in a sinful world. But each member of the family should have a genuine concern for every other member.

Marks of love

What are some marks of a loving family?

One is the honest recognition of existing differences and an attempt to work them out. All too often, one member of a family will be hurt by something another member does, but instead of facing the matter clearly, he will bury it under a show of "niceness." Can other people tell whether a family is honestly loving or just "nice"? They certainly can! "Niceness" rings a bit hollow; it is artificial. Honesty develops the kind of relationship that is solid and real.

Another mark is loving acceptance of a family member who goes astray. Christian husbands and wives have been known to be unfaithful. Christian young people have ended an evening in the police station.

How does the family react to such situations? If the erring member is ostracized, or made to feel he is no longer accepted, the family has failed. For Christian love, like God's love, is unconditional. Without condoning the sin, the rest of the family should make it clear that the sinner is still loved, still very much part of the family. Such concern, when expressed in forgiveness, is impressive to those who look on. In fact, the reaction of a Christian family in such a time may be the most positive witness for Christ they can give to their neighbors. Morality is important, but forgiveness is the heart of the gospel. When people see forgiveness in action, they wonder what causes it.

Love reaches out

But a Christian family's love will not be expressed only within the family. Christian love reaches out to others, as God's love reaches out to us. It embraces neighbors, whether they are the nicest people imaginable or miserable cranks.

All too often, Christian families wave to their neighbors and say "Hello" when they see them, especially on Sunday morning as they drive off to church while the neighbors are working in their yards. But the years go by and the relationships remain cordial but distant. Then the man next door has a heart attack, and all they can think of to say is, "Please let us know if we can do anything to help."

Christian families need to take the initiative toward those around them. Nonchurchgoers tend to be a bit afraid of a family that goes to church every Sunday. Consequently they are not likely to take the first step. If the barriers are to be broken, Christian love must do it.

This means that Christian families will have to be ready to go out of their way to get involved with those around them. People have to be taken as they are. Offers of friendship which carry the unspoken suggestion that friendship will cost conformity to the standards of the Christian family are not likely to be accepted.

If you recall how Jesus was at home among all sorts of people—dining with publicans and sinners and talking with immoral women—you may be able to convince yourself that such associations do not necessarily constitute compromise with your Christian standards. On the contrary, they may be convincing evidences of genuine Christian love.

Real Christian love will also lead you to become concerned about some matters that aren't very "spiritual." When your neighbors are affected by matters like sewers, zoning changes, and the like, you cannot cop out by telling yourself that your concern is limited to spiritual things.

Concern for justice

Suppose a home in your all-white neighborhood is up for sale. Immediately you are faced with the question of loving a neighbor whom you do not yet know. Will you love him if he belongs to a minority racial group? Will you give him whatever support and assistance he needs to feel he is accepted in your neighborhood?

In some neighborhoods that is no academic question. You may live in a neighborhood which is now feeling the impact of minority persons moving in. What are you doing?

Love is the first of the fruits of the Spirit. It is first not only because Paul lists it first, but because the entire New Testament indicates that love is the most basic Christian virtue. Both Paul and James specifically state that he who loves his neighbor as himself has fulfilled the requirements of God's law.

Moving from deeds to words We must recognize, too, that our responsibility goes beyond a nonverbal witness. Our neighbors need to hear the message of the gospel, and deeds alone cannot proclaim that message. Deeds may indicate that we have something worth sharing. Generally speaking, our actions are a necessary foundation on which a verbal witness can be built.

But how do we get from deeds to words? How can we present the gospel most effectively to those around us?

First of all, let us make this a matter of family concern. Witnessing is not merely the obligation and privilege of the various members of the family. The family as a unit is involved and ought to be involved. If one member of the family is aware of an opportunity which seems to be opening up, the whole family should know of it and should pray about it together. Even the small children should be included, so that they may realize that the whole family is concerned about sharing Jesus Christ with others.

A second step might be a family conference to talk over the situation. The more specific we can be about witnessing, the more effective we are likely to be. If we simply ask the question, "How can we reach our neighborhood?" we may find it difficult to come to a satisfactory conclusion. But if we ask ourselves which neighbors we think we should concentrate on first, and then discuss how to approach that family, we are more likely to find a workable answer.

One important question to consider, as we talk together about another family which does not know Christ, is where that family "hurts."

The parents may be having marital problems, or there may be a serious gap between parents and children. At this point it is a matter of taking the initiative—tactfully. For example, if the problem seems to lie between parents and teenage children, we can look for opportunities to talk to the other parents about it, and our teenagers who know Christ can try to do the same with the neighboring teens. If in such contacts we show real concern for our neighbors, there is little likelihood that we will offend them.

Here the vast difference in neighborhoods must be considered. In a suburban neighborhood, where friendliness is considered a right and natural attitude, making contacts may be quite easy. But the same is not true in a city neighborhood, particularly in giant apartment complexes. A minister in an inner city apartment building discovered that he could only meet his neighbors by "drilling wells"—that is, by establishing situations in which people could meet around interests they already had. His answer was a series of discussion groups for neighbors on art, modern poetry, and other subjects which were not specifically Christian.

Within a large apartment building, almost all conceivable interests will be represented. Often a notice on a bulletin board or in a laundromat is all that is needed to get together a group of people who have your interest in common. Once the group is together, it can become a bridge over which you travel to make personal contact with the other members.

In the less reserved neighborhoods, Christians can use the transient nature of our society to good advantage. When someone moves into your part of the community, why not be the one who invites the neighbors to your home to meet the new people? This not only introduces you to the newcomers as people who are ready to accept them, but it also increases your opportunities to meet the other neighbors, to get to know them better, and to gain more understanding of the ways in which you can begin to approach them with the gospel.

Suppose you are the family that is moving? In many cases there will be expressions of friendliness by your new neighbors; be sure to reciprocate as quickly as possible. And though it is common for the old residents in a neighborhood to welcome the newcomers, there's no law against new residents taking the initiative! The important thing is to make contact with your new neighbors as soon as possible. If you get to know each other personally before they have a chance to stereotype you as a "religious" family who ought to be avoided, you can remove many barriers which otherwise you would have to overcome later.

God has established us in families. He has put us, as families, in neighborhoods and communities. And he has given us, as families, the responsibility to be his witnesses. When the neighborhoods in which we live and work, and the communities of which we are a part, see and hear God's love from Christian families, we may expect to see a new interest in our communities in the church of Jesus Christ.

How can we get next to our neighbors? *Philip E. Armstrong*

Witnessing is one of the main tasks of the church. Practically every Christian periodical features some article on the art. I am not complaining; I need all the admonition and advice that I can get. But there is another lost art in the church—neighborliness.

The royal law of Scripture according to James 2:8 (KJV) is: "Thou shalt love thy neighbor as thyself." If you fulfil this, you do well. To love your neighbor is a command. Witnessing is a result of a promise of power. Loving is your responsibility; the power to witness is his.

Paul put it this way: "Owe no man any thing, but to love one another: for he that loveth another hath fulfilled the law" (Romans 13:8, KJV). I tried to be nice to the man next door so I could witness to him. I loaned him my ladder. I painted his ridgepole. It turned out he was a Christian. But he outdid me with niceness and didn't even try to testify. Ask yourself, are you loving your neighbor so you can witness? If you are, he will sense it. Or are you witnessing because you love him? The Scripture is clear—you are to have no debts but one: that one you can never repay. It is love.

Who is my neighbor?

The lawyer asked Jesus: "Who is my neighbor?" The word literally means "nigh-dwellers." Often we are more inclined to witness at some distance than we are to love those who dwell nearby. Consequently, we become specialists at witnessing on planes, trains, or in other parts of town. Because it is so easy to travel, we go to church outside of our neighborhood. At church the program is so full it often keeps us out five nights a week. We conduct services at the mission and the jail; we run a Sunday school bus and do visitation. All good, but they have nothing to do with our neighbors.

Are you your brother's keeper? If so, he may wonder why you pull out of your driveway every Sunday morning. You haven't told him. Come to think of it, you haven't seen him since September. Or was it November? If you share my concern, let's keep our homes from becoming drive-ins and make them dwelling places.

Are you serious about winning the man next door? You say, "I have talked to him; he's not interested." Ask yourself why. Are you interested in him? You say, "I don't know him very well. He drinks; they do a lot of things we couldn't do as Christians." That has nothing to do with Jesus' demand. He said, "Love him!"

The art of being interested

You say, "But I can't get next to him." Let's try. Not to win the man next door, but to love him. Let's start here: he has interests, find out what they are. He may like his anonymity. This is evidenced by the trend toward apartment living even in the suburbs. He likes his freedom; he spends his weekends on the road or at the lake. But he has some sports or hobbies he enjoys. Find them. Jobs you may enjoy, he may consider drudgery. Try to "divvy" up.

Look for common interests—children, pets, car or tool pools. Look for any occasion to know your neighbor. My wife joined the Garden Club instead of the Ladies Aid. Her coin collecting and Questers, a national antique club, introduced us to neighbors we never would have met.

Take another couple with you to the next PTA. Or just take a long walk around the block. How come you never met those people before?

As you look at your neighbors, don't overlook those who are interested in other religions. Those who work at it the hardest may be the most hungry, and may make the best disciples of Jesus Christ. The man who is neutral may be very appreciative of your friendship but completely passive to your presentation of Christ.

Try a check-up on yourself. Did you know when your neighbor went to the hospital? Where are their children in school? Have you seen their slides from their last vacation? Each of these are entrances into warm friendships. Use them.

Next, his needs. He has needs you have been too busy to know. Let's start with simple things. Jesus talked about a cup of cold water in his name. It may mean making a casserole for the couple who just moved in. It may mean fixing a faucet. Most of us are too busy to be bothered.

His needs may not be very spiritual, but if you are not concerned with these, how will he come to you for eternal life, or peace, or forgiveness? An international student described a campus Christian who attempted to witness to him: "All he wants to do is to save my soul from hell and he doesn't care what happens to me." What he was really saying was that he had needs his friend was too blind to see. Every man has a hunger in his heart. Bear the burden that is obvious, and he may later speak of the hunger that is hidden.

The art of listening

How do you find this out? By listening. Dietrich Bonhoeffer in his book *Life Together* has said:

Listening can be a greater service than speaking. Many people are looking for an ear that will listen. They do not find it among Christians, because these Christians are talking when they should be listening. But he who can no longer listen to his brother will soon no longer listen to God either; he will be doing nothing but prattle in the presence of God, too . . . There is a kind of listening with half an ear that presumes already to know what the other person has to say. It is an impatient, inattentive listening that despises the brother and is only waiting for a chance to speak and thus get rid of the other person . . . Christians have forgotten that the ministry of listening has been committed to them by Him who is Himself the great listener and whose work they share. We should listen with the ears of God that we may speak the Word of God.

Many Christians give their neighbors the feeling they have no needs. Sophie Muller, a missionary to South America, speaks of one of her converts: "Rafela, who died in Christ, used to sit at my feet and brush the flies off my legs and sympathize with me for being so far from my parents and not having anyone to take care of me. The one thing that will open hearts to you and the gospel more quickly than anything else, perhaps, is their sympathy."

A fire broke out in the home of one of our missionaries in Japan. The whole town came to their rescue, carrying out their furniture and belongings. Afterward, the missionary saw the attitude of the village change. What before had been icy acceptance now turned into friendly inclusion. How many times a catastrophe in the home of a Christian has brought about the sympathy and understanding of neighbors, which that believer never could have known by trying to meet his neighbor's need.

The art of witnessing

Do not make the mistake of putting off identifying yourself with Jesus Christ. Let us not be so tactful that we never make a contact. Even his name dropped into a conversation may somehow identify you as one of his own. However, this is not enough.

If you have really won the affection of your friend, sooner or later you will want to make a personal presentation of Jesus Christ. Paul called it a "door of utterance." One of the most successful soul-winners I know recently joined an overseas team from his company. Although he was dubbed "chaplain" the first week, he waited three months to win a hearing with his superior officer. Then, under the very obvious direction of the Holy Spirit, he personally confronted this man with the claims of Christ.

When we get to this stage, we hedge. Here are some pointers. First, get the other person to ask about Christ if you can. If he doesn't, be very sensitive to the Holy Spirit. You will know when the time comes. Don't pass it up; that moment may never come again.

Our fear is that we won't handle the situation right. After building such a friendship, we don't want to hurt it. If your friendship is right and you confront him in love, you should be just as close afterward, whether or not he accepts Christ. There may be an offense taken to the gospel. Our problem is to see that it is only the gospel that offends.

The opposite may occur. By this time, the man next door may be so indebted to you for your good works that he is not free to make his own decision. Douglas Sargent mentions this in his book, *Making a Missionary:*

As we present the gospel we are to show complete respect for the personality of the one to whom we are speaking . . . There must be no force used apart from the power of love.

Our hearer must be completely free to make his own decision after we have faithfully presented Christ to him. Any undue pressure in no matter what form it is brought to bear, in the end will be self-defeating.

Perhaps this is the acid test of our understanding of the command of Christ. Must we need to see them saved? Would our attitude toward them change if they did not become Christians? What we are really testing is whom we love. If it is only men, our love may be fickle; if it is Christ, he will permeate every relationship.

Think of what such love would do for the neighbors you know. The world is full of neighbors with needs; God can meet them. The whole world is looking for a little bit of love. God has a lot. Can we spare a little?

YOU DON'T NEED A PIE TO SAY HI!

Say hi to your new neighbors! No need to change clothes and fix your hair. More important, put a smile on your face. On arrival, welcome them with a big hi. Offer a helping hand. You don't need a pie to say hi. Just bring along a pot of coffee.

In a day or so, when the movers are gone and hubby and the kids are off to work and school, stop in and get acquainted. Maybe she would like to know where to shop for good buys. Perhaps she would just like to talk. If she has a baby, offer to watch it for her for an hour.

What a lift you can give. Anyone can scrub the cupboards, lay shelf paper, and wash and wipe the dishes. Misery loves company. And suddenly an awful chore to stare in the face becomes fun as the work is shared with a neighbor who says hi. Just knowing there is a neighbor nearby, someone to talk to, borrow from, and share joys and sadness gives the new neighbor a lift.

You can do many things to make new families feel welcome. Invite the whole family for a meal. Take over a freshly baked loaf of bread during the busy days of settling. Have a neighborhood coffee to help her get acquainted. Invite the children to Sunday school, Mother to Circle meeting, and the whole family to church. Say hi to your new neighbor. Don't delay. Do it today! DELORIS A. PAPKE

What if our neighbors are relatives? *Mary Alice and Harold Blake Walker*

Now and then a man will say to his prospective bride, "But I am marrying you, not your family." He is about as far from the truth as he can get. She is linked to her family by emotional ties that keep her in its orbit, disturbed by disturbances in the lives of her family, concerned by the concerns of her family, and sensitive to what happens back home. Both he and she marry a collection of peculiar relatives when they stand at the altar to be joined in holy marriage.

Usually families want to be helpful. Their mistakes are unintentional and if they create problems for the newlyweds, they often are not aware of it. Normally, the mistakes that cause trouble come as the consequence of good intentions that went wrong.

It is well to begin marriage, then, expecting the best and not anticipating the worst. Relatives and in-laws can be fun and they can be wonderfully helpful. One couple whose three pretty daughters are married to men of assorted abilities seem to have preserved a remarkable rapport with both the daughters and the sons-in-law.

After five years of marriage one young man remarked, "When Jane and I were married, I made up my mind that I would love Jane's people as I loved my own." He confessed that once or twice he had bad moments and got annoyed. But after five years he has no better friend than Jane's father and no bigger booster than Jane's mother. Of course, he started right, namely, on the assumption that he married not only Jane but her family, too. He began by expecting to have relations of affection with those who were closest to the wife he loved. He got what he expected.

To be sure, if he expects the best of her family, she had best expect the best of his family. There is no place for comparison: "If only your people were like mine, everything would be fine." That is an invitation to trouble. Keep searching for the best; the worst will show up of its own accord. Keep expecting the best; the unpleasant will turn up now and then unassisted.

There are plenty of good things to be said even for the worst in-laws, and most in-laws are by no means the worst variety. Any wife gets a big lift if her husband says, "Your dad is a wonderful guy." He feels warm and pleased all over if she says, "Your mother is lovely." Just leave it there without any "buts" to mar the promise of a pleasant evening.

Set up a separate establishment, not too close to either family. Then start making your decisions and choices together and independently. You need not consult either family every time you turn around. Consult each other, think together, pray together, and plan together. If you have established a relationship of independence and equality with your parents and you want their judgment as one factor to help you make up your mind, well and good. But if the relationship is one of dominance, make up your own mind and report the conclusion when you have arrived at it.

Stand on your own feet financially, too. Maybe your parents and in-laws are able and willing to make things easy for you. But too much help from the old folks is a poor bargain. It undermines both your self-respect and your independence. You have to do some respectful listening when your meal ticket speaks his mind. You are not altogether free, and you can't be, if you are leaning on the in-laws or using your own parents as a crutch to make life easier for you.

Struggle never hurt anybody. On the contrary, struggling together and building together inspires togetherness of spirit and deepens love and affection. One young couple, refusing to be subsidized and moving away from home to a strange city, settled in a single room where they ate and slept and cooked. "We don't have much," she remarked without apology, "but we have each other and we're having a wonderful time."

To be sure, there are exceptions to every rule. A young man in medical school with a wife and family is being helped by his parents. He is by no means living a life of luxury, but with a little help in addition to his scholarship, he can stay in school. "What I'm getting from dad is a loan," he remarked, "and not a gift." Then, as if in afterthought, he added, "Dad never will press me to pay him back, but as soon as I am able I will press myself."

One generous father sent a set of furniture to his son and his bride. He had selected it himself and thought it just what they should have. They returned it collect. He commented wryly: "That's independence for you. But I love them for it." He should have loved them. They were happily standing on their own feet and making their way on their own.

Such drastic measures usually are not required. A quiet talk with overindulgent parents ordinarily will settle the issue. Parents want to be helpful. They have no wish to be problems, and if their help is hurting, they will give up without too much of a struggle. They may be a little hurt at first, feeling you are ungrateful, but nine times out of ten they will come through wiser, with new pride in you and what you can do on your own.

The disapproving in-law is more of a problem than the overindulgent parent or in-law. One young woman noted that she and her disapproving mother-in-law never had gotten along. "The minute I saw her, I was upset," she reported. "I resented her and came close to hating her." When the mother-in-law's husband died, she came to live with her son and things went from bad to worse. "I prayed plenty," the young woman reported. "I read books I thought might help. My home was rapidly falling apart. Then I saw there was no hope unless I could love my mother-in-law and daily act as if I loved her until I could honestly do it." What happened was a miracle. "Now," the young lady reported, "we get along swimmingly. She is a grand person and she thinks I am tops."

The whole problem of the disapproving mother-in-law is complicated by emotional and psychological factors that can't be ignored. Ordinarily, the disapproving mother-in-law wouldn't approve of anybody her son married. Emotionally, she wants to hang on to him. She makes him feel her need for his love and consideration, and he feels frightfully guilty and remorseful if, in the interests of his marriage, she refuses what consideration he thinks his mother needs from him. On the other hand, if he caters to his mother, his wife makes him miserable. He is in trouble, no matter which way he turns.

There are two things that can be said, however, and said to the wife. The first is that your husband needs help and understanding. He is being pulled apart. If he is tied to his mother's apron strings by her constant cries for him, it is because she thinks he has been taken from her. The more her son is kept from her, the more she schemes to claim his time and thought. On the other hand, if she can be loved and led to feel that instead of losing a son she has acquired a daughter, she will find security and confidence and less need to possess her son.

The second thing to be said is that the more a young bride loves her husband's mother, the more the husband will love her. The more she understands his predicament and helps him to deal with it, the more essential she will be to him. If she puts increasing pressure on him to put his mother in her place, she intensifies his tension and inner conflict and makes life unbearable for him. Usually it is not love for his mother that holds him. On the contrary, it is a sense of duty she has imposed upon him.

If that seems to put an undue burden on the wife, it should be said that the husband has an obligation too. He can't expect his wife to solve his problem alone. If there is any possible way of providing for his mother without bringing her into his home, he ought to find it. It will be infinitely easier for his wife to love his mother if they are not living under the same roof. He can be wise enough to recognize that his mother is a real problem for his wife. His wife is not just being unreasonable and inconsiderate.

When children arrive, if you have in-law problems, by all means keep those problems out of sight. Children can add fuel to the fire or they can be an asset in the solution of the difficulty.

One man put his feeling simply when he noted, "I never have cared much for my son-in-law, but he is the father of my daughter's child and I'm going to like him and maybe someday I can love him, too."

Then, too, if the grandparents are not too far away, they can be wonderfully helpful during the days while the children are growing up. Maybe they will have a hand in spoiling the children a little, but the damage won't be serious. Most grandparents are wise enough to go along with the schedule for the children, even if they once did things differently. If, now and then, grandma suggests she doesn't approve of the way you are raising Willie, take it in your stride. Her mother or mother-in-law probably said the same thing to her twenty years or so ago, and she did as she pleased.

Wisely managed, grandparents are real assets to the new family. Of course, they have their limitations and should be used sparingly. But if grandma rocks the baby when you think she shouldn't, there are some child specialists who say it won't hurt in the least. Don't worry, little Willie will live through it and won't be any worse for the rocking. The two generations can have a wonderful time watching Willie grow if you don't take grandma's rocking too seriously.

So, accept your relatives, your parents, and your in-laws for what they are and make a serious effort to understand them. They have virtues you can discover, knowledge and insight you can use, and affection to give if you can manage to accept their faults and rejoice in their virtues. After all, you are trying to build a life and a home with somebody they love and cherish as much as you do. It pays to keep things as harmonious and happy as good sense and tenderness can manage.

Have we forgotten hospitality? *Joy A. Sterling*

The work of evangelism often conjures up mental pictures of house-to-house visitation, handing out tracts, or housewives sharing Christ with neighbors over coffee. But we need not let our imagination stop there. If coffee and doughnuts can provide the setting to present Christ, think of what could happen when you ask people to come into your home for a meal!

Opening your home to others is scriptural. It is, in fact, one of the qualifications for a good pastor; he must enjoy having guests in his home (1 Timothy 3:2; Titus 1:8). 1 Peter 4:9 admonishes us to cheerfully share our home with those who need a meal or a place to stay for the night. Throughout the Old Testament, the people of God are instructed to offer hospitality—food and lodging— whenever needed. As a clincher, Hebrews 13:2 tells us that besides obeying God's Word, we might be entertaining "angels unawares" (KJV).

Soul-winning takes time, and most of us are too busy for long contacts. By the time we work, sleep, eat, and spend time with our family, our day is gone. But we spend an hour or so eating, so why not share this time with someone who needs what you can offer—food, fellowship, love, and Jesus. Barriers are broken down easier over the table than anywhere else. (Why do you suppose fellows often take their girls out to dinner when they plan to propose?) Breaking bread together puts people on common ground.

I have seen extremely uncomfortable people backed into a corner in their own homes, while a dedicated witness crammed the plan of salvation down their throats. There is a place for house-to-house witnessing, but if you question the etiquette of invading someone's home uninvited, asking them to your home is the perfect solution. I feel more comfortable discussing what I choose within my own home.

Besides the mental security of my own home, I have the knowledge that my dining room table is pretty well sanctified! It's been committed, prayed around, and used by the Lord so many times that I feel I'm on hallowed ground when I set plates on it. Not that it is such a grand table—far from it. But I know that the Holy Spirit is alive and working in that dining room just in the same way that I've seen him working at the altar of my church.

"But I'm not a fancy cook, and our house isn't nice." Who cares? Surely not people who are crying for someone, anyone, to care about their hurt. Not old Mr. Thomas down the street: he probably hasn't eaten a meal with anybody for five years. He doesn't care whether your furniture is Early American or Early Attic, but oh, how he'd love some homemade biscuits!

This brings us to the food. So who needs a gourmet meal? Out of literally hundreds of spur-of-the-moment guests I've had, I've never had a single one who didn't at least act like they'd rather have canned soup and a grilled cheese sandwich with company than a five-course meal by themselves. If you think you can only serve fine meals on lovely tablecloths to company—then perhaps you have a bit of a pride problem. What are you sharing, anyway? The fancy food, or love and concern and Jesus Christ?

It does help, however, to keep a mental list of easy things to fix on a moment's notice. Some of the menus I whip up with no advance preparation are waffles, grilled ham and cheese sandwiches, pizza, hot dogs and beans, and spaghetti. (Incidentally, I use soybeans in my spaghetti, and it doesn't bother me a bit. Never once has a guest said, "This sauce tastes funny with soybeans in it." My kids, yes. My guests, no.)

Nearly every homemaker keeps ingredients on hand for a favorite casserole. Mine is macaroni, tuna, and mushroom soup, topped with the potato chip crumbs from the bottom of the sack. Tuna and macaroni? For company? Sure. And I can have it on the table in thirty minutes. I sometimes even serve it on a plastic tablecloth, with paper napkins, and we have a great time.

It isn't the extravagant or elegant menu, the polished silver, the grand (or even immaculate) house; it is love and concern that count. Let your guests set the table and help with the dishes if they want to. Remember, most people don't have fancy lives, and those who do might like to see how the rest of us live!

"But who should I ask?" If you are serious about this, the Holy Spirit will guide you. One way to start is to invite people home from church. Every church has lonely widows, young couples away from families, people who have problems, or just people you've seen in church for years but have never really gotten to know.

How about people on your street? The old man in the next block is alone most of the time. Why not ask him? Or the widow whose child has been in so much trouble? What about Mrs. Brown whom you worked with at vacation Bible school, but never really established a relationship with? Or the new family you met when you were doing church calling? Ask at the local nursing home or children's home—they are full of lonely people.

"But what do I say to strangers?"
Witnessing isn't pushing someone in a corner
to get them to listen to you. It is
communicating the love of Jesus. That means
you share your feelings, your dreams, your
disappointments, and your victories. Then
they are free to share theirs, and what an
opportunity to tell them about your Savior and
Lord! A word of caution: never, whatever you
do, serve roast preacher or fried choir. Being
critical will undo all the good your invitation
might have accomplished.

Your guests won't be the only ones to
benefit from your hospitality—you will be
ministered to in ways you wouldn't expect. A
few weeks after our four-year-old son died, a
couple passing through town came home from
church with us. They found out about our
recent loss, and shared how they had lost their
young child a few years earlier. Only someone
who has lost a child knows the depth of the
ache, and they ministered to us in a way that
no one else could have.

Another time when we were battling a
problem in our church, we invited a young
man to our home who was in town for a few
weeks to sell an investment program. He had
come from the West Coast, and was eager to
share the things God was doing there. During
our afternoon, he shared ideas that were
beautiful solutions to some of the church
problems we'd been grappling with.

Your children will profit from exposure to
different people other than those within your
small circle of friends. Many entertain only
people with similar backgrounds and interests,
but inviting others to your home will open new
worlds. An added benefit for us has been that
our children feel free to invite their friends to
stay for a meal, and some of these kids don't
have many opportunities to see how a

Christian home works. I'd rather have my son drop in with three buddies for lunch than to have the best-regimented eating establishment in the world. I'm glad they know that caring about people is more important than caring about things.

Maybe my way isn't your way. Perhaps you aren't geared to spontaneous guests. That needn't keep you from inviting people; ask them ahead of time. Set aside a regular night each week or each month to have someone in. Or take them out to a restaurant, if you just can't cook for them. But give this idea of spaghetti evangelism a try.

Someone has said, "Evangelism is one hungry beggar telling another where to find bread." Sitting around a dining room table seems a fitting place to do it.

Listening effectively means that when someone is talking, you are not thinking about what you are going to say when the other person stops. Instead, you are totally tuned into what the other person is saying. H. NORMAN WRIGHT

Love is listening. Love is the opening of your life to another. Through sincere interest, simple attention, sensitive listening, compassionate understanding, and honest sharing.

An open ear is the only believable sign of an open heart. You learn to understand life—you learn to live—as you learn to listen. DAVID AUGSBURGER

234

Are we for real? *Winnie Christensen*

Listen to this incident which just happened as I was writing. Today is such a gorgeous, clear, spring afternoon. You can almost see the leaves growing on the trees. The playground is filled with shouting children playing ball. Even our dog was barking exuberantly until the phone rang. The steely voice on the other end of the line threatened, "You keep that damn dog of yours quiet, or we'll burn your house down!" The receiver clicked.

I hung up the phone slowly, trying to place the voice in my mind. It had to be one of our neighbors close enough to be thoroughly bugged by our dog. That doesn't surprise me. The dog bugs me too. He just gets carried away and can't seem to quit barking. Most of the time we bring him inside so he won't bother anyone. This once I hadn't brought him in soon enough.

What troubles me is the ugliness of the threat. The caller can't separate irritation at an animal from hatred for its owner. Somehow it seems so typical of all the violent attitudes in our society. We hate people because we don't like their ideas or philosophies or clothes or manner of life. We have lost the ability to reject ideas or life-styles without rejecting the person as well.

One evangelical minister, whose church had made a much-criticized departure from the usual pattern of operation, commented regretfully, "If you shift your methods, your theology is questioned."

The same sort of reaction is often evoked when we bring up the subject of social action. Because we have lived securely in the framework of the evangelical church's prime responsibility to proclaim the gospel of salvation through faith in Jesus Christ, we have tended to withdraw from social involvement. We're told that two-thirds of the world is starving, but we're in no position to do much about that. Of course, we could find out about the people in our own church and community and see what their needs are, but why should we? We have to look out for ourselves. We earn our own living, mind our own business, pay our taxes. Why can't other people do the same? Why should we be reponsible for their welfare?

But Jesus said, "You shall love your neighbor as yourself."

James makes it even more pointed:

Dear brothers, what's the use of saying that you have faith and are Christians if you aren't proving it by helping others? Will that kind of faith save anyone? If you have a friend who is in need of food and clothing, and you say to him, "Well, good-bye and God bless you; stay warm and eat hearty," and then don't give him clothes or food, what good does that do? . . . Faith that doesn't show itself by good works is no faith at all—it is dead and useless (2:14–17,TLB).

The crippled city

A brilliant young lawyer who lives and works in Chicago, and who donates a great deal of his time and legal services to representing deprived and exploited people, said, "Chicago is a very small town when you get involved. You keep meeting the same small group of concerned people all over the city. They seem to be the only ones who care."

What can the evangelical Christian do about the problems of the inner city? Dr. Howard Hageman, pastor of the North Reformed Church in Newark, New Jersey, who has worked for twenty-four years in that city, said,

First of all, if we are going to be effective

*witnesses in the inner city, we had best get
over the . . . hang-up we have about working
in the ghetto. I have no sympathy whatever
with those who claim that hunger, poverty,
bad education, and bad housing are simply
social questions with which the church should
not be concerned. The Christ in whom I
believe is concerned about human wholeness,
the needs of the body.*

A pastor and his wife and young children
decided to move back into the city from their
comfortable home in the suburbs. They got an
apartment in a typically old building. There
had been riots in that very area just before they
moved. This young minister walks the streets,
talking to the people in the ghettos, frequenting
hippie hangouts, and talking to kids who have
"dropped out" or run away from home.

Dick and Audrey chose to remain in the city
rather than move out. They have five children.
Audrey, a nurse, is often called on by her
neighbors for emergencies or even to read a
thermometer for an illiterate mother. "Our
well-functioning, loving family life makes an
impression in the community where family
living is not the rule. Other families don't
work together. Also, I don't feel our children
are being cheated educationally. It takes more
of our time as parents to supplement their
education, but it's well worth it. We're happy
in the city because God put us here."

**" . . . in
prison,
and you
came"**

Ruth and Bob were typical suburbanites with
four young children. They started going to jail
to paint.

"I hate to paint," Ruth laughed as she
recounted their experience, "but we heard that
Chaplain Erwin needed help, so Bob and I
came to help. We painted, laid tile, put in
ceilings, and loved every minute of it."

Ruth's husband, Bob, is an executive in a

large department store, but he changed into old clothes and went to the jail after office hours night after night to work.

Inmates also volunteered to help. One of them was Tony, a drug addict and a "con artist." Tony worked hard, side by side with Ruth and Bob. He talked to them by the hour as they hammered, painted, and laid tile. He had never met people like these. Imagine—an executive, on his hands and knees doing menial work! Why, even the chaplain was there in work clothes working until midnight.

Tony had met Christians before who had tried to beat him over the head with the Bible. They would preach and talk and hand out tracts and leave, but these people showed they really cared about men like him. They talked about Christ and the Bible, but it was different with a paintbrush in their hands. This was living Christianity.

After many conversations, Ruth asked Tony, "Have you ever thought about accepting Christ?"

"Yes," replied Tony, "but I don't know how." Ruth sent him a New Testament and told him to read John 3. Tony did. But he didn't accept Christ until the day he was released from prison. "I purposely held off," he said, "to show that I really meant business. I didn't want anyone to think I believed just to get special favors while still in prison."

Tony made a profession of faith in Christ because people who lived their Christianity had communicated Christ to him.

The Apostle Paul said, "The kingdom of God is not just talking: it is living by God's power."

The youth explosion

We like to be able to put things in convenient pigeonholes. "If you raise your child this way, he will turn out to be a responsible adult." We want simplistic formulas so that we can be sure of success. The only problem is that sometimes human nature just doesn't work that way.

The casualty rate in good Christian homes seems to be rising steadily. People whose children have been absorbed into society and are considered "acceptable" tend to have pat answers. Those whose children have made a departure from the so-called "norm" have few answers, especially when they have sincerely sought, with the Lord's help, to be good parents.

A college senior told me, "A lot of young people are turned off on 'success' because they have lived close to successful people. The criterion for judging a 'good family' has been if they are churchgoers, if their kids get good grades and are athletic. And I don't think that's a valid basis for judgment. I think 'success' in a family is determined by interpersonal relationships. Is there harmony in the home when no one else is around? Are the parents geared to producing spiritually mature families?"

Here was a young man who objected to the Christianity he had seen while he was growing up because it was mechanical. People went through the motions. But it was all so hollow. Is this a valid criticism? How many of the spiritual motions do we go through because that's what is expected, rather than because we're motivated by genuine love for Jesus Christ?

Young people look for the real and the genuine. They are also highly critical—and always have been. Seldom do they admit that something is all right. It can always be improved their way.

Christian adults need to listen to young people, no matter how radical their ideas may seem.

One mother of five, three of whom are

teenagers, said, "My daughters and I may have been cross with each other all day, but at night they always say, 'Come on, Mom, let's talk,' and we do—about everything. They know they can trust me not to share their confidences with anyone. The girls are fifteen and sixteen now. I hope this line of communication stays open."

A Christian high school counselor said, "Many of the kids I see on drugs are looking for peace. They face so much tension and unrest in their homes that they look for a way out. They don't see their parents facing up to problems and solving them. Their parents move when the issues get too knotty in a community, or escape to Caribbean vacations and leave the kids on their own. And I believe," the counselor went on , "that unless a parent involves God in the whole family's life, he isn't going to find any workable solutions."

I talked to a lady recently who has taken into her home a college-age girl from a Christian home who is on drugs. "You can't imagine the criticism I have gotten from other church people for doing this," she commented.

Other families have done the same thing for young people who have become alienated from their parents and local churches. In some instances, the parents have strongly resisted the efforts of other Christians to help their children because they felt it was pointing up their own failure as parents. This is no time for pride to get in the way of God's working. We should thank the Lord for every person who cares enough to make a positive contribution to our sons or daughters.

An elderly lady in our church prays for every single family in the church by name every single day. "And I pray for all the young people twice a day," she said, "because I feel their problems are so great." Because she prays for them so faithfully, she says she finds it's a lot easier to talk to them when she sees them. No communication gap here. She cares, and they know it.

During a recent disturbance on a large university campus, a man in a nice business suit was trying to talk about Christ to the students milling around. Though he was very sincere he was making no headway. Another Christian fellow, looking like a hippie, with long hair, came on the scene. Seeing the man was having trouble, he decided to help him out. He took over the microphone and said, "Look, what this man is saying about Christ is true."

A voice from the back of the crowd challenged, "If your Christianity is true, then give me your sweater. I'm cold back here!"

Without a moment's hesitation, the young man had his sweater off and passed it through the crowd. From that point, he had their complete attention.

The same challenge was thrown at the man in the nice suit, but he disappeared into the crowd.

Yet if those two men came to your church, which one would you be most inclined to welcome? Which one communicated the message of Jesus Christ most effectively? A sure way to lose any audience, but especially an alert young audience, is to fail to back up our preaching with our actions.

Christian parents, Christian adults in a community and church, can contribute a great deal to the welfare of their children and young people by first of all being genuine Christians themselves.

God doesn't expect everyone to do everything. But he does expect each of us to do something. "Let us stop just *saying* we love people; let us *really* love them, and *show* it by our *actions*" (1 John 3:18,TLB).

8

How should we choose a church home? *Stanley C. Baldwin*

In our highly mobile society, the number of families who have to search for a new church home is large indeed. According to the U. S. Census Bureau, seventy-two million people moved from one house to another in the four years between March 1970 and March 1974. Some stayed in the same general locality and so had no need to change churches. But more than thirty-eight million moved far enough to require them to find a new church home.

The following checklist is offered as a guide to finding a new church. Have each member of the family grade the church independently and then compare results. You could learn some interesting things about your family as well as about the respective churches.

Location. A Christian should weigh the advantages of attending a church near his home. If the church has a full program of activities and your family is to take full advantage, it could involve a lot of travel. You'd either need to buy an interest in a gas station or curtail participation.

Too, it can handicap your Christian witness to attend a church at a distance. It makes it difficult to invite your neighbors. They either have to travel too far to attend your church, or they have to go to a nearby church without your being there to welcome them properly.

Good Sunday school. Certainly if you have children, you want a church with a thriving and effective Sunday school. You want your children to enjoy going, learn biblical truths when they get there, and develop Christian character and proper attitudes toward sacred things.

But Sunday school is not only for children. A stimulating adult class can enhance your grasp of biblical truth and help you personally apply its implications. On the other hand, who wants to sit through an hour of tedium every Sunday morning?

Good youth work. The teen years can be tough, for kids and parents alike. Since it's an age when a teen's peers affect him most strongly, many parents consider a good youth work to outweigh all other considerations when seeking a church home.

And what's good so far as youth programs go? Solid Bible teaching, understanding leaders (not necessarily the flamboyant type), and a group spirit, with key young people themselves being committed Christians. Beyond that, here is one place where numbers are often important. The youth "group" that consists of four girls and one guy is, generally speaking, in trouble already.

Strong preaching. The apostles of Christ said, "It is not desirable for us to neglect the word of God in order to serve tables" (Acts 6:2, NASB). Important as other duties were, they refused to be diverted from primary emphasis on their study and ministry of the Word.

Seek a church where the ministry of the Word is given this priority. However, not all "biblical preaching" is worthy of that name. "The word of God is living and active and sharper than any two-edged sword" (Hebrews 4:12, NASB). If preaching is deadly dull and passive and about as sharp as the edge of a dill pickle, it's a travesty of biblical preaching, however much lip service to the Bible is given.

Brotherly love. Few things are more devastating to a church than divisiveness among members. Look for a church at peace, where the warm spirit among the people testifies that for them the glory of Christ which they share (John 17:22) far outweighs their differences of opinion.

Positive, outreaching spirit. Look for an evangelistic church. But some churches that say and honestly think they are evangelistic don't reach out to people. How can you tell whether a church is reaching out? A better indication than the evangelistic flavor of the pulpit messages, as good as that is, may be the friendly spirit of the congregation. Do they reach out to you as a visitor? Do they try to make you feel welcome? (If you dash for the door before the benediction ends, don't blame the church for being unfriendly; give them a chance.)

Acceptable doctrine and worship forms. Denominational identity is not considered so important as it once was. Individual churches vary greatly within single denominations, and in some areas independent churches abound.

But don't assume that denominational distinctions are now a matter of indifference. The differences could turn out more important than they at first seemed.

Scripture says, "Can two walk together, except they be agreed?" (Amos 3:3, KJV). Total agreement on everything is neither possible nor desirable, but if there's disagreement on basic teaching or procedure that you consider vital, you'd best seek another church.

Lay participation. This one can be tricky. Some Christians have been overworked in a previous church and see their move as a chance to find a large church where they can attend without being put to work. One basic question should be faced by every Christian: Shall I seek a church that needs me or one that meets my needs?

The precise answer must be sought carefully

and before the Lord. But some principles from the Bible are clear: you should both give and receive in the Lord's service. A church that doesn't meet your spiritual needs and build you up is failing in its most basic purpose.

However, you are also supposed to minister to others. So, find a church that will meet your spiritual needs in such a way that you in turn will be able to minister to others, not necessarily within the church structure but wherever and however the Lord wants you.

Worship. God is seeking true worshipers (John 4:23, 24), and you need a church that provides for and encourages worship, not just activity. Since true worship must be in spirit, look for a reverent, worshipful atmosphere. Since it must be in truth, look for a firm commitment to Christ and to the Bible.

Adequacy. A church should have adequate facilities to house an adequate program operated by an adequate staff. An inadequate staff means some work poorly done or not done at all, or a serious overload on the workers, or both. If the program is inadequate, the places where the gaps come may be just the places you and your family most need help.

The witness of the Spirit. The checklist here is not intended to be decisive in showing you what church to attend. Some items may be much more important to you than others. And no church is perfect. Furthermore, your observations may not be entirely accurate; God may give a church a good mark on the same characteristic you marked bad.

Pray about it. And be sensitive to the witness of the Holy Spirit. He may want you in a less-than-ideal church, as a catalyst for improvement. Or he may not want you to join a particular congregation, even though your checklist suggests a green light.

"If any of you lacks wisdom, let him ask of God, who gives to all men generously and without reproach, and it will be given to him. But let him ask in faith" (James 1:5, 6, NASB).

CHURCH EVALUATION CHECKLIST

Desirable characteristics in a church	Good	Bad	Marginal
Close to our home			
Has a good Sunday school			
Has a good youth work			
Preaching is biblical and challenging			
Harmony: the people love one another			
Positive, outreaching spirit			
Doctrine & worship forms acceptable			
Lay participation encouraged			
I can worship there			
Adequate facilities, staff, & program			
I sense the Holy Spirit's witness that this is the church for me			

Are we serving the church but losing our children?
V. Raymond Edman

The boy across the desk from me was in trouble. Half-defiant, half-repentant, he was not trying to fool me or to be funny. But I was unable to find any point of contact that would bring a favorable response. Then I said, "You know how highly I regard your father!"

"Who is my father?" was the immediate and burning retort. "He doesn't have any time for me. He doesn't care what I do, or what becomes of me."

The outburst astonished me. His father was a leader in evangelical Christian circles!

Without success, I tried to persuade him that he was incorrect in his estimate of his father and in his attitude toward him.

Unfortunately, this case is not unusual.

A freshman girl was in for counsel. While she was deeply attached to her father and wrote regularly to him, she had not received a reply since school had opened. Twice a day she had gone to the college post office in expectation of some word. Although March had brought the first days of spring, no treasured letter arrived. Sharing her sorrow made me speechless.

The impressions that I have gathered from conference and prayer with young people who appear to be disillusioned, even embittered, because of their parents are varied. Some believe their difficulty is simply this: The work of the church is more important than we are!

Young people have the impression that their parents have so many responsibilities in causes which are intrinsically good that there is little opportunity for fellowship with them. There are committee meetings without number, conferences, church services, dinners for Christian causes that must be prepared or partaken...all of which leave very little time for life and leisure of the whole family together. Children are left to shift for themselves.

My second impression is that some youngsters feel that other children are much more important than they.

They gather that their parents, busy helping other youngsters at Bible conferences and rallies, in youth work near and far, are quite unconcerned that those of their own household may be lost.

These impressions gathered over the years call for soul-searching questions on the part of Christian parents today.

What is meant by "seeking first the kingdom of God and his righteousness" with the result that "all these things shall be added unto you"? Truly God comes first in every life and each parent must decide in the light of God's Word and the illumination of his Spirit what is meant by that basic and primary relationship. The children of believing parents are dedicated to the Lord; how then should one care for them?

I believe that if mothers and fathers earnestly seek to know the meaning of full consecration in God's service, they also will have clear guidance in the rearing and education of their children.

Correct them

What constitutes neglect? The Word says clearly, "The rod and reproof give wisdom: but a child left to himself bringeth his mother to shame" (Proverbs 29:15, KJV).

The correction needed by a child may be gentle or quite severe, depending upon the personality of the child.

One of the saddest words in all Scripture is

the divine declaration regarding Eli, "For I have told him that I will judge his house for ever for the iniquity which he kneweth; because his sons made themselves vile, and he restrained them not" (1 Samuel 3:13, KJV).

This awful Word of God given to Samuel, who himself hesitated to tell it to Eli, should have been sufficient warning for him all his days. But Samuel allowed himself to become too busy in religious activities to give adequate attention to his own boys. Eli had been both judge and high priest in Israel—too many responsibilities for any one man—and when Samuel came to maturity, he attempted to carry the same unbearable and unnecessary burden. The result was that "his sons walked not in his ways, but turned aside after lucre, and took bribes, and perverted judgment" (1 Samuel 8:3, KJV).

We parents would do well to consider whether or not fewer responsibilities in God's service would not make us more efficient, and at the same time give us more evenings at home, more time with the Word for ourselves and around the family altar.

The Word of God is very plain in its injunctions of parental discipline. Solomon observed sagely, "Withhold not correction from the child: for if thou beatest him with the rod, he shall not die" (Proverbs 23:13, KJV).

Correction must always be just and equitable; for not without cause does the Word say, "And, ye fathers, provoke not your children to wrath: but bring them up in the nurture and admonition of the Lord" (Ephesians 6:4, KJV). Andrew Murray counsels in his choice little volume, *The Children for Christ:*

Before the child knows enough to refuse the evil and choose the good, simple obedience is the law. As he grows out of it, it is still a parent's influence that must train the young will to exercise the power on which in after-life everything depends; he must now be trained to refuse the evil and choose the good himself.

**Play
with them**

Beyond the correction that is both firm and kind is the matter of playing together. From earliest childhood, little folks should be accustomed to family activities. At first, games and activities cannot be too strenuous. When still quite small, children enjoy walking with parents in the woods (or in the park, if they are city dwellers). There need not be extensive plans or preparations. Often, I recall walks in wooded New England hills where my little fellows imagined that they were reenacting the story of Billy Goat Gruff or were intrigued by stories about Peter Rabbit and his escapades.

Correct spelling (a sad lack in many quarters today) can be improved greatly by anagrams played on the kitchen table. Arithmetic can be improved by elementary lessons in multiplication and division played at mealtime. Vacations can be especially meaningful to family unity.

If I had those days to live over again, I would give a good deal more time just to being with my children, not necessarily always doing things for them or with them, but just to be there. Such memories linger long in little hearts and help condition them for stormy days ahead.

**Pray
with them**

Not only should we play together, but also pray together. I have had young people say quite wistfully that there has been little or no time for a family altar, for group participation in which each member of the family could be a part. Admittedly it is difficult to arrange a time in the day when all the family can be together for the reading of the Word, better still for memorizing that Word and for the fellowship of prayer. But the effort is infinitely worthwhile.

Work with them

We can work together. A great many children are city bred and lack the opportunity and privilege of having chores on the farm. More than one father has said to me, "I can't give my boys the benefit of the jobs that were mine when I grew up in the country."

By careful planning and real effort, however, we can assign duties in connection with the household for which the individual child is responsible. It will pay out in the end.

If nothing else, we can study together with our children around the kitchen table. To be sure, there will be interruptions, questions to be answered, and problems to be solved. But those hours together will long be remembered and the benefits derived well worth the efforts.

Plan with them

For all these delights of praying, playing, and working together, there is the necessity of planning together. Everyone is helped by the family council. We may have very clear ideas as to what should be done, and the ideas of the youngsters may be very erroneous and inefficient, but the wholesome result of taking children into the reasoning behind family action will pay out rich dividends for you and them in the years to come.

Appreciate them

Above all, young people need to know that their parents at home are deeply interested in their progress and in their problems, and to be assured that correction is approved if needed and that appreciation is expressed for accomplishment.

Children are the heritage of the Lord. They

are the greatest investment God has ever given anyone. Our part is to devote more interest, attention, and devotion to them than to our investments or industry and our multiplied service in the church. Investing in our children will bring us the highest rates of interest in time and in eternity.

When the ten-year-olds in Mrs. Imogene Frost's class at the Brookside, N. J., Community Sunday School expressed their views on "What's wrong with grownups?" they came up with these complaints:

1. Grownups make promises, then they forget all about them, or else they say it wasn't really a promise, just a maybe.

2. Grownups don't do the things they're always telling the children to do—like pick up their things, or be neat, or always tell the truth.

3. Grownups never really listen to what children have to say. They always decide ahead of time what they're going to answer.

4. Grownups make mistakes, but they won't admit them. They always pretend that they weren't mistakes at all—or that somebody else made them.

5. Grownups interrupt children all the time and think nothing of it. If a child interrupts a grownup, he gets a scolding or something worse.

6. Grownups never understand how much children want a certain thing—a certain color or shape or size. If it's something they don't admire—even if the children have spent their own money for it—they always say, "I can't imagine what you want with that old thing!"

7. Sometimes grownups punish children unfairly. It isn't right if you've done just some little thing wrong and grownups take away something that means an awful lot to you. Other times you can do something really bad and they say they're going to punish you, but they don't. You never know, and you ought to know.

8. Grownups are always talking about what they did and what they knew when they were ten years old—but they never try to think what it's like to be ten years old right now. SOURCE UNKNOWN.

How can we succeed with family worship? *Tenis C. Van Kooten*

Our society is witnessing a certain disintegration of home life. Each member of the family seems to be going his own way. Each is not only working at a different job, but each seeks to find his real life with those of his own age or kind. Even parents do the same. They look for a group with the same occupation or recreational interest.

But in a Christian home, life together should be meaningful enough to heal this separateness. And that is where the family altar stands central. Building better family altars is the best remedy for the erosion of the life of the home.

When

When is the best time to conduct the family altar? Mealtime seems to be the answer. This is when the whole family is most likely to be together.

Of course, it is not always possible to get all the family together at every meal—sometimes not even at most of the meals. Then the next best must be done: whoever is present should conduct worship. If Mother is there with one or more of the children, family worship must not be interrupted. Never think there are too few to make the time worthwhile. Such sessions should be geared especially to the needs and the capacity of the child. When properly conducted, these small sessions by only part of the family can build a valuable intimacy, and can furnish some lasting instruction and inspiration.

Take time

There must be a willingness to take the necessary time for an interesting and instructive gathering at the family altar. It is not a matter of spending long hours at the altar. It is a matter of a few minutes, regularly, unhurriedly, and intelligently devoted to worshiping God. If a family has come to the point where they have no time to sit down and quietly listen to God, it is long past time to drop everything else and "take time to be holy."

Work at it

It takes work to build the family altar, just as it takes work to build anything worthwhile. Also, the spiritual exercise at the altar itself is work. Listening to God's Word, prayer, and constructive discussion takes effort. Even in listening to the Word, one is not entirely passive. The living Word must be actively received into the hungry soul. God's Word is not a set of instructions for the manipulation of moral robots.

Read the Bible itself

The Bible must be central on the family altar. Not infrequently it is shunted from the main line and left to stand idle on a side track, replaced by stories, dramas, and devotionals about the Bible. Some of these may be used with profit, but the difficulty is that in many instances they have entirely replaced the Bible itself. Those that are fed on such a diet indefinitely often have only a conglomeration of scattered notions as to what the Bible says; there is little or no system in their understanding as to what the Bible teaches; they have not been sufficiently confronted with the Word itself.

Everyone participate

Everyone should participate in the worship program. Participation makes for better attention and greater benefits. Everyone should follow the reading of the Bible in his own copy. As soon as a child can read reasonably well, he should be given his own Bible. Everyone should also be given opportunity to read. The procedure for reading can be varied. Each may read in turn, or each may read for a few days or for a whole week. Even young children can be asked to read short passages. The important point is that everyone participate meaningfully.

Do they understand?

The question asked by Philip of the Ethiopian should be asked at the family altar: "Do you understand what you are reading?" (Acts 8:30, RSV). In fact, that question should be kept in mind constantly, and every means should be used to insure that a positive answer can be given. That requires that the Bible be read "interpretatively." This will demand explanation, analysis, and application.

There is no single procedure that need be followed in reading the Bible at the family altar. In fact, variation is advisable, for it stimulates and challenges. Do not allow practices in conducting the family altar to congeal into an inflexible form, so that the bare procedure becomes a religious ritual.

Varied programs of Bible reading

What are some of these variations? Sometimes one will take the lead in reading, then another; responsive reading of a Psalm or some other poetic book; questions that challenge listeners to apply the Word; children and youth expected to ask pertinent questions and to make pertinent application on a given Scripture; a short preparation expected from one member of the family; current events and social problems looked at in the light of God's Word; personal duties and responsibilities discussed; personal faith analyzed; reading from various parts of the Bible so that there is a balanced use of the Old and the New Testaments.

Selective reading of the Bible can also make for variation. This will mean that the Bible will not be read through from beginning to end, but rather that the order of reading will be by selection. It may be simply to alternate between a New Testament Gospel, an Old Testament historical book, a poetic book, a New Testament letter, and an Old Testament prophet. Or one might want to read the various books in the order in which they were written and in their historical context. Such reading of the Bible facilitates the understanding of God's message. The proper order to read the various books can be determined by looking up a chronology of the Old Testament period. Such a chronology can be found in a Bible handbook or a Bible dictionary.

The same procedure can be followed in reading the New Testament. One could read the book of Acts and then the various letters at their proper place. While reading through, one of the children could be required to look up in a Bible dictionary every city touched upon.

There are other variations. During the season of Christmas, Lent, Good Friday, Easter, Pentecost, Ascension, and Thanksgiving, appropriate Scriptures can be read. A list of such Scriptures can be found in a Bible handbook, a chain-reference Bible, or a topical Bible. Appropriate Scriptures can even be read for the Fourth of July and Labor Day.

Another very profitable variation is to observe special events in the home with the reading of an appropriate Scripture. The special occasion might be the birth of a child, someone's birthday, a holiday, a great good that has been experienced by one or more of the family, or even a death or some tragedy.

At the beginning of every month, someone should check the occasions to be observed during that month. The other special events can be added as they take place. If this program is to be successful, some responsible person must be looking for and marking Scripture passages pertinent to these occasions.

Discuss

Generally there should be some discussion following the reading of the Word. But first an emphatic don't as to that discussion! Don't hold debates on obscure passages and technical details. The discussion should always be directed toward acquiring a better knowledge of what God's Word says, and the integration of that truth into the life of everyone gathered about the Word, so that everyone may be nourished unto dynamic Christian living.

Once a week it can be very profitable for the family to study the passage that forms the Scripture lesson for some meeting that one or more members of the family are to attend. If it is a Sunday school lesson, have the children do some preparation.

A family might take a subject, a doctrine, or a concept and read all Scriptures related to it. Children and youth should be asked to suggest what they would like to study. Each could also be expected to find a news item that would relate to the concept being studied. This would teach everyone to see the Scriptures as relevant to life today.

Other subjects could be the parables of Christ, the miracles of Christ, or character studies. The latter can be very interesting and instructive. Each member of the family could select his own character and then be expected to find all the related scriptural material.

Store up the Word

The Word should also be stored up by memorizing it. The value of memorizing materials is questioned by some educators. But the simple fact is that the only way really to know something is to know it in such a way that you can produce it when the information is needed. Before any Scripture is memorized, that Scripture should be carefully explained. The value of that particular Scripture should also be pointed out, indicating why that passage is to be memorized.

Scripture memorization should follow a plan and a program. Regularity in learning small sections over a period of time will accomplish the most. Single texts or entire chapters can be learned. The important point is that everyone knows why certain passages are being learned, and what they mean. For example, it is well to have everyone familiar with passages of Scripture that give comfort in distress and courage in danger. Psalms 23, 46, 121 have been laid up in many hearts and have poured comfort and courage into many lives. The same is true of John 14 and 17, and Romans 8.

Memorization at the family altar should be made interesting and challenging. Read the texts in unison to facilitate learning them. A family might spend the better part of an entire week on one chapter, and all would know it the rest of their lives.

Three verses to keep in mind for your family altar:

"Understandest thou what thou readest?" (Acts 8:30, KJV).

"Thy word have I hid in mine heart, that I might not sin against thee" (Psalm 119:11, KJV).

"Let the word of Christ dwell in you richly . . ." (Colossians 3:16, KJV).

Can we claim our family's salvation? *Theodore H. Epp*

God's dealing with the Philippian jailer has some very instructive matters for us to consider with regard to family or household salvation. The account is found in Acts 16.

Paul and Silas had been placed in prison for preaching the gospel. They were severely beaten at the order of the cruel magistrates. Then their sufferings were compounded by their being put in stocks in the inner prison. Yet the missionaries sang God's praises, and God answered by sending an earthquake. The foundations of the prison were shaken. The doors were opened, and every prisoner's bonds were loosed.

The jailer was awakened out of his sleep by these remarkable events. He was about to commit suicide, thinking all the prisoners were gone, when Paul called to him not to harm himself.

The prison keeper was brought under sore conviction by all these events. When he brought Paul and Silas out, he said to them, "Sirs, what must I do to be saved?" They answered, "Believe on the Lord Jesus Christ, and thou shalt be saved, and thy house" (Acts 16:31, KJV).

Then it was that they spoke the Word of the Lord to the jailer and to all that were in his house. That same night he "was baptized, he and all his." Following this he "rejoiced, believing in God with all his house" (v. 34).

Several times in these few verses, the household of this jailer is spoken of. This is very significant.

When he asked how he might be saved, he was told to believe on the Lord Jesus Christ. This is the only means of salvation, whether for the head of the house or the members of his household. It is this faith that brings a family to salvation.

Paul challenged the keeper to a personal faith in Christ, and then assured him that this same faith exercised on the part of each member of his household would bring him (her) to salvation also.

There is no question but that an individual needs personal faith in order to be saved. But if that person is a parent, how can his faith bring a family to salvation? On the basis of this Scripture, we can say that the same faith that saved the individual can bring the family to saving faith.

The order in this section of Scripture is— first, the parent believed God for his own salvation. Second, he believed God to bring the family to salvation. In order to get the full-balanced scriptural view on this, we must note certain Bible passages. For example, in John 6:44 (KJV) we find the Savior saying, "No man can come to me, except the Father which hath sent me draw him: and I will raise him up at the last day." It is clear from this that no man can be saved until he is drawn by the heavenly Father.

Now see what John 12:32 (KJV) says. Our Lord again is speaking. His words are, "I, if I be lifted up from the earth, will draw all men unto me."

In the third place, the parent trusts God to grant the children saving faith. The parent must believe God for his own salvation. Then he believes that God will bring his family to the place of salvation. Just as the parent was drawn to Christ for salvation, so must the family be drawn. So then, the parent must trust God to grant the children saving faith. Faith is a gift of God. No one can believe unless God gives him that faith.

In the first place, we believe for our own

salvation. In the second place, we believe that God will bring our family to salvation. But it is right here that a definite responsibility must be met by each member of the family. In this passage in Acts, we see that the promise was made to the jailer that if he believed in the Lord Jesus Christ, he would be saved and so would his house. Then we learn that the apostles spoke to him the Word of the Lord and to all his house likewise. So all heard and all believed.

In Acts 11 we have another example of household salvation. Cornelius had been instructed by an angel to send men to Joppa "and call for Simon, whose surname is Peter; who shall tell thee words, whereby thou and all thy house shall be saved" (Acts 11:13, 14, KJV).

All through the Scriptures we find this method indicated. We find it with Noah. He not only believed God for himself, but he believed that God would bring his whole family to the place of faith. In exercising faith, he built an ark not only for himself, but for his whole house. Eight souls in all were saved— Noah, his wife, his three sons, and their wives. He believed that they would come to the place of trusting. They did—and they were all saved.

We find in Exodus 12 that God instructed the Israelites through Moses to slay a lamb and apply its blood to the doorposts of their houses. This was for the physical salvation of the family. The father had to begin the act of faith, and the children also had to believe if they were going to stay in the house under the protection of the blood.

The same truth is seen with regard to Rahab. She protected the spies whom Joshua sent into Jericho. She asked them that she and her family would be spared when the Israelites conquered the city.

The answer of the spies to Rahab was: "Behold, when we come into the land, thou shalt bind this line of scarlet thread in the window which thou didst let us down by: and thou should bring thy father, and thy mother, and thy brethren, and all thy father's household, home unto thee. And it shall be, that whosoever shall go out of the doors of thy house into the street, his blood shall be upon his head, and we will be guiltless: and whosoever shall be with thee in the house, his blood shall be on our head, if any hand be upon him" (Joshua 2:18, 19, KJV).

These all had to be under one roof in order to be spared. But before this could be done, they had to be persuaded that their safety lay in believing what Rahab had told them. She in turn had to believe that they would believe and do as she said, and thus not die when Jericho was conquered.

After the city was taken, we read: "And Joshua saved Rahab the harlot alive, and her father's household, and all that she had . . . " (Joshua 6:25). The only reason these were saved was that they were in the place of safety. They had to believe that safety lay in being with Rahab in her home. But she believed for them to begin with, and that is what got them to believe her. The personal responsibility factor cannot be overlooked in any of this. Joshua emphasized that clearly when he reminded the Israelites that they must choose whom they would serve. As for him and his house, he and they were going to serve the Lord.

How could Joshua say this that involved his whole family unless he believed that his would be a believing family? God honored his faith.

According to the incident in Acts 10, after Peter and his friends reached the home of Cornelius, the centurion called in his kinsmen and friends. Then it was that he believed, and they also believed and were saved. Cornelius, however, started this cycle of faith.

This is where parents often make a mistake. They pray that God will save their children, then start worrying and wondering whether God will hear their prayers or not. Where there is worrying, there is no faith. Where there is faith, there is no worrying.

The remedy for this whole situation lies in Philippians 4:6, 7. There we are told to come before God with thanksgiving and make our requests known. It is when we ourselves believe for our children that God will bring them to faith. So claim this great prayer promise: "Be careful (anxious) for nothing; but in every thing by prayer and supplication with thanksgiving let your requests be made known unto God. And the peace of God, which passeth all understanding, shall keep your hearts and minds through Christ Jesus." Apply this to your own life, to your family and their salvation, and God will give you peace.

Faith comes by hearing, and hearing by the Word of God. So we must witness concerning the truth of Scripture to our loved ones. We must not only tell them the story of Jesus and his love, but believe that God will bring them to saving faith. It is said concerning Catherine Booth that she prayed, "O God, I will not stand before thee without my family." And God brought her family to saving faith.

Jonathan Edwards claimed his family for God. God honored his faith and most of his family was saved unto the third generation. Can you trust God for your family?

Am I my child's biggest problem? *S. Bruce Narramore*

I once asked a woman to describe her father. She replied, "He is loving, kind, just, and a fine gentleman . . . but I feel he is so distant." Some weeks later I asked her to tell me about God. She replied, "He is loving, kind, just, and omnipotent . . . but he seems so distant." She used almost the exact words in describing God and her own father! This is not uncommon.

A child's image of God is strongly influenced by his relationship with his parents. Since God is an immaterial person located in a seemingly distant heaven, he is hard for a child to comprehend. Foreseeing this problem, God created the family structure to teach us about his own nature. We live in a natural, physical world. There is also a spiritual world. To bridge the gap between the two, God uses concepts from our physical world to teach truths from the spiritual realm. He uses light (John 8:12) to represent the True Light, and he uses a father (Hebrews 12:7–10) to represent the True Father. As a child grows, he learns about the love and justice of his earthly father. When he is told about God, he begins to understand. His unconscious reasoning goes something like this: "God, whom I have not seen, is a heavenly Father. He must be like my father. Now I can understand what God is like."

The carry-over from earthly to heavenly Father is clearly shown in Matthew 7:11 (KJV) where Christ said, "If ye then, being evil, know how to give good gifts unto your children, how much more shall your Father which is in heaven give good things to them that ask him?" This passage indicates that a child can expect to see the virtues of his parents magnified in his heavenly Father. Where few of these virtues exist, it is hard to build up a positive image of God.

Loving and mature parents make it easy for children to understand God's character. But anxious, inconsistent, or domineering parents instill a poor father image. Children of these parents may see God as distant, unconcerned, punitive, or weak. The exact image depends on the attributes of their earthly parents.

The teenage daughter of a harsh, critical minister once came to me for counseling. She was severely depressed. In her suffering she tried to commit suicide to end her misery. While talking about her relationship to God, she said with great anger, "Don't give me that ------ about God is love! If he were love, I would see it in my father!" This reaction and others like it are rehearsed daily in counseling offices around the world. Many people look for God, but their vision is clouded by an earthly parent.

A story is told of a father who put his young son on a tabletop and said, "Jump to daddy." When the boy jumped, the father stepped aside and let him fall to the floor. "That will teach you never to trust anyone!" the father stated firmly. This parental action is extreme. But children often learn they cannot trust. We spank a child in anger and tell him, "This is for your good," rather than admitting, "This makes me feel better." We make a promise and fail to keep it. Through this, our children are gradually learning not to trust. When they become Christians, they want to trust God. But somehow it is hard. They have trusted many times before and have been let down. Now their feelings whisper, "Be careful. You can't depend on him. You may be used, or you may be hurt."

My experience in counseling neurotic adults has invariably shown that their image of God has been colored by negative experiences with parents, God's representatives on earth. This is not to say that biblical teachings on God's character fail to influence our spiritual relationships. They certainly do. But negative emotional reactions stemming from childhood interfere with our ability to apply biblical knowledge. Think of your own Christian experience. Haven't you had difficulty believing God's will was best for you? Have you resented God's direction or discipline? Most of these feelings are emotional hangovers from childhood.

In a real sense, God has given us a divine opportunity to shape our children's lives for time and for eternity. It is beautiful to realize we can actually teach our children the love and character of God. It is awesome to know that our own hang-ups can drive wedges between our precious children and God, our Creator.

Father power is different from mother power and your child needs both to develop properly. One of the reasons that many fathers feel unnecessary is that they see an impenetrable emotional wall around the mother-child relationship. The fact that the mother is deeply involved with the child subtly means to many that the father is to be excluded.

While mothers frequently make a serious mistake in presenting the children's father in a very feeble light, father himself needs to be reeducated. There is much pressure on today's man to define his masculinity in terms of his job or economic value to his family . . . Regardless of whether your job pays $6,000 or $600,000 per year, whether you are the bottom man in a company or the top, you should never be satisfied to define yourself solely in terms of your job. Always think of yourself as a multi-faceted person—a father, a husband, a career man, a citizen, and an individual with varied talents and interests. This can, little by little, be passed on to a child. If he develops a strong sense of self-esteem and independence, he is already on the way to possessing a high degree of achievement motivation.

Do I have to be perfect?
Keith Miller

Both my wife and I have always said a prayer
with each of our children as we tucked them in
at night. We had a standard prayer ritual of
"now I lay me down to sleep" followed by the
"Godblesses" (God bless Mommy, Daddy,
Sister, Grandmommy, the dog next door,
etc.). One night as I was going through this
with one of our daughters, I realized that I
wasn't actually praying with my children. I
was trying to teach them to pray instead. It
dawned on me that they had never heard any
real confession or petition from me about
things that were real in my life.

The next evening I was cross at the dinner
table and glowered at their mother during the
meal. That night, as I lay on our five-year-old
middle daughter's bed, I prayed, "Dear God,
forgive me for being fussy at dinner tonight."
There followed a kind of awed silence. Then
very quickly, she went through the familiar
prayer. The next night, "it just happened," I
was also cross during dinner. Again, in my
prayers, I said, "Dear Lord, forgive me for
being cross at dinner again tonight and help
me not to be fussy again. I really don't want to
be that way. Please help me to try hard not to
be." There was the same silence. Then with
eyes clinched shut, my little girl said, "Dear
God, forgive me for teeteeing out in the
backyard under the big tree last summer." I
almost laughed and cried at the same time.
This was real confession at a five-year-old
level (of a behavior which is against the rules
at our house).

I saw that, from Christ's perspective, one
does not teach people to pray; he prays with
them out of his own life as Christ did (see
Luke 11:1 f.). They learn by example. Of

course, one must pray about things a child can understand and handle emotionally, like happenings around the house or neighborhood. If you have a $75,000 note due at the bank Monday morning and don't know how you're going to pay it, I would not pray about that with a five-year-old. She would have no way of understanding anything about your problem—except possibly the note of terror in your voice. We have fallen into new rituals at our house. But prayer is at least more meaningful than it had been, and some real changes in our lives have come out of this different perspective regarding our prayers at home.

For one thing, I had often wondered what I ought to do about talking to the children regarding Christian commitment, but I didn't want to manipulate them. One night we were having an adult dinner party. I came in to say prayers with our (then) ten-year-old. Being in a state of turmoil about a vocational move I was contemplating, I closed my prayer by saying something like, "Lord, I want you to take my future and show me what you would like for me to do with it. Amen." My little girl looked up at me very thoughtfully. "Why did you say that, Daddy?" I looked down at her in surprise, not realizing at once what I had prayed. "Well," I replied, "I'm just trying to give my life to Jesus, honey, so he can show me the best way to live it."

"Oh," she said.

A few minutes later, I was alone in the kitchen when I seemed to feel two little eyes peeking in through a crack in the door. As I looked around, she pushed the door open, came running across the room and threw her arms about my legs. "What is it, honey?" I asked. She looked up at me thoughtfully. "Daddy," she said, "I'd like to give my life to Jesus, too."

She had heard the words many times that God loved her and that Christ had died for her. But that night she felt different about them. Right there I explained to her that what she was doing was telling God that she wanted him to be her Lord, that she wanted to get to know him and love him, and that she would like for him to show her how to live her whole life for him. This she did. Now, I don't know what this will mean in her adult life, but it meant something then. And she came to it in the context of her everyday living, hearing us pray sincere prayers out of our real needs.

This is not as easy as it may sound—to begin to be open concerning your own needs, vulnerable in your own home. At first I said to myself: "If my kids see that I am not strong and have to pray for all kinds of strength and help, they won't respect me as a father. I may have some real discipline problems on my hands. Who am I to be telling them to straighten up when I have trouble 'straightening up' ? "

It is never easy to apologize when we really mean it, but experiences in our home have convinced me that children already know about our weaknesses. Our faults show. And when we as parents refuse to confess them, our children do not think that we're strong (as I had supposed) but that we are either phony or can't recognize our weaknesses. More generally, I believe they simply learn to imitate us and to keep their own needs hidden and bottled up. I began to realize that unless my children learned from me that they were acceptable to God with all of their incompleteness and missing of the mark (even when they have tried hard to do right), they may never learn it at all. And they will have missed the good news that our acceptance is dependent on God's righteousness and not our own. Of course, I realize that paradoxically we are called to be perfect (Matt. 5:48), but I am stating that our justification is based on grace, on Christ's integrity and not our own (Rom. 3:23, 24). And in this respect at least parents are on equal ground with their children—all must depend on that same grace.

HE LIFTED ME UP

My father never wrote a book, never starred in a major revival play, never sang a magnificent aria, and yet he is and will always remain the principal influence on my life. He is an ordinary man by most standards, but to me he has always stood tall against a background of the Bible, Christ, and the church. He introduced me to all three at a very early age, and I have never regretted it.

My memories of childhood are vague and disconnected, except for a fleeting one of struggling vainly to carry a four-foot doll into our house. About the time I got to the back steps, Daddy came out of the house, lifted me and the doll into his arms, and proceeded to carry me into the house, where supper was steaming on the table.

The memory of those strong arms lifting me and my burden into strength and assurance carries a strong allusion even today of Christ lifting the burdens of the world.

Now I am a junior in college. My father's faith has given me a strong foundation on which to anchor myself as I face the buffetings of the world.

Oh, I have great memories. The best are recent, ones that included a hard struggle for truth, the reaching out for a solid foundation on which to stand. I found it in my father's faith.

Then, and only then, did I realize what he had been trying to say: Christ is the answer. I believe that with all my heart. And though I may stumble and fall, his hands will be there to pick me up and carry me to safety, just as my father lifted me and that doll into his arms that breezy autumn day! REBECCA BRUNSON

Which answers never change? *Stanley E. Lindquist*

"Aren't you going to do anything about your boy? He's crying!"

It was my dad speaking. He was referring to our first son, two weeks old. I patiently explained that if we did something each time he cried, he would be spoiled. I knew the books—and presumably dad didn't.

"You children weren't treated that way," he answered simply.

Years later, I wondered about how we seven children were reared. A doctor's degree in psychology was completed—but I wasn't as sure as I had been as a new father.

One of my students, a woman returning to school to earn her teaching credential, emphasized the question. She asked, "Who writes the books on child-rearing? When my first child was born, I was supposed to keep him on schedule, never pay attention to his crying unless it was mealtime, never hold or rock him. When the second one came, I thought I knew what to do, but they had rewritten the books! For this one I was supposed to feed him when he cried, follow his schedule, rock him to sleep, and love him a lot. Which way is right?"

I couldn't give her the answer. All I knew was that this kind of change didn't occur in my parents' family. There was consistency.

What made the difference?

I believe the essential factor was that Dad followed a guide that didn't change: the Bible. Any new concept of child-rearing that came along was evaluated according to that standard. Sharp vacillations in procedure were not possible.

What validity do biblical concepts have in light of today's psychological principles? Is there much difference between the two?

Look up in a concordance all the scriptural references relating to children. There is relatively little reference to the way children should be reared. Proverbs 22:6 is fairly typical:

"Train up a child in the way he should go: and when he is old, he will not depart from it."

The implication is that the parents already know how to rear their children! In other words, the knowledge has come from *their* parents. This leads to the essential teaching, represented in verse after verse, that children should be taught the Scriptures. The essential elements of moral understanding that form the basis for personality development are in the Scriptures.

This emphasis is especially important in view of current thinking about relative standards and the deterministic philosophy of Freud and others. Determinism holds that a person is shaped by his environment, and therefore has no direct responsibility for his own actions—they just reflect the way he has been reared. If the essential feature of the environment is to do what everyone else is doing, there are no clear moral standards.

A psychiatrist recently described a phenomenon that he had discovered in several clients. These people, lacking moral principles, were well-educated, wealthy, seemingly well-adjusted, but suffered from a lack of purpose in life. Therefore life had no meaning for them, was uninteresting and almost unendurable. His first task was to help them regain the moral standards of life.

If their parents had taught them principles from the Bible (Deuteronomy 4:9, 6:7; Psalm 78:4, 6; Isaiah 54:13; 2 Timothy 3:15, etc.), there would have been purpose in life, and they in turn would have taught their children. The first principle is to help the child to accept God through Christ, and to follow the basic moral principles as set forth in the Scriptures. "Train" in Proverbs is "catechize." In other words, the training should be intensive. When the child has internalized this, his life has meaning and purpose.

A boy was brought to me for counseling, a juvenile delinquent who had already been in jail. His father decided to seek professional help.

The boy's story was a familiar one. Love had been lacking in the household. His mother, whom he remembered only dimly, had been an alcoholic. She left, and though the father tried to make up for her absence, he seemed unable to demonstrate his affection. The boy had moved into a little house at the back of the lot where he spent hours by himself. He started sniffing airplane cement. No one really cared for him, he was sure.

This boy had been denied his birthright—the security of love and affection—because his parents had failed. He did not know of the greater love of God embodied in the principle, "We love God because he first loved us." Had God not loved us first, we could never be capable of love.

Parents often feel that they love their children, but that their children do not understand that love. Invariably, an investigation of the background indicated that the love they thought they demonstrated was a possessive, selfish love—identified by the child as such, and consequently not accepted.

Psychology is emphatic in teaching that love is the child's birthright. A child should be loved for what he is, not for what he does—just as God loves us for what we are, not for what we do. We could never merit God's love; it is a gift. Why should we expect our children to merit our love? This is our gift to them, without reservation.

The danger comes when parents confuse this kind of love with license and permissiveness. The truly loved child is firmly taught to fit into the standards of society and Christian life. No child can make this adjustment without suffering a bit, and true love does not withhold the disciplining necessary.

If a child has never gone through a period of structure in which he recognizes that limitations are placed upon him, and in which he has had to curb his desires, he will never know what security really is. Never having known how far he can go or what he can do, he will not have any guide points. Therefore, he will always be looking for the limits to what he can do.

Parents who think they are showing love by granting every whim of the child are failing to prepare the child for life in a structured society. Certainly this is not the teaching of the Scriptures. The "way" of Proverbs must mean positive direction which helps the child.

True psychological teaching and the Scriptures do not disagree. The problem is finding what "true" psychology is. If a principle of child-rearing is at variance with the true interpretation of the Scriptures, we can be sure that it is not true psychology.

Parents need to learn as much as possible about child-rearing. But such instruction must always be compared with biblical standards in order to find and maintain the consistency of training that is necessary to bring a child to spiritual strength and purposefulness of life as an adult.

9

& Other Questions

What makes mealtimes fun? *Merla Jean Sparks*

A traditional picture of a closely knit, happy family is of a smiling brood gathered formally around a massive, feast-laden table. But perhaps that sort of dream situation is a bit out-of-date in this hurried, "grab a hamburger" era. Now there are tiny, efficient kitchen nooks, sleek restaurant counters and stools, and modern, gala patio sets.

Is this change in tastes bad? Of course not; styles have always been changing. But it is an indicator of the growing informality of our lives.

Although there is nothing basically wrong with this switch to the casual, it is a contributing cause to the breakdown in family solidarity.

It is important to realize that the spiritual growth of the individual members has definite correlation with the unity of the family. A lack of fellowship and communication on the home level breeds misunderstanding between adults and children and makes regular Christian training impossible.

Therefore, mealtime, when most often the family is together, can be a rich opportunity to cement bonds of family communion, which will, in turn, nurture a fertile atmosphere for spiritual growth.

To establish a program of increased family loyalty, it is not necessary that radical measures be adopted to insure that at all three meals a day there is 100 percent family attendance. Varied individual schedules make this impossible for many families. But a desirable plan would be for the whole family to be able to sit down together for a least one meal a day.

This may necessitate some adjustments.

Mother may have to give up her wish for an early supper, even though it means doing dishes later in the evening than she prefers. If because of necessary irregular schedules complete cooperation is not possible every day, then several times a week would be a second-best alternative.

However, the value of mealtimes even when only part of the family can be present should not be overlooked, for they can be utilized in special ways to give important individual attention. A child who comes home from school for lunch can blossom out under the special, undivided attention that is possible for an otherwise busy mother. A father and teenager who must eat an early breakfast alone can find that this is a good chance to share ideas that could never be discussed in the noisy atmosphere of a regular meal. Mother's peaceful meal alone with a preschooler gives a chance for him to share his small interests without competing with the grander exploits of older sisters and brothers. A quiet meal for Mom and Dad after young children have been put to bed can give an opportunity for much-needed communication.

But there is no substitute for the mealtime when the whole family is present. It may be noisy, but it is a high point of the day—when exciting events are recorded, ideas shared, and plans made.

The following suggestions can make family mealtimes more enjoyable and profitable:

1. *Strive for an unhurried atmosphere.* Since this is primarily the result of a relaxed mental attitude, we can cultivate this even if time is limited.

2. *Allow no negative conversation.* Combat criticism, complaint, and argument. Take advantage of the time together to make necessary group decisions and plan positive

family projects and activities. This is not the time to discuss individual problems or deal with frictions in specific areas of disagreement.

3. *Guard against one person monopolizing the conversation.* Bring out quieter members with directed questions. Guide the conversation so that the older children's exciting recitals of their activities do not swallow up the younger's "just as important to me" stories. It is especially important that we parents do not dominate the conversation.

4. *Encourage free discussion on a wide variety of subjects.* Avoid controversial items that lead to family quarrels.

5. *Delay disciplinary action in almost all cases until the meal is finished.* Nothing ruins a meal faster than parent-child confrontations. Avoid these by:

a. Ignoring petty infractions. Many of these are a result of childish awkwardness anyway, not of deliberate disobedience.

b. Delaying action whenever possible. For example, when a child deliberately misbehaves, instead of dealing with the problem right then, we might say nothing until the meal is over. If there is general family disagreement, we must stop the discussion and set a later time, after the meal, for it to be continued and the problem worked out.

c. Using quiet methods if misbehavior needs immediate attention. Send the child (or children) to another room, rather than give a public lecture. If we must deal personally with one child, take him to another room, so the rest of the family may continue the meal in comparative calm.

6. *Give training in table manners.* At the same time, we must not let this dominate the atmosphere. My interest in proper manners gave rise to a habit of nagging. But it was hard

to keep quiet when the children's table manners seemed unbearable. We worked out the following compromise that works most of the time for us.

a. We discussed the problem outside of mealtime.

b. We decided together on the basic table manners we would stress. My husband and I would not nag about small "deviations" if the basic rules were being followed.

c. We established that this was a "training" area, not a "punishment" one. Therefore, if we had to point out when the children were violating a basic rule, they were to remember we were only reminding them, not blaming them. Our part was to see that our tones conveyed this.

d. We agreed on a couple of signals so we wouldn't have to verbalize the matter too often, especially when there was company or we were eating out. Two fingers raised for the "peace" sign means to cut down the excessive talking. A raised index finger means to slow down the gobbling.

7. *Make the saying of grace a meaningful activity.* It helps if we use varied forms: singing, spontaneous prayers, memorized verses. A good custom, especially in families with young children, is to join hands during grace; this gives physical force to the idea of a spiritual bond (as well as keeping active little hands still). Rotate the responsibility of leading grace.

8. *Supplement the family worship program with the use of a promise box or a "verse of the day" right after grace.* This could be a springboard for stimulating discussion during the meal.

9. *Take advantage of any established mealtime routine to facilitate a regular family worship program.*

If mealtime in our homes is cheerful, animated, positive, and inspiring, then it will be an important influence in our children's spiritual life.

The family that eats together stays together. Meals are the one time that the entire family meets as a unit with a recognition of different statuses—the youngest child, the oldest child, mother, and father. The children, at mealtimes, learn something about what it means to be Mother and Dad—to fill those roles. Also, without knowing it, children, during meals, build a sense of togetherness and community, where they learn to carry each other's burdens a little bit, to share, to take turns, to talk things out. Most of the family's other relationships are very changeable, not permanent. The shared mealtime, and the relationships that go with it, therefore, add a sense of stability.

Also, the shared meal provides children with a sense of identity. A child begins to feel, "I'm a Smith or a Jones, and my parents are real human beings, with their normal share of human virtues and failings."

Not only is it a good time for sharing conversation, it also is a good time for sharing the work that goes into preparing a meal. Talking things out in the kitchen is much more natural than setting up a time and saying, "Now we will have a discussion." A mother and child wiping the dishes together often wind up talking to each other spontaneously, and a discussion follows. It is not artificial, and it's much less self-conscious than if it had been planned and programmed.

Each family must then decide what is the best time to eat together. Unless this is done, the mother, father, and children sooner or later find out that there is no home at all. REV. JOHN L. THOMAS, S. J.

How can we have a happy family vacation? *Bernice K. Gregg*

"You mean your teenage children actually want to go vacationing with you?" a friend exclaimed. True. They have never objected even mildly.

Certainly it's not because we spend our time at spots like Waikiki. Much of our travel has been to out-of-the-way places, camping and hiking in the exhilarating outdoors. In the past ten years, we've covered 75,000 miles in forty-nine states and a lot of Canada, often for two months at a time.

My husband, who is an optometrist-teacher-writer, has a bad case of wanderlust. That's why he arranged a career permitting long summer vacations. It suits me fine. Our children have a good share of gypsy spirit, too.

We have ten fundamentals which make our family travels easy and rich.

1. *Start when your children are very young.* Family travels build a firm tradition of doing things together. Our kids went papoose-style on their first short trips. There is really nothing like seeing the world through the eyes of your children.

If your vacations are for adults with children taken only because there is nothing else to do with them, no suggestions I make will make your vacation a success. On the other hand, you can get a wealth of fun from family travel at any age if it's truly designed for the whole family.

2. *Expand travel plans as your children grow up.* Go slowly. Take short trips at first, until you learn how to travel together. Once the kids get out of the toddler stage, camp part of the time. Buy travel equipment gradually;

try and test what suits you. No need to have everything at once; rent, borrow, or improvise until you are sure you like camping.

The pattern must change, too. As you get better at camping, try more adventurous trips, farther from home, a new mode of travel, or simply stay longer.

3. *Use the simple marvels of nature to the utmost.* Don't limit family trips to big cities, fancy spas, and the museum circuit. Use them for flavor, but the big outdoors should be the main diet. Scenic grandeur isn't always necessary to charm children; a chance just to be outdoors is all they ask.

I'll long remember the happy gleam in the eyes of my children, Janell and Ronnie, as I watched them catching tadpoles in New Hampshire. It was often like that. A collection of pine cones amused them for hours in Wyoming. A whole carefree day was spent building a tiny dam near our Missouri campsite.

4. *Tent camping does the best job of building family togetherness.* Camping out makes you get along with each other and share the work. But even more, camping provides the biggest share of the outdoors. Trailer life can have these same important qualities if it isn't too much like home. Cabins and lodges? Depends on where they are and how much adult-oriented.

There is something about living right in the outdoors that makes us look forward to each trip. We stay in motels about one night in four for an extra-long shower, a swim, a restaurant meal, and a close-in location to visit cities. Camping, however, is the most fun, and we never tire of it; especially with children to share the pleasure.

5. *Let everyone in on the planning process.* The procedure to follow is simple.

Collect a mass of travel literature; pore over it on long winter evenings. Hunt for unusual and out-of-the-way places. Finally, rough-draft three or four possible trips. Discuss them in a family meeting. A vote decides where to go. You'll be amazed at how much you'll agree. Each plan should include something to everyone's liking.

My husband, Jim, makes proposals about what there is to do each day: for example, relax in camp all day; go fishing; hike around the lake; drive to the top of the mountain for a picnic. Each is discussed and a family vote taken. The children have a part in the decisions. I think this is one of the important reasons why they still like to go with us.

6. *Let everyone help with the work.* As soon as our kids were old enough, they helped with their own clothes. Each has his own clothing list. This goes for all the things we take. Carefully prepared lists eliminate much of the packing chore. As the children have grown, more of the duty has become theirs.

Share the work on the road as well. We use a patrol system. Jim and I are patrol leaders. We change patrol members every day. Each child changes jobs and bosses daily—good for all of us.

While traveling, baggage handling must be smooth and nuisance free. Children should handle their own bags.

7. *Load your trips with variety—plenty of variety.* "Where are we going next year?" Ron asked the other day. There would have been a big letdown if I had replied, "Same old place." Covering new ground most of the time has added challenge and excitement to our travels; spiced them, too, with an air of mystery.

In the Sierras, we climbed to the top of Mount Whitney. In Alaska, we horse-backed up the famous Chilkoot Trail. In New York, we stayed in a forty-story hotel. In Minnesota, we canoed the vast lake country. Train, bus, plane, ferry, auto, houseboat have all taken us around this great land. That's the way to go; try every means of travel.

Neither camp nor stay in motels exclusively. As great as camping is, we enjoy motels as well. But a month straight indoors would never satisfy our children. A basic factor in success of our family travel is that we do many different things.

8. *Relax the routine of family living.* Let everyone take a holiday from some of the rules that apply at home. Bedtime should be when convenient, not by the clock. Let meals happen when hunger dictates. We freewheel— hamburgers for breakfast, afternoon snacks, ice cream at 10 PM if we wish. No one has been sick on a trip; in fact, we show a remarkable display of health.

Somehow on vacation there are fewer needs for parents to say no. This is a good atmosphere for building family relationships.

9. *Be active wherever you go.* "Get out on the trails to really appreciate the wonders of nature," a ranger in Lassen Volcanic National Park told me. That's good advice for traveling anywhere. I remember how Lake Louise was an exquisite sight from the lawn of the lodge on a perfect summer day. Then we hiked the trail to the Teahouse of the Six Glaciers. Now I know its deep and inner beauty.

Keep armchair sightseeing at a minimum, especially traveling with youngsters. Get out of your car, take all the time you need; and, of course, do something to suit everyone in the family. Museums, beaches, campfire programs, lectures, boat rides—take in everything worthwhile with zest.

10. *Make your travel meaningful.* Start in the planning stage. Select interesting places to

visit. Read up in advance; take along brochures and guides to keep informed as you go.

We get souvenirs from every state, collect everything that will help us build memories. I always keep a diary. All this is later edited to make up a trip scrapbook.

There is a great big hidden benefit from applying these ten family-travel principles. Not only do our children still want to vacation with us, but we feel young enough to vacation with them.

How can parents get away —alone? *Valerie Sloane*

Parents frequently become so involved in the child-rearing process that they forget the romantic charm of dinners alone or the luxury of uninterrupted conversations. Dedication to their task causes them to be reluctant to leave tots or teenagers and to neglect the sparkle in their marriage.

One young mother and father recall that they had an opportunity to travel to Japan when their children were eleven, five, and two years old. "We agonized for a long time before friends convinced us that we'd never forget the experience, and our children would not suffer permanent psychological damage from our absence. Having made the decision to go, we stifled our occasional guilt pangs and organized for our journey."

This couple developed the following plan, which can be used as a model for parents planning a trip without children.

Hiring sitters

The first thing these parents did was look for a competent sitter. With grandparents and relatives thousands of miles away, they needed to find totally reliable substitutes.

After many phone calls and interviews, they hired a woman with an excellent reputation for child care. She was willing to stay at their home, where the everyday surroundings would provide security for the children. The familiar faces of neighbors and friends might also provide a lift for a lonely tot.

To avoid the trauma of leaving the children with an adult they had never seen before, the sitter arrived a few evenings before the start of the trip.

The parents discussed their lists of instructions with her well in advance of departure to give her an opportunity to raise questions, such as "Are the children allowed to stay overnight at a friend's house?" and "Do they like to be read to at bedtime?"

Lists, lists, and more lists

The Japan-bound couple provided as many answers as possible to any questions related to the smooth running of their household.

They compiled an emergency guide containing their home address (including the names of the nearest cross streets), and the names, phone numbers, and addresses of doctors, police, fire department, and hospital. Also included were the names and phone numbers of neighbors and close friends. They hung this framed guide by the telephone.

Other vital information made available for the sitter and a neighbor was an itinerary of the trip, the name of the family lawyer, and the location of important documents . . . just in case.

They left forms granting permission for emergency treatment by the doctor or hospital personnel, and written permission for the children to ride in the sitter's car.

Lists of the routine schedule of activities were designed to provide order and security in their children's lives. They felt that their absence was no excuse for their children to become sloppy in their habits or behavior. They hoped that beds would be made, clothes would be picked up, and eating would be confined to the kitchen.

They listed such things as bed- and nap times, usual mealtimes, and school, carpool, and bus schedules.

Vision of sedentary children watching TV for three weeks prompted this couple to list the amount of television normally allowed.

Other parents suggest that the following information be included in lists of instructions for sitters or grandparents:

Indicate the days for collection of trash and recyclable newspapers, bottles, and aluminum cans, and whose responsibility it is to get these items to the curb.

Provide for the care of plants. One mother neglected to inform her sitter that it was her ten-year-old's responsibility to water the houseplants. Because the sitter didn't know it, the greenery received double drinks and the results were catastrophic.

Avoid coming home to broken washing machines and mountains of dirty laundry by leaving the names and numbers of dependable repair people. Authorize the sitter to call them in case of emergency.

Give careful thought to the children's needs and try to foresee every imaginable problem.

Anticipate stuffy noses and leave instructions for the administration of medication. Anticipate birthday party invitations and leave prewrapped gifts such as bubble bath or model airplanes.

Meal planning

Food is another area of concern for departing parents. One mother returned from a trip to find that her chubby children had grown even chubbier. Learning that they had consumed too much cake and macaroni and cheese, she suggested nonfattening meals next time. She left cupboards stocked with low-calorie foods, and money designated for fruits and vegetables rather than cookies and candy.

A father was angered to learn that the sitter had forced his children to eat vegetables they didn't like. "The only accompaniments to entrees which they like are green salads, carrots, and applesauce," he said. "The next time we traveled we told the sitter not to bother buying or cooking spinach, green beans, or succotash."

Extra preparations

Another couple, excited about their first trip to London, wanted to make it an educational experience for their children as well as themselves.

At the library they found books about London and its famous attractions, such as Westminster Abbey and the Tower. They read A. A. Milne's well-known poem "Buckingham Palace" to the children.

They discussed the difference in time and explained that while they were eating dinner, the children would be sound asleep. "Piquing the children's curiosity produced unexpected side benefits," they said. While they were gone their sixth-grader's chart on time zones won an honorable mention in the school science fair.

They talked about traditional English food and bought kippers and mix for preparing Yorkshire pudding.

All these little extras helped parents and children feel a long-distance rapport despite the thousands of miles between them.

A Michigan family suggests that parents prepare a calendar for children, illustrating days in flight with a picture of an airplane and the day of their return with a red gummed star.

The parents purchased inexpensive surprises such as jacks and balls, toy baking sets, or balloons with cardboard paddle feet. Before they left, each lettered, wrapped item was put in a box and a letter placed on the children's calendar. On the day when B appeared, they picked the corresponding gift from the box.

"This advance preparation causes the children to anticipate our departure rather than dread it," the father stated. "Eyeing the bulging box, they are more likely to ask, 'When are you leaving?' than 'Why can't you stay home?' "

Communication Children need to understand that adults need trips with each other as well as with the entire family. They also need to hear repeatedly that their parents have confidence in them.

One mother and father think their final verbal communication with their sitter helps her and the children get along well with each other. Their parting words, within earshot of their children, are: "These are good kids, and we know you will have their full cooperation and respect."

Carefully planned written communication with youngsters is also important.

Parents plagued with a last-minute trip to the pediatrician were ready to get away from child care and responsibilities and relieved to be away at last. However, they smilingly recalled that during their first hour of flight they found themselves talking about their kids. Nevertheless, they were careful not to convey this instant loneliness in their letters.

To their seven-year-old they wrote cards about things to which she could relate. For example:

Dear Perri,
We visited Holland today. Count the number of red tulips that you see on this card. We thought you would like this stamp with the queen's picture on it.

Love, Mom and Dad

And to the kindergartner they wrote:

Dear Hal,
The windmills are as big as the tree in our front yard. They go around and around.

Love, Mom and Dad

This couple also arranged to receive mail from the children. They had learned a valuable lesson from a friend's unfortunate experience during her first trip to Europe: "I was gone three weeks, and each time I arrived at a new hotel I checked for mail. Finding none when I got to Switzerland, I burst into tears. Neither the snow-covered Alps nor the cheese fondue could take my mind off my children. I cut the trip short and flew home."

To prevent this total lack of communication with the home front, purchase aerograms at the post office and preaddress them. Indicate when the letter should be mailed in order to arrive on time and mark it "Hold for arrival."

Some children develop communication plans of their own too. Two girls look forward to their parents' trips and secretly tuck "We love you" and "Have fun" notes in their mom's and dad's luggage, hidden in pockets, shoes, and socks. These surprise love messages are very comforting to their parents.

Also comforting to traveling parents is the knowledge that they did everything they possibly could to ensure their children's physical and emotional well-being. Exhaustive pre-trip efforts add immeasurably to the pleasure of parents and their children.

In the majority of unhappy marriages, the partners do not have satisfactory joint recreation. Use of leisure time should be planned as the handling of the finances—much more carefully than many of us plan our budget!

Young couples who have moved into a new community after the wedding need particularly to build up a normal social life, which they may often do by joining a Young Married Couples group in the church of their choice. These groups, which have had such a remarkable growth in the last generation, have actually, and silently, saved many marriages.

It is hard to overestimate the importance of the social and recreational life in marriage. Merely improving it often takes enough of the hostility and alienation out of the partnership, so that the couple agree better on everything else. Attention to it should be almost the first concern of anyone trying to improve a marriage, whether the effort be made by a professional counselor, a clergyman, or a relative or friend. PAUL POPENOE

How is college affordable?
Frank L. Keegan

Let's assume your son or daughter is prepared for college. He or she has completed high school, scored high on the college boards, and knows which of the private or public institutions of higher learning (now almost 3,000 in number) he or she would like to attend. Your child is prepared for college. The question remains, however, are you?

College costs have risen extravagantly in the past few years, yet enrollments continue to rise. Whether because of poor employment conditions, the normal indecision of young people, or the very real values still to be gained from college attendance, it is more true than ever that most young men and women look forward to attending a college or university. When the children turn to you, the parent, for counsel about college, what do you say?

You must try to balance their high school records and interests against the bewildering array of institutions, on the one hand, and against your savings account and other assets, on the other. You may indeed feel that struggling with calculus and the causes of the American Civil War was easy homework compared to the mysteries and the malarkey connected with selecting the best college for your son or daughter.

Because I have had some experience in this matter, both as a former college president and as the father of ten children, I am prepared to give you some advice, including several tips on how to face this momentous decision and how to survive it with both your equanimity and your pocketbook intact.

My first rule is: Estimate your income and assets carefully. Are you secure in your present position? Is there likely to be a raise in your future? Remember that for a four-year period your income must remain stable. And, if you have other children in college now or soon will, your financial condition must be healthy enough to support them as well. As you consider these questions, remember that many colleges have a "guaranteed cost" plan, which ensures that annual tuition and other costs will not escalate over the four-year period. Just ask the college admissions office about it.

If your health is good, you already have an asset; you can insure your life for an amount equal to the cost of a college education. In the event of your demise, your children will still make it through college—cost free.

As you review your assets, don't forget your relatives. Almost every family has a kindly, often single, Aunt Jane or Uncle Jim. They may not even be relatives. Now, when the financial crunch is on, they might translate those elegant and costly graduation and Christmas presents to your child into a percentage of those high tuition costs. Ask them. They may be flattered.

Your other helpmate is the federal government. Be sure to ask the admissions office about the National Direct Student Loan Program and the Work/Study Program, both of which are campus-based. The first lends money at 3 percent interest, payable after graduation; the second pays wages for campus work. Or you can apply directly to the federal government for the Basic Educational Opportunity Grant (BEOG). Don't assume that because your income is over $20,000, your child will not qualify; it's the combination of circumstances, like the number of children you have and what mortgages you hold, that determines eligibility. Give it a try.

My second rule is: Be realistic about your son or daughter. Your child's goals should be clear, and both of you should see how college attendance will really advance them. Maybe your child shouldn't go to college. Other young people wait a year or two before starting college. After four highly competitive high school years, some students need time to relax and to reassess things. Don't push them (they will love you for it), and your savings account will grow larger.

Help your child discover whether a two-year or a four-year institution is best for him or her. Some fields, such as dietetics and practical nursing, require only two years of college, while the computer programming and electronics fields require only one year in a proprietary school. Does your child need four years of college? Maybe two years is enough.

Discuss with your child also whether he wants to go to a small or large college, to live in a dormitory or in his own room or apartment. Does he want to commute? Should he commute? How often? In many colleges, class schedules can be arranged for three days rather than the usual five, so that commuting and other costs can be reduced. The rearranged schedule also allows for a two- or three-day job, which will save even more money. These are the questions that you, your spouse, and your child are best able to answer. And how you answer them makes a real dollar difference.

My third rule is: Select both the best and least expensive college for your child. Let me warn you right now that your own alma mater may not be the best, or the least expensive, place for your child. Some children don't want to follow in their fathers' or mothers' footsteps —and they shouldn't be pushed. Costs have probably skyrocketed since you attended anyway, and it is certain college admissions standards are tougher.

My second tip under Rule Number 3 is not to be disdainful of public or "commuter" colleges. They have a number of assets. They are usually close, permitting your child to live at home, thus saving room and board costs. Their faculties are constantly improving; overall, average salaries are higher at public than at private institutions. Finally, they are undoubtedly the least expensive to attend.

In recent years, public institutions have greatly improved in both quality and accessibility. The best college for your child is not necessarily a private one—nor indeed a public one. Again, be realistic about your son or daughter. It is my firm conviction that an alert and ambitious student can get a good education *anywhere*.

When comparing costs at public institutions, note carefully the differences for residents and out-of-state students. Harassed legislators are now increasing public college tuition for those from out of state. Even so, hardly any private institution is less expensive than a public one, though these differences can shrink if your son or daughter wants the best transportation available (car, gas, insurance), the best clothes, and the best tape deck in town.

As you examine particular colleges, look carefully for special scholarships and cost-cutting plans. The college catalog is your best index for local scholarship aid. Because you are an alumnus, a state or city resident, a musician, a General Motors employee, or a member of a minority, your child might qualify for a sizable scholarship. Some colleges, such as Antioch and Berea, have five-year work/study programs, enabling students to earn some income when not in school.

Other colleges offer a five-day boarding plan to reduce food costs. Did you ever hear of a three-year bachelor's degree program? It cuts costs by one-fourth. Furman, Emmanuel, and Carroll colleges, among others, have this plan. If your child wants to be a lawyer, dentist, doctor, or architect, some universities have a plan to admit them to graduate school in their senior year, and even before, if they are exceptionally bright. A quick acceleration into graduate study results in a big undergraduate saving. Remember that professional schools have their own sources of scholarships and grants-in-aid, often for research activities. Check them out.

My fourth and final rule is simple: Hustle! In every college, there are a number of "insiders' jobs." It may be as secretary to a popular department chairman, student director of a minority program, or maintainer of the tennis courts or swimming pool, over the summer or whenever. An ambitious sophomore (it takes a year to discover them) will find these jobs. And every campus town has a host of undergraduate salespeople. Florsheim, Kawasaki, or McDonald's franchises may be available with only a little push. I know three students who purchased a trailer for $3,000, used it for four years, sold it at graduation, and ended up paying nothing for their room expenses for four college years.

Can we escape the debt trap? *George Fooshee, Jr.*

Fly Now! Pay Later!

Sounds easy. And fun! Consider these slogans widely used on TV, billboards, and in direct-mail advertising:

> Presenting: The best friend your checking account ever had.

> Introducing: The "peace of mind" checking account.

> Now: An easy solution to tax and insurance problems.

These friendly phrases have been used by bank credit card companies to promote the uses of their plastic cards. What are these painless answers to your financial problems? Have these credit card companies discovered some slick way for you to spend more money than you have in your checking account?

No! No!! No!!!

They are presenting you with so-called convenience checks. When you want to spend more than you have, you simply fill out your convenience check. Instantly you have secured what they call a cash advance. The check you have written has been an instant addition to your bank credit card account. You have borrowed that money at an annual percentage rate of 18 percent. The best friend, the easy solution, the peace of mind add up to one word which the advertising neglects to mention: debt!

What is debt? Why do those who sell easy credit fail to use this word in their ads? Why are the adjectives commonly used for debt left out of descriptions of the new state into which you move when you borrow money? When I looked at all the adjectives listed for debt in Roget's College Thesaurus, I quickly understood the reasons:

*indebted; liable, chargeable, answerable for,
in debt, in embarrassed circumstances; in
difficulties; encumbered; involved; involved in
debt, plunged in debt; deep in debt; deeply
involved; up against it; in the red; fast tied up;
insolvent; minus, out of pocket; unpaid; un-
requited, unrewarded; owing, due, in arrears,
outstanding. Slang—in hock, on the cuff.*

Were you uncomfortable as you saw this
list? Did you notice the negative aspects of
each word and phrase used to describe debt?

A good rule for borrowing is: Never borrow
to buy depreciating items. Such things as cars,
furniture, clothes, appliances, boats, and
luxury items should not be purchased until
money is available to pay for them.

Debt violates God's commandment for our
lives. "Keep out of debt altogether . . ."
(Romans 13:8, *Phillips*). God says Keep Out!
The sign is clear. Keeping out of debt
certainly isn't easy. But the Bible gives a
definite way to avoid the trap—"make do with
your pay!" (Luke 3:14, NEB). Individuals I
know in the debt trap all took exactly the same
road to get there—they spent more money
than they made.

Debt is costly. Why are so many people
blind to the pitfalls of easy credit? They do
not count the cost. The Bible instructs: "But
don't begin until you count the cost. For who
would begin construction of a building without
first getting estimates and then checking to
see if he has enough money to pay the bills?"
(Luke 14:28, TLB).

What is the cost of debt for a family
earning $12,000 annually and consistently
overspending its income by $1,000 a year, or
$83.33 each month? Assume the interest rate
is 10 percent. At the end of ten years the total
debt amounts to $10,000. The interest for just
the last year is equal to the amount borrowed

that year. Paying only the annual interest, the cost of their folly has amounted to $5,500 in the ten years. And they still owe $10,000. That's costly!

Freedom is lost. "Just as the rich rule the poor, so the borrower is servant to the lender" (Proverbs 22:7, TLB). The person in debt is in bondage to his creditors. A portion of his pay is committed to pay back the debt; choices as to how to spend his pay are lost.

Other freedoms are also involved. I've noticed that money that is borrowed with a smile is usually paid back with a scowl. Debt is often a thief of joy. But I've seen hundreds experience the relief and joy that comes when they've allowed God to lead them out of the debt trap.

Jesus said, "What is impossible with men is possible with God" (Luke 18:27, RSV). Escaping from the debt trap to the glory of God is a tremendous objective. Here are the steps to help you work out your own plan for escape.

1. *Set a goal.* Think for a minute about the benefits of getting out of debt. Such action will: reduce your expenses; delight your creditors; provide financial freedom; and please God. Since a clear goal will put you out in front of ninety-five people out of every 100, you are well on your way to becoming debt-free. Incidentally, I've never seen anyone get out of debt by accident.

2. *Start giving a set percentage of your income to the Lord.* Most Christians abandon their giving along the path into the debt trap. God says, "But seek first his kingdom and his righteousness, and all these things shall be yours as well" (Matthew 6:33, RSV).

Do you want God's blessing stamped on your get-out-of-debt project? Then don't be foolish and keep going into debt with God.

3. *List all you owe and all you own.* The headings on the "What We Owe" list would look like this: Who We Owe; Total Amount Due; Monthly Payment; Interest Rate; and Percent of Total Debt.

Now list "What We Own." This list would include most of the things bought with borrowed money.

Take a good look at both lists. Under "What We Owe," did you include any amounts due relatives? Put them on your list. Have you included everything you own—musical instruments, collections, guns, sports equipment, or hobbies?

4. *Have a sale.* Study the list of things you own. Which of these can you do without? One couple who counseled with me recently discovered they could eliminate 20 percent of their total debt by selling one car. Then they were able to apply the amount of the car payment to further debt reduction. Don't think about how much you will lose of what you paid for the item you are selling. Think how much you will gain which can be applied to your debt reduction immediately.

Your attitude will determine your success. One young lady came to me about her financial mess. "Could you get along without your car?" I asked her. "Impossible!" she exclaimed. But transportation was very convenient. Neighbors and fellow employees had offered her rides to and from work and church. Also, shopping was convenient to her house. With her attitude, it was really impossible to clear up her financial plight. Within a few weeks, she had lost her job because of repercussions from her personal financial irresponsibility.

5. *Set a monthly debt-payment amount.* Squeeze this money out of your monthly income. Be realistic, brutally so. Don't waste

money—stick to your plan.

6. *Add no new debts.* Gather your family around, take a large pair of scissors, and deliberately cut each credit card into tiny pieces. Make a list of all charge accounts. Call or write each store and tell them to close your account. The key to your success in avoiding new debt will be to do without.

7. *Establish a time goal.* Write down the number of months according to your plan that it will take to become debt-free.

8. *Cut the goal in half.* That's right! If you have determined that it will take you four years, or forty-eight months, to get out of debt, then write down a figure of one-half that time.

The only way I know to save money in paying off debts is to pay them off faster. The faster you pay, the less it costs. Your solution to the problem will depend upon your family's creativity.

For example, consider housecleaning. Domestic help now comes under the Federal Minimum Wage Law—that's $18.40 for an eight-hour day. Another alternative would be to have the whole family clean a house on Saturdays. Remember the magazine salesman —"I'm working my way through college"? Maybe your family slogan could be, "We're working our way out of debt."

Other family projects might involve baby-sitting or working for temporary campaigns such as health foundations. Many churches are willing to pay for part-time jobs in the kitchen, in the church nurseries, or even part-time custodial help.

If you have teenage youngsters, then allowing them to have a part in the debt-repayment program would be excellent training.

Finding dependable janitorial service is

often a problem for small business offices that require cleaning only once or twice a week. Inquire of churches in your neighborhood. Keep your eyes open for lawns that need mowing or shrubs that need trimming, right in your own neighborhood. You'll be surprised how much you're worth if you're only willing to invest a few hours a week.

9. *Develop a repayment schedule.* Usually writing down your plan will help you to achieve it. After you've made your payments, write down the amount paid and the balance due. Watching the balances diminish will give you an excitement that will help you stick to your goal.

10. *Take or send a copy of your repayment schedule to your creditors.* I promise you that they will be very impressed with the fact that you have made out a plan. They will be even more impressed as you send them the regular monthly payment you have promised.

I have worked with hundreds of credit grantors. I have yet to find one who will not go along with a person who makes an honest effort to pay some amount regularly on his bill.

11. *Stick to your plan.* You'll be tempted again and again to quit. Don't do it! Each missed payment will set you back on your goal. Life is littered with dropouts who quit when the going gets rough. The Bible has a very specific word of encouragement as you escape the debt trap: "Having started the ball rolling so enthusiastically, you should carry this project through to completion just as gladly, giving whatever you can out of whatever you have. Let your enthusiastic idea at the start be equalled by your realistic action now" (2 Corinthians 8:11).

PARABLE OF THE CHARGE ACCOUNTS

In the beginning the man took unto himself a wife. And lo, they did live happily, even unto the thirty-first day, when many charge accounts rained upon him, yea, as in a flood:

For lo, though the husband did make sufficient bread to keep body and soul together, yet had the wiles of the spoiler ensnared the wife, calling forth grievous wants from her breast. Color television, myriad appliances, and innumerable credit card purchases had multiplied fruitfully, which came high unto sinking the ship of matrimony. For the winds of inflation blew upon the land, and each one lusted after his neighbor's goods. And the man was sorely angered and spoke forth bitter words, from which his wife took great sorrow, but not unto repentance. For upon the first day of the week she went forth again and spent abundantly.

Then it was that the man was sorely pressed, and he took unto himself a second labor by the light of the moon, and his wife likewise, and their lives did pass like ships in the night. Behold, the time of the paying of bills returneth, and the man saith unto his wife, "Yea, though I moonlight and work my fingers to the bone, I cannot get ahead of thee!" And his wife beateth her breast. "Truly," she saith, "I am now filled with remorse. Let my bed be empty if I mend not my ways."

Then gave she ear unto her husband and they took counsel together that they might be of one mind in their values, and beat the system, yea, and build for their future according to a budget. And so did they walk prudently before the Lord, who knoweth our ways and pitieth those who cannot make ends meet. JAMES G. T. FAIRFIELD

Will someone please explain the fine print? (A short course in reading legalese)
Roger Dean Duncan

Tom and Shirley Hoffman liked to make a game of stretching their dollars. And they were usually pretty good at it, too. Even before the energy crisis hit, they decided to trade in their sedan for a compact car. After shopping around, they found a friendly dealer who could beat every other price in town. In fact, he even offered to finance the car himself to save the Hoffmans the hassle of going to a bank. The interest rate was reasonable, so the couple chuckled to themselves and signed the contract.

Then Tom accepted a job in another state and they moved. Four weeks later, they received an official-looking notice from their friendly auto dealer demanding that the balance of the contract—about $2,600—be paid immediately. Tom fired off a hasty note saying that they had never missed a single payment and had no intention of coughing up the full amount in a lump sum. Yet before the month was over, the car had been repossessed and the Hoffmans were still obligated for the $2,600.

Why?

The loan contract they signed with the dealer plainly stated they were not to take the car out of the state without the dealer's "express consent." They violated this provision by moving to another state for Tom's new job. Other provisions in the contract said the Hoffmans were in "default" if they failed to perform any obligation of the agreement, and that if in default they could be required immediately to pay everything they owed.

Perhaps the auto dealer didn't turn out to be so friendly after all, but he was perfectly within his legal rights to demand full payment and then repossess the car. The Hoffmans, like millions of other Americans, could have spared themselves plenty of dollars and disgust if only they had read and understood the fine print.

Many family management specialists say that next to imprudent credit buying itself, ignorance of—or outright disregard for—the terms of legal contracts is what's getting more and more consumers into financial hot water. There's no need for any of us to fall victim to fine print, because with some basic (and simple) guidance we can translate almost any credit contract into plain English. Let's try it with a few of the legal phrases most commonly found in credit contracts.

Agreement to pay

Buyer agrees to pay to the order of the seller, his successors, or assignees ...

Obviously, when you buy something on credit, you agree to pay. But the clincher of this phrase is that you allow the seller to sell your obligation to pay to a third party, such as a finance company or a bank. Then you're sent a coupon payment book and are required to make payments directly to the third-party lender. Under the laws of most states, this transfer decreases your rights. You must continue to pay the lender even if the product fails to work or is returned because of any other problem.

Security interest

The seller reserves a security interest in the merchandise sold until the purchase price is fully paid.

This means the seller continues to own the goods until you have made all payments as agreed. If, for any reason, you fail to make a single payment when due, the seller may take back the merchandise—and he's not obligated to give back the money you've already paid.

As long as he doesn't "breach the peace," the seller may take back the merchandise without a court order. A breach of peace occurs when the seller's efforts to repossess the collateral without a court order provokes physical action on your part to prevent repossession.

For example, if you won't allow a dealer into your home to repossess an appliance, he must get a court order to avoid breaching the peace. When the sheriff's representative comes with the court order, you must let him have the appliance or be faced with a contempt of court citation that could result in a fine and/or imprisonment.

Limitations on buyer's use of secured goods

Buyer shall not sell or transfer the merchandise sold or take it out of the state without the express consent of the seller.

This is the sort of provision that brought Tom and Shirley Hoffman some unpleasant surprises on their car deal. It protects the seller's right to take goods back if they are not paid for as promised. It keeps him informed of the whereabouts of the merchandise and keeps it within the jurisdiction of the courts of that state, should legal action be required to regain possession. If you plan to move secured goods out of your state or drive a secured automobile across state lines, you have agreed under this provision to get permission of the secured party (the original seller or his assignee) before doing so.

Acceleration clause

If the buyer defaults on his obligation under this contract, the entire remaining balance shall become due and payable at that time or at any time thereafter until the contract is paid in full.

Of course any contract should clearly define what is meant by the word "defaults." Many of them actually spell out several definitions designed to encompass nearly any eventuality imaginable. The Hoffmans will vouch for the fact that the moment you default—either in payment or in the performance of any agreed-upon obligation—you can be required to pay the remaining balance in its entirety.

"Default" also may include making any inaccurate statements on the loan application; loss, theft, or substantial damage of the collateral (if your bought-on-credit TV is stolen, you may have to pay up immediately); or even the business problems of your cosigner (one young couple had their mobile home repossessed when the bride's father, a cosigner on the loan, closed his dry cleaning firm).

Exclusion of oral agreements

Nothing said by the salesman nor any representations made by any agent of the company will be binding unless they are endorsed herein.

It is assumed that a written contract contains the total of all provisions of the sale and payment agreement. No agreements made orally will be considered a part of the contract, and no oral agreements will be enforced by the courts. If you want certain conditions to be a part of the agreement, you must put them in writing. Even if the contract does not contain this provision, it still applies. So if a seller's promise is not put into writing, it isn't an enforceable part of the agreement. Don't be misled by the friendly salesman— no matter how sincere he seems—who waves the flag of a "gentleman's agreement." Even honest people sometimes have short memories.

Insurance waiver

Credit life and disability insurance is required to obtain this loan. This insurance coverage is available at $——— for the term of the credit. I do desire credit life and disability insurance as a part of this loan. Buyer's signature:———

The seller may require you to buy credit insurance or other insurance to secure the loan or the collateral for the loan. But he cannot require you to purchase that insurance from him, although a careless reading of the clause may give that impression. You are free to buy the insurance from any insurance company licensed to do business in your state. In fact, you'll often get more for your insurance dollar that way. Initialing or signing a statement like the one above authorizes the seller to provide insurance coverage as a part of the contract.

Cognovit note

A cognovit note in a contract usually contains all four of the following provisions:

1. Power of attorney—*Buyer authorizes any attorney-at-law to appear in an action on this note, at or after the note becomes due, in any court . . .*

Here you have given the seller permission to select the attorney who will appear in court as your proxy. This "power of attorney" is to be used only at or after default occurs. Yet when you authorize a power of attorney, you waive your rights to speak and act for yourself. A power of attorney clause should specifically state what the authorized person is allowed to say or do in your behalf.

2. Confession of judgment—Here the buyer authorizes power of attorney to— *confess judgment in favor of the seller.*

The power of attorney authorizes an attorney selected by the seller to confess in court that you are guilty of all claims against you which the seller may make. Following a court judgment, this confession of guilt may result in the powers of the court being used to collect amounts due, plus court and collection costs from you (or your employer through garnishment of your salary) regardless of any claims—however legitimate—you have against the creditor.

3. Waiver of notice . . .*Buyer waives the issuing and service of notice in any action taken on this note.*

4. Waiver of right to appeal . . .*Buyer releases all errors and waives all appeals in actions taken and judgments made concerning this note.*

Under this provision you have literally given up your constitutional right to ask that the court action taken against you be reopened or appealed to a higher court. You have also given up your right to question and seek correction or restitution for any errors the seller may have made in regard to the contract you signed.

Buyer acknowledges terms

I have read and understand all of the terms of the above contract and consent to them all as evidenced by my signature.

Even if this provision is not included in the contract, it is generally assumed that your signature is evidence of your agreement to all the terms.

If you object to certain clauses of the contract, through mutual agreement with the seller such terms can be crossed out. The initials of both of you must appear beside the crossed-out provisions to show that each has agreed to their removal.

Oddly enough, this is one provision that nearly everybody seems to read yet still ignores. It usually appears just above the line for the signature. Strangely, the buyer reads the provision; then, even though they're right before him in print, he asks the seller what the terms are. He usually gets an answer like "Oh, just a bunch of legal mumbo jumbo. But don't worry about it, I know you're honest."

And the buyer probably is honest, too. Yet he's not very smart, or he would carefully read and understand what he signs before he signs it.

Not all the provisions discussed here will be found in every consumer contract, although they often are. Since individual contracts differ, you need to read yours carefully to see which clauses are included. Provisions are frequently worded in different ways, too, and differences in wording may affect your rights and responsibilities.

While these pointers can help you understand many provisions in contracts, you may still encounter clauses that are unclear to you. Agreeing to terms you either ignore or don't understand can lead to serious problems later. Caution is much less expensive than trying to take corrective action later. If you have doubts about a contract, just don't sign it. Ask for a copy of the contract form that is filled in and ready for signing. Then take the copy to an attorney for his appraisal and advice. His fee will be nominal (probably less than $20) compared with the costly kind of lesson learned by the Hoffmans.

The smart rule is simple: Do not put your signature on a contract until you fully understand its terms and are willing to abide by them. It's your money, so take your time and know what you're signing.

What is TV doing to our family? *John W. Drakeford*

Suppose you know a smart, fast-talking man who makes a good living by questionable deals in which he gives a distorted picture of the goods he sells to unsuspecting customers. This voluble, lovable half rogue takes a keen interest in your ten-year-old son. While you hope he appreciates your son for his own worth, you suspect he is setting you up, seeking to get at you through your son.

Would you let your ten-year-old spend up to fifty-four hours per week with this character?

Well, suppose no more.

This is no fiction or fantasy, but the grim reality of the advertising pitch aimed at today's children. Your child is fed one commercial every four minutes of television viewing time—about twice the commercial diet of adult programs.

One television ad salesman claims that 70 percent of the kids ask their parents to buy products advertised on television and 89 percent of the parents yield to the pressure of their children.

When a parent yields up his better judgment and buys a "triple-powered Whamo," his guilt at spending so much money on trivia may be assuaged by the realization that he has brought joy to his child's heart.

But don't be too sure.

When the gadget fails to work after the first week, the disgusted child suspects that the whole advertising pitch is a gyp. In fact, he may begin to suspect much of all that he is told by adults. Possibly it is the start of the "credibility gap" that leads him to cynicism about the world of adults.

In the course of some experimental work, I

spent an afternoon with a group of people at different levels of a hypnotic trance. The work was fascinating, and as I left the office to drive home, I was grateful for the opportunities of my work as a psychologist.

My poodle met me at the door and wagged his way into my heart. As I proceeded through the den, I saw my son sitting with eyes glued to the television screen.

I greeted him with a casual, "Hi!" There was no response.

A trifle annoyed at his bad manners, I retraced my steps.

I stopped and examined him carefully. He was in a hypnotic trance!

Yes, there it was—the same immobile body, glazed eyes, complete lack of interest in anything but the matter of his concentration.

Hypnosis is the process whereby an individual concentrates on just one idea, eliminating everything else from his mind. He then comes under the sway of the suggester and follows his behest almost without question.

Television monopolizes the viewer. It refuses to let him do anything but focus on its message. The victim easily sinks into a comfortable hypnotic trance, his will to act almost dissipated.

Children are the most susceptible subjects of all, and television takes advantage of them. A child will spend more time with the TV set than he will with his parents, at his school, or in his church.

For better or for worse, television is undoubtedly the greatest single educational force in society. The typical American high school graduate will have spent some 11,000 hours in the classroom, but during this period he has been exposed to 15,000 hours of television.

What does all this time spent in front of a television set do to your child? Research offers these findings:

—Apparently it has little physical effect on him. There is no reliable evidence to show it will affect his eyes or posture.

—He will spend thirty minutes a day less at play than did his pretelevision counterpart and will lose some valuable interpersonal experiences.

—While well-validated studies do not show he spends less time reading, I can personally vouch that my pre-TV child always read much more than his younger brother.

—The experience of a family gathered around the fire on a winter night with father reading seems to be gone. Television has effectively replaced sessions of reading and storytelling.

—"Video boy" is increasingly a spectator of the events of life; life at its best should be lived, not just observed.

—His vocabulary may be extended, but will it be of much value for him to know all the ways of describing deodorants, beer, and toothpaste?

However, the paucity of studies on the effects of television viewing on children has been noted, and we may have to draw some conclusions of our own. When this is done, most people discover just what they are looking for.

This is nowhere more clearly seen than in the discussions of violence on TV and its effects on the viewer. In one city, TV stations in one week carried 7,887 acts of violence, and on Christmas night one western program demonstrated peace on earth and good will toward man by showing thirteen homicides.

One research team spent two weeks

watching three network stations from 4:00 P.M. to 10:00 P.M. each day. They counted 790 persons killed or injured during the programs, or about five casualties for each program.

Perhaps the most disquieting aspect of this study was that the typical persons committing the acts of violence were young unmarried or middle-aged men. The victims were generally older people.

If your child is an average viewer, in the years between five and fourteen, he may see as many as 12,000 human beings violently destroyed. What does this do to his idea of the worth of persons?

Conclusions regarding the effect of exposure to TV violence may be grouped in three main categories.

1. The catharsis group. This group argues that every individual has a certain residue of hostility within him, that it is natural for men to murder and destroy. Through programs of violence, the viewer can vicariously live out his hostilities. This gives him a safe outlet for his feelings.

This catharsis concept is coming under fire from many psychotherapists. Some of these, including this writer, have seen persons more upset and hostile following a catharsis experience than they were at the beginning.

2. The middle-of-the-road group. Violence on television does not cause crime or aggression, but it can be a factor. According to this argument, only when the child has some type of emotional disturbance is his aggressiveness or hostility aroused by his viewing.

This argument has an element of sophistry in it. If the program arouses the impulses within the child, is it fair to say it did not cause it? We may say the video violence motivated him.

How does this fit in with the idea that each man is his brother's keeper? What of the Pauline concept of concern for a weaker brother and that which causes him to stumble?

3. The deeply concerned group. This group believes that children constantly exposed to violence on TV may come to feel that this is a normal way of life. These children may have little compunction about reproducing the activity they see so vividly demonstrated on the screen to gain their own ends.

For years children are fed the idea that force, deceit, fraud, manipulation, and seduction are the means of getting one's own way. They develop a skepticism about the "square" world which calls for self-discipline, delay in satisfaction, and hard work as the pathway to success. The problem is obviously psychological.

While the process of personality development is complex, one important component is identification. A child grows into adulthood by identifying with some adult.

In a home where there is no father, and the mother is away for most of the day, TV becomes the baby-sitter. With whom will the imaginative child identify? The slippery, glamorous thief or the dull, muddleheaded Fred Flintstone? Few TV models will help the child to become a good citizen.

A clinical psychologist placed a nine-year-old boy in a theater and attached wires to different parts of his body to measure respiration, skin moisture, and heartbeat. He then ran a series of movies of the type frequently seen on TV. During the performance he carefully measured his subject's reactions.

One of the most disturbing tentative conclusions was that TV may be creating what

he calls "violence addicts." Constant exposure
causes them to become completely insensitive
to ferocity and force. We may be producing a
generation of viewers who can participate
unemotionally in acts of brutality.

Any plan to use TV more effectively must
proceed on these fronts:

—Decide you are going to act. Almost all
   authorities agree that children's viewing
   habits should be limited. Yet one study
   showed that less than 5 percent of
   families do anything about their
   children's time with TV.

—Limiting of TV viewing should take into
   account the amount of time spent with
   TV and the type of programs viewed.

—One expert has suggested one hour a day
   is ample time for a child's viewing.
   Others suggest one evening a week,
   perhaps Friday at the conclusion of
   schoolwork.

—Beware of using TV for reward and
   punishment. If the child is punished by
   not being allowed to view TV, he may
   come to think his parents value it so
   highly that they reward him by allowing
   him to watch.

—Try some viewing with your children.
   Point out strong and weak points of
   programs and help them make their own
   selections.

—Spend some time with children on the
   commercials. How is the sponsor trying
   to sell his product? What factors should
   viewers have in mind when they decide
   what they will buy?

—Only the family can provide some
   experiences vital for a child's
   development. Parents should not use TV
   to keep children "out of their hair."
   Every home needs moments of quiet

when parents sit down and talk with their children.

Exercise your influence at the programming level. Sponsors are sensitive to the reactions to their offerings.

Be fair. When a good program is aired, write to the network and commend them. When objectionable material offends, write, write, write. Mention the good program, then express disappointment in an offensive program or commercial.

Make a triple approach. Write to the networks, the manager of the local station, and the sponsor. Remember the sponsor. He wants to sell his product. If he feels he is antagonizing prospective customers, he will change.

Lamenting the influence of TV, a parent said, "When it was mainly the movies, we could insist that our children not go. Now that movie to which we objected is piped into our house."

There is also an advantage in this situation. In the home, parents can view a movie with their children and decide whether it is suitable.

All parents really need is to want badly enough to do something about TV. They can do it. If they do not, they may have a monster that will educate, tyrannize, and finally control their children and their homes.